PONIES WITH WHEELS

Sue Millard

Jackdaw E Books, 2022

JACKDAW E BOOKS
Daw Bank
Greenholme
Tebay
Penrith
Cumbria
CA10 3TA
http://www.jackdawebooks.co.uk

E-book ISBN: 978-1-913106-21-8
Paperback ISBN: 978-1-913106-22-5

Table of Contents

INTRODUCTION

I've contributed a lot of material to the Recreational Equine Driving List over the years. It is a discussion forum about carriage driving which began on Yahoo and is now on Io.com. I write about driving and harnessmaking and the fun I've had with Fell ponies.

It was quite a shock to realise that even a modest selection of my posts there amounts to a novel in length. To these I have added some of my blog posts, where the content is relevant to ponies and driving. The dates in headings refer to the date I when posted on the forum or the blog.

Some of my posts, as you will see, are continuations of discussions on the RED list with other members. Where they were comparing leisure driving to competitive driving, I referred to the Federation Equestre Internationale (FEI) rulebook at the time of posting, but a lot of rules have been updated since then! Still I've tried, in editing, to retain the conversational tone of the forum posts and their contemporary references, rather than tidying everything up.

It's more fun that way.

Sue Millard
  Greenholme, September 2022

Sue Millard is a member of the North West Driving Club on whose committee she has served at various times as Chairman, Secretary, Treasurer, Webmaster, Press Officer, and Vice President.

She serves on the Council of the Fell Pony Society and is its Webmaster and Magazine Editor, as well as scripting and speaking the commentary for the FPS Display Team's performances at country shows. All the diagrams and modern photographs are the copyright of Sue Millard or Jen Bernard.

How I became a harnessmaker, 23 March 2004

I got interested in Fell ponies in 1968 when I went pony trekking in Cumbria. They impressed me so much that I worked with Fells for the same family business for five summer seasons, 1972-1976.

I started driving in 1984 after Clive Richardson, former Secretary of the Fell Pony Society and the North West Driving Club, asked me to illustrate a book he was writing, *The History of Horse Drawn Vehicles*. As I did the work, some of it from photocopied pages from existing books on driving, I became intrigued.

In 1984 I owned a 4 year old Fell pony mare whom I had bought as a riding pony, but she had been broken to drive, so I asked Clive how I would go about trying her. He lent me some harness and a cart, and showed me how to harness up. Clive's harness was a good one as exercise harnesses go, made of well padded good grade buffalo leather (John Willie was the make, an English firm who were well respected in their time.) It fitted Rosie well as it had been made for another Fell of similar proportions. The cart too fitted, for the same reasons.

We drove the mare together up and down a field with a husky friend as a helper (Paul Metcalfe, now vice-chairman of the Fell Pony Society). We drove her down the road and she didn't put a foot wrong. I mean, seriously, as in, "Yeah, yeah, I know this job, big sigh." After they'd gone home, I bought more books. I learnt a lot by reading them... and then I tried putting it all together with the young pony. On my own.

I was lucky, I think. Rosie was a thinking pony and although young she "knew better" than me, because she had driven lots of times and I had sat in just once! My husband told me later that the cart only had one wheel bearing, the other wheel making odd clanking noises as it turned. Also, there was no step to get in and out, which you had to do by climbing over the shaft (Clive's legs are longer than mine). Rosie decided that she was not going to stand still for my awkward getting in and out, and so I never actually drove that vehicle, which was probably a good thing.

We didn't get our act together until I was lent the "bits" of a vehicle that needed reassembling, for which my husband did the welding and created the necessary woodwork for me to sit on safely. I returned Clive's cart and, reluctantly, the decent harness, and bought instead a very cheap nylon webbing set. When I came to try it on and fit the rebuilt carriage, Rosie was distinctly upset, and despite my husband helping out, she was quite jerky and unhappy. Yet I knew she had been driven and trained quietly by our blacksmith, who had a good reputation for turning out sensible drivers, so where was the problem?

Well, I thought about it and the following evening I harnessed her as before but without the blinker bridle. I put on her open ordinary riding bridle. Then I brought the vehicle up behind her, just to watch her reaction. I swear she looked round, gave a big sigh, and totally relaxed. "It's not scary now I can see it. Put those silly blinkers away!" So we repeated the exercise of the night before, and she was relaxed and happy in her open bridle, and for the next five years Rosie and I drove locally and in small driving club competitions with no blinkers. She was rock steady, would outface a truck on the road if she felt it necessary (or a flock of sheep, or a herd of cows), and although not really fast, she went forever. She would take the wind out of know-it-all riders though by pretending to bolt, and was only suitable for experienced kids who knew enough not to show off or bore her with endless "schooling".

(Is it really that long since 1984? Doesn't time fly when you're having fun?)

I was so dismayed by the nylon harness I'd bought though, by its cheapness and bad design, that I vowed I could do better – so I tried. And used the result successfully.

The blacksmith came one day and said, "Sue, why is your harness hanging on the washing line?"

"Because I have just washed it," I said, thinking this was obvious.

"But you don't WASH harness," he said, horrified.

I explained that polyester webbing WAS washable. So, being a reasonable man, he looked it over, and shortly afterwards he put me in touch with another man who wanted fourteen sets made, of assorted sizes; he was willing to buy me a heavy sewing machine and pay me for making them. And that, gentle readers, is how I turned into a harness maker.

We copied good ideas where we found them. I measured a lot of sets of old harness and a lot of horses. Most of the intended wearers of this new equipment were newly broken Fells and Fell crosses, and they were certainly not the calm product that my blacksmith friend had turned out – they were pretty much just mouthed, harnessed to an exercise cart and let go. By the end of the fourteen sets (I think I only made twelve for him, in fact) I had learnt a huge amount by observation and testing, about what worked and what didn't – because what didn't work, the green horses broke! I sold my own first set and made another for myself. I kept on learning, and applied my learning to what I sold. I still have all the card index cards with customers' horse measurements on, just in case I ever go back to harness making! (And yes, most Fells have the same measurements, within half an inch or so – apart from the variations in girth between Fit and Fat.)

I went on refining, and experimenting, and improving, until locally my harnesses were well known and sometimes you'd go on a drive, or look round the class at a competition, and there were more harnesses of my making than of any other type.

After the Fell mare came the Welsh section C cob. He was a very athletic lad, not the best conformation wise but very fast, clever and keen, and although he was a bit nervous, he soon settled down (I have this gift of laziness which seems to calm nervous horses... sadly I don't do quite as well in galvanizing idle ones!) I used him mainly for driving in local cross country competitions, which he loved and did very well, and my daughter rode him for fun and at a few little local shows.

We'll fast forward here a little to gloss over the purchase of the Fell x Arab colt with the gorgeous legs and the paranoid dislike of strangers.

My present pony, little "Mr T" is a 13.1 black Fell, whom I bought for his kind eyes and nice nature. He was broken to drive already (which was necessary for my nerves after the Fell x Arab!) and we have been together for 11 years now. He isn't as cunning as the Fell x Arab, but he likes to please, and he understands what pleases me, and so long as I don't overdo it he will produce exactly the right goods in the "posh" show ring class, an exercise cart show class, a pleasure driving "do these exercises accurately" class, or a cone driving class, and even (steady, Rob! I know you hate them) a cross country competition. Of course, being a little short legged chap, he doesn't get the times on the marathon and I don't press him to, since what we both enjoy is ducking and diving through the obstacles, so again, we have compromised, in that I don't ask for speed over the course, and he reserves a lot of spirit and gusto for his "games" with the posts and the red and white flags. You only have to look at his ears when he sees them, and you know that for all his short legs, HE thinks that he is a racehorse.

His other skill – oddly – is dressage. I once took him to a local show titled "Best of the Rest" where (as a sort of bet with myself to see if we could do it) I drove him in the exercise carriage in a 20 by 40 metre RIDING size dressage arena, in a ridden dressage class with a riding dressage judge. She placed him 3rd out of 15. I have used him quite a lot for teaching, and for introducing newcomers to driving. I don't do this so much any more, partly through lack of time but also because for every lesson I teach with him, I seem to spend another lesson reminding him that *I* am in charge once again and he can't just slop along taking advantage of the beginner driver ... and these days, because I am driving just to enjoy myself and him and the fresh air, I don't want to have that nice balance altered, which I know is selfish.

It was quite a lot later that I discovered my great-grandfather had been a domestic coachman in Cheshire, though by then I was well "hooked"!

Oh and the other thing I do (this will surprise you) is write, so I wrote a novel about the struggles of horsemen in Victorian England when the new railways decimated the coaching trade. *Coachman.*

Sue in the English Lakes

Intelligence is no defence against one's own stupidity

MR T "THE YES MAN"

T walks away, August 2003

Well, I had a funny morning. T and I have been a team for over 10 years now and I thought I knew all his little foibles. Ha!

As background, we're having our house reroofed and the slaters usually arrive at 8am. I go to work normally at 8:15am and have been working my Fell pony in the evenings (Britain is pretty hot right now so after 8pm is ideal weather for driving – earlier is too hot). But tomorrow I am going to drive at a big show – Lowther Country Fair – which has a very big 3-day driving event. It's run under UK National and Federation Equestre Internationale rules; also known in the USA as a Combined Driving Event. It began today, Friday, but we are competing in the "Private Driving" class tomorrow which is separate from the main event and run under British Driving Society rules. It has a 5 mile drive and a show in the main arena. Mr T and I have been working daily short distances with his new collar to get his shoulders toughened and the collar "broken-in", and I have arranged a day off work today to wash horse, clean brass and trap and load all the gear, you know the story.

I thought I would work him really early today so he'd have done a little before his show bath, and we'd get all that over before the slaters arrived to work on the roof (they worry him ... He's never seen birds that big up there.)

Got him hitched and drove down the road to the field gate. Hopped down to open the gate. Blow me, there he is, following me and rolling one wheel up the gate stoop! So I grab him and push him back and realign him and we walk through OK. Then I have to close the gate; there's stock in the field so the gate has to be shut, but it's a bit tight so he can't turn around so I have to let him stand there, and the reins aren't long enough to reach so I leave those too. By the time I've shut the gate he's slonking off, at that steady, unchanging, going-somewhere Fell pony walk that means his mind is on other things than work ... totally ignoring my commands to to Hoo-hooo STAND. ... No panic, no trotting, just that "I'm off now and be buggered to you" 4-mile-an-hour walk. He finally stopped for me on the other side of the field, but not until he'd put the vehicle sideways on to a 35 degree slope.

It might have been worse: our fields are pretty rocky in places and there are steeper slopes than that! I led him off there, climbed in, worked him, and he went fine, big poncy trot when I wanted it and bending nicely either way; we drove back to the yard and had no trouble with the gate (it's easier going home).

Just goes to show that you can NEVER trust 'em totally. I was lucky not to have been picking up the pieces of my vehicle and worrying about retraining. Wonder what he will think of doing at the show tomorrow …

… and the slaters have still not arrived … maybe they have all gone to the Country Fair!

Sue in the English Lakes

Intelligence is no defence against one's own stupidity.

In defence of Horse Driving Trials (2004)

Rob, after reading your criticism of at Horse Driving Trials (HDT) I must stand up for the standard of driving that I see there in Britain. As an introduction to my points, let me explain that I regularly spectate at Lowther HDT, a big national event with huge entries each year. (I am often there in other capacities too but that's irrelevant.) To fill in the background: There are NO novice classes at Lowther; you have to qualify out of Novice to get into the Singles class there for Horse or Pony; and you have to have driven a single horse or pony in Open level classes to be allowed to drive a pair in ANY National competition.

I will admit that at lower levels in driven eventing, not all is perfect. But to tar the whole sport with the same brush is to reckon without some great talents at the top end, and some wonderful exponents of the art of driving at its best.

> *BUT, a big BUT for recreational drivers, it (a dressage test) does not teach you how to drive in consideration of, and to indicate your intentions to, other road users! Have you ever seen a hand signal in a Combined Driving Event?*

Well, Rob, *yes*, there are requirements for drivers in dressage tests to drive one handed, as they would have to if they were to give a hand signal on the road. Various movements in different tests DO require this, including 20 metre circles at collected trot, and deviations from the outside track, changing the horse's bend twice, on leaving and returning to the track. And, during the cross country phase, carriage drivers are out on the roads and MUST communicate with car drivers and pedestrians whom they encounter, just as we all do when out driving recreationally and meeting traffic on four wheels or two, four legs or two.

> *not possible when the driving style resembles*
> *Cassius Clay taunting Sonny Liston!*

Not every HDT driver drives in this fashion. I am sorry if some people you have seen have driven this way, but you can't extrapolate from those that ALL competitive drivers do so. I can think of a great many drivers who take great pains to persevere with the English coachman style and use it to good effect in the dressage arena of HDTs. Would you like a list? It starts with George Bowman ...

> *if you come driving with me, the first thing I*
> *will show you is how to harness to advantage*
> *(for the horse). I will show you balanced*
> *draught. I will explain how to harness for*
> *draught efficiency, and horse comfort as top*
> *priority. And we will go drive down the road,*
> *with other road users, and also pacing our horse*
> *appropriately, things that just don't happen in a*
> *CDE, where there is no traffic, and you are*
> *driving to a set pace.*

Again, Rob, you misunderstand the purpose of the HDT. It was based on the principle of the coaching era where horses had to bring the coach in on time over a set stage of 10 miles or so (though if they were early, there wasn't then a vet asking how it was done or checking for abuses). In a HDT you adjust your speed for the terrain, to come in within a window of time. That means where the going is excellent you can stretch out, and where it is poorer you are more conservative. You are not (or should not be) batting along at full speed the whole time regardless of the conditions underfoot. If the going gets difficult on the whole course, the technical delegate will adjust the required times accordingly.

> *... every time you drive, it will be the same*
> *thing, horse comfort and efficiency, pacing him*

for the drive, taking turns correctly, fitting in
with the traffic. You are not going to get ANY of
that in a CDE!

Again, *yes* – you are going to get quite a lot of this, in British conditions, because often several of the phases, including the fast Section C trot, take place on public roads and tracks. I'd take your point about balanced draught and horse comfort and efficiency, but even so, there are HDT competitors who drive in full neck collars and set good examples.

> *Vehicle choice, well please believe me the CDE*
> *vehicle, and a good recreational vehicle are*
> *miles and miles apart ... You won't see a good*
> *rec vehicle at a CDE!*

I'd tend to agree with you, at the levels where people are compelled to comply with FEI standards and drive their single horses/ponies to four wheelers; the tendency to go with breast collar harness and the low line of draught does make for poor efficiency. But see above ... and when I take part in small local events I drive using the same harness and carriage that I use for my everyday work, properly balanced, with a true line of draught to the axle of my carriage from a well fitted neck collar.

> *... dressage can be very impressive, but you can*
> *practise it every day, in a quiet, not repetitive way,*
> *in your drive to town, you don't need an arena! But*
> *rather than rote learning, try making decisions that*
> *are relevant to the moment, and carry them out*
> *correctly.*

Yes Rob, I agree that dressage is simply good training (which is what the French word means) and that a well mannered horse will probably turn in a good dressage test. Prince Philip's original vision for the driven dressage was that it should resemble figure skating, testing accuracy of paces and accuracy of figures to reveal good basic training and good driving on the day. Training a horse for a dressage test in a HDT (as for a ridden test) should NOT be rote learning of the patterns and anyone who trains in that manner either has very bored and resistant horses or very stupid ones that will put up with it… Fells, I can tell you, will not! Yes, I train successfully for regular, rhythmic paces just going down the road... OTOH that doesn't mean that nobody can learn anything from watching a dressage test.

Go on Rob, pick the bones outa that! :-) You know I love to tease you.

Sue in the English Lakes

The Tebay Rail disaster, 15 February 2004

It probably isn't quite fair to post this as a "progress" post, as my Fell (Mr T) is 17 and thinks he knows it all, but we have not done much work during the winter – maybe 4 outings since October 2003 – so a nice fine sunny Saturday and Sunday here in England have seen us rubbing off the dust in more ways than one!

OK, the harness was clean – but Mr T was concreted over with mud, and his mane, tail and feather tastefully decorated with dead weeds from happy rolling in the paddock … and the little robin who roosts in the shed has been pooping all over the cart in spite of its waterproof covers. So we were not at our spick and span best when we ventured out on Saturday (yesterday).

Things worked out OK though. We went a mile down the road and a mile back and sorted out the annual Spring argument about who defines the pace, as in, do we stand and update our mental database of local objects, or do we go forward? So we got that out of the way early and with no spectators (it looks so bad when dust rises from your pony's coat as you give that artificial aid …)

Sunday has been another bag of worms! Nothing to do with the pony who, having got over the annual Spring argument yesterday, behaved splendidly. I drove out around 10:30 am and immediately found that our normally very quiet local road was like Piccadilly Circus, with traffic coming not in the usual ones and twos every half hour, but in fives and sixes every few minutes. When I realised I'd counted 5 police cars in a mile of walking, it began to dawn on my dim brain that something might just be going on that was out of the ordinary. By then we were about 1.5 miles from home so I thought turning back might be the best idea. We met more cars, and pickups, and police cars, and even a motorbike (Mr T is usually afraid of motorbikes but he just stood with his neck up and stiff, and drew back his lower lip, and waited while the bike went by. I have become very familiar with the sight of his lower incisors as motorbikes approach; also the springy adrenalised trot that follows their passing).

I met some of my neighbours out for a walk and commented on the huge increase in traffic. They told me that there had been a terrible accident on the railway line. A tracklaying wagon had been allowed to get loose during maintenance work in the early morning and had run four miles until it smashed into another work gang at Tebay. This stretch of line (Shap) is one of the steepest grades in the country so the wagon must have been going one hell of lick. Four men (at least one from the local village) were killed, another is in hospital and three more were injured but allowed home. The wagon went another mile before it actually stopped. The police had closed the main road to allow all the emergency services to the scene – which is on the edge of Tebay village.

All the diverted traffic was coming past our house and along the roads on which the pony and I were driving. It made for a good training experience, but it was one I would rather have done without, than have had those men killed and injured.

As one of my neighbours said, "Aye, live each day as if it was your last, because YOU NEVER KNOW."

Sue in the English Lakes

Intelligence is no defence against one's own stupidity

A young carriage driver, 6 June 2004

My young neighbour Christopher is coming on a treat as a carriage driver. He's keen to ride as well, and has had a go, but he is not yet secure in the saddle, which means carriage driving is really the safer option for him to do daring things like trotting and (gasp) cantering. We have been out for a couple of drives, learning about rhythm, contact, and how to relax his back, hands and shoulders and really feel when he's communicating with the pony's mouth and what is coming back to him from there. We also learned about balancing the carriage up and down hill and discussed whether certain gradients on our route were safe to drive up or down. He thought one might not be, as he always brakes down it when riding his bike, but Mr T copes with it OK.

Today Chris started to learn to steer more accurately by building and then driving through a simple cones course. He's still driving two handed at the moment but I shall be teaching him to drive in English coachman style before long (in the USA that translates into "Achenbach" of course; but here in Cumbria we just call it "coachman"). It seemed to me that coachman style and contact were two concepts so he would find it easier to learn them separately, and I wanted him to understand contact – feel – before I wanted him to attempt classic rein handling.

He's learning the right order of harnessing up and unharnessing, and the names of the harness parts (and remembering them too), and in between all that we tell each other terrible horror stories, and learn the names of the wild flowers and animals we see while we're out driving, and discuss the ethics of such things as myxomatosis (he is an unusually tenderhearted child, so I didn't push the financial details of bunnies vs sheep too strongly; kind 12 yr old boys are hard enough to find!).

If only my daytime students – the "cool" 18 year olds who are studying computing – could string reasoned thoughts together in as articulate a fashion as my weekend driving student, who is so much their junior!

Sue in the English Lakes

RUBY "THE MAGNIFICENT"

I have a new horse, 8 August 2004

I have a new horse. "Ruby" is a bright bay Fell mare, 13.3 hands high; and when she arrived she was 78" around the middle – we are working on that! She has a lovely eye, and a quick brain, and the big thing is, she has been handled right from the start by people who understand Fells and their clever and keen nature. Her owner said she was "always a free spirit" and many years later I happened across this photograph (*next page*) of her at Windermere show, when she'd been recaptured after enjoying a solo "jolly" round the showfield.

At the moment, aged 9, she is a typical cob shape – head like a lady, bottom like a cook – or as more than one person has said, "she's built like a brick outhouse!" She has bred 2 foals and although she had been broken to ride she was just being a pasture ornament and so came up for sale. Don't assume though that this mare is a dead-broke, placid plod – far from it; she is a long striding, quick stepping, BIG pony.

I took a big gamble on her as she was only "backed, ridden and lightly shown", not broken to drive; and I have not ridden for some time. But, she's a Fell, and bred from some similar lines to my first mare who was a smashing driver and is STILL doing it well, if more slowly, at the age of 24; also carrying lines going back to relatives of my present old boy Mr T, who just wants to please you; so it was a pretty good bet she would take to it.

I took delivery last Sunday night. Ruby was raging in season, so she jumped into the horsebox thinking her birthday had arrived! She was a bit confused when we got to Tebay, because though there was indeed a stallion about, responding to her whinnying, she was immediately taken indoors and didn't get to meet him. So for the last 7 days, she has been dieting (a little), listening to the stallion shouting (quite a bit), and learning (A LOT) about carriage driving. The yard where she is staying is about 4 miles from my house.

DISCLAIMER

What follows here is a true record of what we've seen happen this week. It's NOT a recommendation of a schedule for breaking every horse. It's just an amazing example of an intelligent, mature animal learning extremely fast because she already had secure foundations. Read on with that in mind!

My friend David Trotter has tamed and taught a lot of utterly wild Fell ponies over the years – unhandled, straight off the high fells with almost no experience of humans. Thanks to his expertise and confidence, and Ruby's maturity and intelligence, we – Ruby, David, our helper Chaantallaimy, and I – have made huge strides this week.

By Monday night Ruby had worn and accepted all the major parts of the harness, including the crupper, which must have given her a bit of a shock; in the last five years, she has only ever been transported away from home to the stallion – so a crupper will not have been quite what she expected when a strange man lifted her tail. She long-rein-lunged to David's voice commands, and he said she hardly needed the reins. We think that – since her previous owner had bought her first Fell from David – that David had taught *her* the commands for him, and *she* had then taught the same to the young mare, and now the mare was working with the originator of the commands and everything had come full circle!

By Tuesday night Ruby had stood between the shafts, in an open bridle, and been walked about in David's vehicle inside the building. It's a low exercise cart made of piping with pneumatic tyres – not what I would choose to use for regular work over any distance, but easy to handle and very easy to get in and out of. It has lots of room for the horse's ribs and hips, though the shafts were a bit of a "nip fit" at the tugs for her "plumpitude" – but she thought nothing of it. By evening she had gone steadily down the yard to the (quiet) road and back with the (empty) cart, being led by David with Chaantallaimy handling the plough cords "just in case" and keeping an eye open for any traffic. THAT was the bit that shocked me when I heard it... going out in the carriage after a day and a half... but I know David would not have done it if Ruby had not shown him she was taking everything in her stride.

She did the same again on Wednesday, and then went a bit further down the road in long reins without the carriage. You could see her thinking things through and making sense of what was going on. We were all quietly excited and pleased about her progress.

Thursday, David's busy day travelling on his fruit-and-veg round, I worked with Ruby in the same pattern as David, with Chaantallaimy helping us and David supervising for the first twenty minutes until we got out of the yard (safely away from the stallion); then with Chaantallaimy "leading" – in reality just walking beside with the attached lead-rope in her hand, to give the mare confidence – we drove down the road for a couple of hundred yards, and then back, with me sitting in the cart and giving Ruby the commands to walk on, turn, halt and stand still. Then we took the cart off and went for a really long walk with Ruby on the long reins. She met traffic and passed excited young stock in fields, and met another horse in a carriage, and she behaved sensibly. We kept telling her how clever she was! We kept talking to her, reinforcing all those commands in "my" voice rather than David's. She didn't want us to leave at the end of the session; she wanted to go on doing things, because that way she'd have our company.

Friday, again she harnessed and yoked no problem, and this time I got into the cart and drove her over the same route as we'd walked on Thursday; up and down a decent hill to the next stableyard and back, accompanied by Chaantallaimy on foot; she passed the daft young horses and traffic and people with dogs, all in her stride, if somewhat talkatively. Then, in long reins without the cart, we walked to the motorway roundabout to watch the heavy traffic. She had one minor tizz about a big truck that revved as it went by, but nothing else – other than wanting to eat grass as she walked!

Yesterday David drove her the same distance, without a leader because Chaantallaimy was then sitting in the cart beside him!

Today Ruby whinnied when she heard me arrive (I think she had eaten all her hay <VBG>). I harnessed and yoked her up by myself and drove her about inside the building (yes it is quite big, but not big enough for a horse to get up any speed if problems occur). She has learnt the routine now and is feeling pleased with herself, and after a few circuits she was waiting for Chaantallaimy to appear to open the sliding doors and let her be going! However, our young lady was not there, because she was spectating at the Lowther driving trials with David. Ruby was being so helpful that I might well have been tempted to take her out by myself, but the stallion yesterday had been getting rather frustrated because this new "bit of totty" was being led in and out under his nose every day and she wasn't allowed to have anything to do with him! Although she is not in season any more, David had made me promise not to try to handle the sliding door and the gate and the mare and the cart and the potential stallion advances on my own, so I didn't (damn, I thought I WAS Superwoman). David has now come back from the driving trials (which finish today) so I daresay that Ruby will be going down the road again with him and Chaantallaimy, as I write.

Well, I really didn't expect to have so much to report, when I came home with my very sweaty in-season mare, only LAST Sunday.

Like I said earlier, "don't try this at home, kids"... this is remarkable progress by a very intelligent and mentally well balanced, mature and physically strong mare, who already knew the commands we were using, and who is bred to co-operate as well as thinking things through for herself. She was ready to go on and learn. We're not rushing her; SHE is pushing US.

The other good news – progress of a different kind – is that my older Fell gelding, who has been a touch lame for six weeks, positively asked me to yoke him up this morning. He whickered and squared up for the carriage as soon as he saw I was bringing it out of the shed! He walked sound and trotted sound on the road. He IS showing his age though, and will be more than happy to let Ruby take his place in the public eye, and himself retire into being a much loved and respected schoolmaster.

Ruby is progressing, 11 August 2004

The new mare, Ruby, is proving a real gem (excuse the pun). She is driving out in a mullen mouth Kimblewick, and the "half cup" racing blinkers that I like for everyday exercise. She is proving game and kind and relatively unflappable.

Here's the current turnout. It's called "I'll slim into it" – ladies, you all know where I'm coming from here.... She's just practising in this shot; able to see the vehicle behind her and know exactly what is going on. Obviously, I am also checking the harness and vehicle fit. Photographs are a great help.

Several things will be improved shortly when she has lost enough weight:

The shafts can drop on the backband, which will let the carriage ride level. At present they would rub too much on Ruby's rib area! I could widen them, but I think she will drop a lot of weight once I get her home and start doing longer drives, and she will be able to go out in the pasture and play with my other Fell. (At present she is stabled to keep her away from the stallion in my friend's pasture.)

I will be using this vehicle for both my Fells on occasion, and it fits Mr T well, so I don't want to do much more than I have already done, in lengthening the shafts to their maximum. At the moment, from the box seat Ruby looks like a moving bay sofa, but by golly she can go! Yet, she is very sensitive to what I am asking her to do, so I am really looking forward to having her muscled up and fit!

Dropping the shafts will bring the swingletree more into the correct line of draught. At the moment there's a break there. It will also correct the breeching line. Balanced draught won't happen till I get Ruby into a full neck collar. I have one that I believe will fit her a few weeks down the line, but at present her crest is too big for it and I don't want to buy yet another just for a few weeks' work (I have acquired five collars over the years and although I am loath to part with any I could do without buying a sixth.) Hence the wide, well padded (and quite high) breast collar. An old friend of mine, Fred Todd, who is a highly experienced whip once said, "Fit your breast collar where you think it should go – then lift it two holes higher. God put the windpipe well out of the way – it's much less vulnerable than the point of the shoulder." My breast collar always looks higher than people expect, but I never have a sore or jibbing horse … and I have, as I say, lots of neck collars!

The seat is currently set forward on the cart to allow my assistant to stand on the backstep. That too will balance better when Ruby has lost enough weight to allow the shafts down a bit more!

The other amusing thing that I have found out about Ruby is that she loves massage and manicures. She is a "posh girl" who ASKS to have her hair done and be groomed, and goes all droopy while you do it. And when you've gone round her once she asks you to do it again! Talk about "My Little Pony"... I am used to Fell geldings who prefer to be scruffy and think hoof oil is not "butch". It will be quite a novelty to have a pony who might actually enjoy being bathed to go to a show.

Sue in the English Lakes

Intelligence is no defence against one's own stupidity

Drive with Ruby at Tebay, 12 August 2004

It has been raining. That's an understatement – Britain has been undergoing the aftermath of Hurricane/Tropical Storm Alex, whose huge volume of water has been suspended over us for several days, held up in its northeastern travel by high pressure over Scandinavia. It rained solidly for 48 hours and put down over 6" of rain on Monday and Tuesday. Today it rained half-heartedly all morning but by lunchtime things looked OK for driving.

I went over to Tebay, to the stable where Ruby is staying at present.

She is already yoked up when I arrive; my friend David likes to teach them standing still by leaving them tied up in his building, with the carriage and harness in place, but no blinkers, so they can see exactly what is going on all around and gain confidence that though it may be irksome, it doesn't actually hurt if you go with the flow. Ruby has " got" this bit and is perfect to yoke and unyoke, but she is impatient for action once you go out, and is inclined to shuffle and dance backwards and forwards. We need to work on this.

I change the riding bridle for my "racing half cup" blinkers, correct the fit of a few harness components (it's my harness and vehicle, so David is less familiar with it than I am), drive carefully out of the building, and then with Chaantallaimy on the back step we head off down the yard.

"Whoa, stand still, Ruby," while Chaantallaimy opens the gate. Ruby is shuffling and wants to go out and work, but she holds the bit gently and waits for me to say she can go. She doesn't go back or sideways, which is an improvement. Well done, Ruby. We wait a little longer than usual after Chaantallaimy gets up on the back step, before moving off. Ruby is compliant. That's even better. What a clever girl.

We drive down onto the road and turn left instead of David's usual right. We walk round the bus stop and the big road sign in a nice circle, then straighten up past the stable yard and set off along the road to Gaisgill. Ruby is really striding along, her broad bay back like a table filling the shafts, and her tail swinging freely. Why am I excited? all we are doing is WALKING. But this is a walk that is worth savouring. She is so relaxed, yet full of go. I can hardly believe that this is the mare who knew nothing about driving only 11 days ago. Her ears are forward, her mouth is soft. She is really enjoying herself. We pull steadily up a long rise, and breech down the next to pass Lynn Winder's stables and Cocklake Farm. Ruby has got used to the young horses in the field trotting down to watch her go by, so she doesn't whinny this time and goes on swinging along, occasionally doing a little soft-shoe shuffle to show that she wants to go faster. I know if I let her she would accelerate gradually and powerfully like a big automatic car. But she holds the bit gently and settles with a good grace to that long, quick and powerful walk.

The roadside gullies are full of rushing water; she flicks an ear, but she was raised on these fells, and knows the noise of running water after storms is nothing to be afraid of. A heron, full of fish from the River Lune, flaps lazily over above us. The clouds are a mix of dark and pale grey, low and tumbled and half threatening, but the rain holds off.

Ruby's still green and unschooled, and she tends to look left and drift right; I spend a lot of time keeping level reins and the whip softly tapping her right flank to make her walk in the proper place on the road. A Land Rover and trailer comes along, and we have to pull in tight to the left hand verge to let it pass; she is steady and attentive. She has travelled in such trailers herself and knows they are not dangerous.

We pass the stables. There's a faint deviation of her body as we pass the yard gate; we have turned in here to come home on other occasions. But with a word from me and a touch on her side from the whip, she accepts that this time we are going further and not stopping. "Hmm, well, that is interesting; after all, perhaps there will be other horses around if we go on?" Here's a nice level stretch of road; I ask Ruby to trot, and off she goes, smooth and powerful, really enjoying herself. We're now into entirely fresh territory; everything is new to her. At the next farm, Raw End, she is a little surprised to see a gang of Shetland ponies all trotting up to the fence to snuff at her as she goes by, but she holds her line on the road – just turns her head to look, and goes straight on. We walk again, as there is a tractor and trailer coming; I talk to her, and she keeps going, listening, trusting. She doesn't rush into trot after it passes, but goes on walking, walking. Past the sheep building at Redgill, with the fat lambs dashing about the yard and the pen gates rattling; another Land Rover and trailer draws up there, behind us, but she just turns her ears to listen and does not alter her stride.

Coming up now is the green horse's big test: Gaisgill Row Farm, where the grass verges abound in spooky stuff. Big slabs of marble intended for kitchen worktops, bought up when the local workshop closed; demounted truck-container bodies with fertiliser stacked inside; tractors; implements; uneaten bales of silage from last summer with frayed plastic wrapping trailing from them; wheelbarrows; roofing materials. Ruby doesn't even appear to see them. She whinnies at a mare and foal but keeps going. Past the cattle building and the house and the milking parlour and the feed hopper, and through the puddles on the road she strides out confidently. "If you say so, then we'll do it." This mare, as grannies say of confident babies, "has been here before". We walk to the next road end, then turn round and head homeward. We have walked perhaps a mile and a half, with short steady trots. She is warmed up and absolutely rock steady, so it is time to think about what else we might ask. I am still keeping her to a straight line on her own side of the road; she is a little left-bent all the time, but that will fade with steady work and schooling.

Chaantallaimy comments on how I change the pitch of my voice to give Ruby commands. I had not noticed it, because I do it by habit after driving for so many years, but I explain that this helps Ruby to know when I mean her to take notice and do something, and when I am just chatting to a passenger in the vehicle. Chaantallaimy also says that my touches of the whip are probably hardly noticeable through Ruby's thick hide; again I explain that I know she is sensitive and will be feeling what I am doing. After all, she can feel a little fly landing, so why not my whip? We talk about Ruby's drift to the right hand side of the road; "You're not in America, Ruby!" Maybe we should have a word that means, "Drive on the left"? Chaantallaimy suggests, "England!"

We walk back past Gaisgill Row; again, Ruby takes absolutely no notice of the assorted decorations on the grass verge. A domestic cat hides with flattened tortoiseshell ears behind a tuft of grass in one of the steep fields, and watches us ride by. We go through the dips and bends by the sheep building, and the road is clear, so I press Ruby to trot. Again, that smooth surge of power, and off she goes up the long rise to Raw End Farm. The Shetlands have decided this is no fun, so they ignore her. We crest the rise and Ruby comes out of draught and feels the breeching. This time she is a tiny bit unbalanced; the cart is now pushing her and she wants to go still faster so she breaks into a gentle canter. The hops get bigger and the bum is coming up higher – "Ruby, no, we're not going to do this." I take rein, softly, and she comes back into my hand, steadying to a trot, nice and level again. Good girl. Clever girl. What a star.

We walk for a little way, then try another trot. This is cut short by another Land Rover and trailer appearing where the road is narrow; Ruby stands quietly close in to the hedge, with Chaantallaimy by her head just in case she steps the wrong way when the trailer is close. But Ruby just watches; she doesn't move. Chaantallaimy gets back on the step after the trailer has passed, I ask Ruby to walk on, and away she goes. We pass Cocklake Farm where John and Ann Cooper are doing something energetic down a drain, with a tractor running machinery from its power takeoff. Ruby doesn't break stride as she goes by; reared on a farm, this is all old hat to her.

Past the stables, the young horses trot alongside, sploshing through wet patches, rattling the rushes, but she ignores them and strides up the hill. I ask her to trot, and she goes forward smoothly. It is fascinating to feel how she tests what I will allow; if you shut your eyes you can feel the power turn on and off as she goes forward, then feels the bit and subtly tones it down; back and forth we converse as she trots up the slope, over the top, and for a little way down the far side. She's "got it" now; she already knows that she must hold the cart downhill when she's walking, and now she understands that she must not allow it to suggest that she goes faster, even if she's trotting; the trot remains a trot. We reach the level and walk again. Let's play round the recycling centre; we make circles round the road sign, walk up the grass verges and over gravel lay-bys. She is calm about it all, although the right handed circles fall in rather. Schooling, and miles on the clock, will cure that.

We arrive at the yard, and the Welsh Cob stallion has come down from the top of the pasture to see whose footfalls he can hear. Chaantallaimy takes my whip to chase him off so we can get into the yard. Ruby has time to practise standing still. She knows we have finished our work; but she can see the gate is closed. Ten yards from the gate, she is standing quiet and relaxed. She is waiting intelligently to be allowed back in, to have the carriage taken off and be given hay and water. I repeat the Stand Still command, and praise her for being so good. She waits for the gate to be opened, and on my word she takes the carriage carefully into the building.

We unyoke and unharness her, and I brush her off. She has done a steady three miles and is barely warm. When I've done brushing her, she nibbles me and asks for more, so I give her a really good working over with the body brush. Her eyes half close in bliss; she leans into my brush strokes; "brush my mane out please.... clean my face.... this is better than food...."

David arrives just as we are tidying up. "Had a good drive? Has she been good?"

"Yes, she was perfect – this is what holidays are about.... "

Sue in the English Lakes

Intelligence is no defence against one's own stupidity

Ruby at Raisbeck, 15 August 2004

Ruby is coping unbelievably well with her transition from "pasture ornament with occasional rides on the fell" (hills and moorland) to "carriage pony".

I drove her on Wednesday, Thursday and Friday, each time going a little further, scaling up from a mile out and back to nearly two miles out and back. Yesterday however I was helping (making contacts and stewarding) at the Fell Pony Society breed show; nearly 200 ponies from all over Britain were there, competing for our breed's top honours on its home ground in Cumbria. I knew it was going to be a long, hot day, satisfying but tiring, so I agreed that David and Chaantallaimy should work Ruby while I was away. They drove her to Gaisgill and back, down into Tebay village to the motorway roundabout, and then into the truck stop among the wagons and coaches! David's phone call, reporting this morning, was almost lyrical – not only does she learn fast and want to work with you but she is "bomb proof". For me, that was her last big test – if she will stand all that big traffic and the weekend motorbikes, she is ready to come home. (Shame

I am back at work Monday! but it's only for a week and then I have a whole 2 weeks off when we can play.)

This morning (nursing my sunburn from the day at the show) I turned up early at David's buildings to get Ruby ready to go out. She had eaten all her hay, and whinnied to me when she heard the gate – "I am starving to death in here, bring me food!" I brought her out of the box and put her on the "chock" tie where we yoke up, and gave her a handful of hay to settle her while I brushed her off. She has lost a lot of weight and is beginning to muscle up, so the quality underneath is starting to show through!

I made some adjustments to the harness (no bad thing with an impatient pony!) – changed a couple of the Swedish hooks for stronger carabinas where I've had to extend breeching straps, and adding short chains to the carabinas on the trace ends. Everything is more flexible for fitting now and though the harness would win no prizes in the show ring I am content that it is strong enough for its job and is adjusted as comfortably for Ruby as I can manage, until she is slim enough to try a full collar. My biggest collar (a 20" x 8") sat 6" up her neck when we tried it on Friday, and she was extremely puzzled by the whole business but went along with it as usual – only doing a small levade as we swivelled the collar at her throat the first time!

I phoned Chaantallaimy to come and ride with me. We yoked Ruby up and checked everything for fit; the shafts now have room to swing a little either side of her, which is a very promising sign that the work and the restricted grazing are doing their job. Ruby was delighted to go out and danced around as we opened the sliding door and the gate. We walked a short way to settle her, then moved up to trot and away she went, ears pricked and stiff as horns, up the first of the gentle slopes and down to Lynn's stables. She held back the carriage at trot without fussing. However, as we drove on towards Raw End she started to wander about the road, and the ears were distinctly saying, "I am fed up with this route. I would like to get into the hedge and eat the ash leaves. I came this way yesterday and the day before and the day before that. I know we are going to turn around somewhere and come home the same way, and *it's boring.*" With some horses, this would have sparked a major resistance. Fair enough! She couldn't know that we had a longer and more interesting route planned! We over-rode her dissatisfaction by simply insisting, gently but firmly, and she fell in with our wishes and went on pretty smoothly although you could tell she was still feeling miffed. (This is a "pony mare" condition, occurring when she doesn't agree with your orders!)

We reached Gaisgill, where the slow, quiet and narrow Old Road meets the New Road, which is straight and fast; she stood sensibly and waited for a gap in the traffic, into which we could cross and turn smartly right for a hundred yards before rejoining the Old Road as it goes to Kelleth. Here, she was on new ground – and her attitude completely changed. Gone was the "miffed" expression; she went into the collar with a will. It's a mile-long steady pull up from the River Lune at Rayne Bridge to the turning for Raisbeck, and she trotted the whole way eagerly, taking in all the new sights and sounds. Chaantallaimy and I just sat and grinned at the energy she generated.

"You didn't tell me we were going somewhere new! Wow, this is good! This is exciting!"

We walked up the next long slope through Wain Gap, and then walked and trotted alternately over the shallowly rolling limestone landscape to Raisbeck. By now she was getting a little tired, but she was relaxed and walking with a swing. After 4 miles, and 50 minutes, we turned in at Newlands Farm. She couldn't believe her luck when she saw that the fields contained Fell mares and foals, and when we got into the yard and met four ridden Fell ponies coming out, she was sure she had arrived in heaven!

Because of the Breed Show taking place yesterday, there were several Fell breeders staying with Mike and Di Slack, the owners of Newlands. Everyone was sitting in the yard around white plastic picnic tables.

Peter Moor from Switzerland (*above*), and George Guy from Gloucestershire, came to look Ruby over and talk about harness and carriage and show classes. As always happens with such gatherings, we all had our own opinions on how things should fit, about the length of a whip, about how to prevent flies bothering our horses and the best way to trim chestnuts and ergots; while Ruby, the fidget at setting off, stood like an old cab horse and listened to all the "words of wisdom" with a patient expression: "I've heard it all before." Of course everyone wanted to know how old she was and how long I had owned her and how long she had been broken to drive. I was proud to be able to say that I had bought Ruby exactly 15 days ago, and before that she had never been driven. And their comments were all the same: there's nothing like a grown-up horse with some riding experience to learn quickly and get the job right first time. No three-year-old silliness here!

George Guy said at last, "Well, I like your pony, Sue. I like her so much I'm going to offer you 500 pounds for her." (This was a quarter of what I had paid for her.)

I just grinned at him and said, "That's damned generous of you George, and I can't think why I'm not tempted by your handsome offer!"

"Well, you've got to try, haven't you?" he retorted, unabashed. "Same as with a woman!"

Ruby, resting one hind-leg nonchalantly, took no notice of these sallies. She washed her mouth politely in the big yellow bucket of water that Di offered her, but did not want to drink. Chaantallaimy and I accepted a beaker of orange squash, and I walked Ruby round the yard to look at the picnic tables and the people sitting at them. Her side-passing to turn in the yard earned much admiration, but as she's had to do this from day one in David's building, she didn't preen herself too much about it; it was "old hat". Having helpfully nibbled up some weeds from the path, she tried licking the top of one table, but didn't find anything nice to eat on it. Someone thoughtfully moved it away from her.... noticing the black soil-smudges her nose was leaving.

After that, we decided we'd better set off back to Tebay, so we said our goodbyes and thank-yous, and turned Ruby up the farm lane back to the road.

With four miles under her girth and three still to go home (we took a shorter route, but with a steep hill to go down), I asked Ruby to walk on and she swung along, nice and relaxed. The warm morning let fall some spots of rain, so Chaantallaimy and I sheltered together under the light waterproof jacket I had brought with me, but the shower quickly passed, and we re-emerged giggling.

We meet little traffic, and Ruby takes no notice of it anyway. The left-bend in her body is disappearing, and the drift to the right of the carriageway with it; it reappears towards the end of the drive, but I don't make an issue of it; she's been a star today. We come to the New Road again and she stands like a rock while the traffic whizzes by, until we see a gap and she pops into a fast trot to take advantage of it and get across safely. We walk and trot, following the Old Road back from Gaisgill to Tebay, gradually letting the walks get longer and the trots shorter, so she arrives home cool. Again, her "standing still" at the gate into the yard is very good. Again, she is pleased to have the harness taken off and be groomed – she leans onto the brush. I rub her shoulders with methylated spirit to cool them; she's not so keen on the smell, but is distracted by a handful of hay from the net that Chaantallaimy is stuffing for her.

Between us we look after Ruby, as her reward for the fun we have had this morning and the pride we have in her progress. Chaantallaimy leads Ruby out to graze outside the main pasture (Rupert, the Welsh Cob stallion, is still keen to make her acquaintance but luckily today the other two mares in the pasture are coming into season and he is otherwise occupied.) I muck out the box and put down fresh bedding – you may think that as I'm the elder of the party by more years than I care to count, I've organised this the wrong way round, but Chaantallaimy is such a help to me and so keen, it would be mean to make her do the mucking out today!

When we bring Ruby back in, she dives into her haynet as though the grass verges had been bare and she were starving (both untrue) and so we leave her, totally engrossed and absolutely not caring whether we stay or go.

What has Ruby learnt today? That even if she thinks the route is boring, there may be nice surprises in store; that she can't have her own way through being sulky (though the display was a very very mild one!). I hope she has continued to find carriage driving fun.

What have I learnt today? That Ruby, like most of the Fells I know, is quick and clever and does not like being bored with repetition. That she is very nimble and capable of putting the carriage exactly where I ask her. That she loves being praised, and if we forget, she is less willing! That she is getting fitter, and is thoroughly on top of "this driving lark". And that the next instalment should involve Ruby driving home to my own stables....

Ruby at home: A work in Progress, 29 August 2004

Ruby, the "hunk of Fell pony", is now at home. I left her at my friend's place during the week when I had to be in work, so that she would get some hacking out under saddle while I didn't have so much time, but as soon as the end of that week came around, I organised Chaantallaimy to groom for me and we set off to bring Ruby home IMMEDIATELY!

When I arrived at the yard I could see a small problem – Ruby, in her gallops up the fell, had loosened a shoe, and she'd cast it in the field. It wasn't unexpected, as this set (her first full set) had been on perhaps 9 weeks and her feet were getting quite long. However, knowing that her feet are pretty hard (more on this theme later!) I wasn't too bothered about driving her home with a shoe missing.

She was, as usual, delighted to see us arrive, and stood happily while we harnessed up and put her to. Given the missing shoe, I opted to take the shorter 4 mile route rather than the longer 5.5 mile one, and so we turned left through the village of Tebay. I have to say, this mare is a Christian as far as manners goes. There was a wedding at the chapel, with cars and crowds of people on the roadside; she just took it all in and kept on walking. The road was quite busy (it was mid-day Saturday), and we had to cross the railway and the motorway on a big bridge with mesh sides, so she saw all the traffic pouring along under her, but never bothered. Then we got onto the narrow side road that leads to my house, and she pulled away up and over the hill – it's a killer, but she just kept on plugging away. Chaantallaimy hopped off to ease the load. We planned to give her a breather halfway up but met a car coming down which promptly pulled off and blocked the lay-by I had meant to use... but Ruby didn't want to stop anyway. Wherever we were going, she wanted to get there! I have to admire the brains of this mare; she is all that my old mare Rosie was in the brains department, and higher class physically. She is what I hoped to get when I bought Kestrel (a Fell x Arab) as a foal; beauty, brains and power. I am just amazed by her. Of course, the big hill knocked some stuffing out of her, as she is just not used to handling a carriage up slopes like that, but she behaved beautifully and did not bother about meeting the traffic on that narrow road, not even 2 motorbikes (which have always been Mr T's Big Horror).

She was blowing hard by the time we got to the top, but coped well. She held the cart back going down the other side and trotted up the final pull to our yard. We took her out of the cart, unharnessed her and brushed her, and put her in the stable with a haynet (which she immediately dived into).

I brought Mr T round from the little paddock and put him in the adjoining box. He was gobsmacked – another pony! and a Fell! and FEMALE! He must have stood there most of the rest of the day, reaching out to touch her, as though he just couldn't believe it unless his nose was resting on her. Ruby, surprisingly, didn't do much squeaking and stamping, but she did tell him a few times that there were more important things in life, like hay. She is such a chunk, she almost makes him look slight, and yet he isn't. She is still slimming hugely; she has lost at least 6" off her girth line in the last 2 weeks and looks all the better for it. She was 78" round the girth when I got her and must be down to 72". All the fat was width, so she doesn't look much different in side-on shots, but the new riding-saddle girth I bought (52" long) had to go back and be swapped for a 46" one before I ever used it! If she goes on slimming she will fit into the 44" one T is currently using.

She was tired out when I looked in on her after supper; snoozing with her chin on the windowsill. Rosie used to doze off sometimes with her chin bone on my shoulder... amazingly heavy, those big bony heads!

Ruby and T have hardly had a cross word so far, although she is currently the Boss Lady. And WHAT a lady ... she has been so good. We have driven out solo twice, and once with Chaantallaimy as groom. I was working on Standing Still yesterday, and today she was foot-perfect whenever I asked her for stillness. I worked her in the field by the river, with some cones set out, to see how balanced she was on smooth turns; she wants to turn quickly at present and over steers. However, we walked and trotted through a few pairs of cones, and then went for a little drive (with one eye on the weather – stormy clouds and rain coming from Shap area!) She attacked the hill towards Roundthwaite well, so I did not take her right to the top, but stopped halfway up and brought her back, as she was blowing quite hard. She is tremendously willing (and FAST!), but still not completely fit of course.

A day or two later we drove the 5 mile triangle between here, the junction down to Orton village, and Scout Green (along the riverside). Chaantallaimy came as groom. Ruby seems to understand now that "England" means "drive on the left!" I think she is more hyped up when Chaantallaimy is there, as you might expect with a 17 yr old. I don't mean she was "like an old dog" with me on my own, by any means, but just sensible and willing. My husband Graham comes out onto the yard when I am on my own, to see me out and see me back in safely with her. I think she charms him with her big brown eyes. She is such a Posh Pony (and amazingly clean compared to T who has always been a greasy, untidy scruff, dearly though I love him. And she is tidy in the stable too, a very big advantage to any owner!)

Danny the farrier came on Monday and put new shoes on her. He was most complimentary about her and also about her feet – "A bit of quality this time eh Sue!" Big grins all round. Watching how hard Danny had to work to cut her feet back and rasp them, compared with doing the same with T's feet, the quality was very obvious. "I could shoe feet like this all day. They're the kind of feet you dream about shoeing." I never worked T for long unshod, but I bet you could do miles with Ruby's tough slate-blue hooves.

There was still plenty of "foot" left after her drive from Tebay to home and a couple of quiet miles out and back on Sunday.

She has only been home with me for 9 days but she has fitted right in. T has got over his unreserved admiration stage, and is now torn between thinking she is going off and leaving him, and being jealous because she eats faster than he does, and so she MUST be getting something *nicer!* and *more of it!* She gets straight into eating hay, and she polishes off all her feed before he is halfway through (though feed, in this context, means enough to make her eat up the wormer... about three tablespoonfuls.) So now, although T is fond of her, and they whinny when they are parted and reunited, he also pulls horrible faces at her at feeding time and when I give them hay. Given that I always take ALL the hay into HIS stable and then throw a share over to Ruby; and that the feeds they get, which both contain medicines of some kind and that's the only reason they get anything, barely cover the bottom of the feed skip; and that Ruby is working 1.5 hours a day and T is doing nothing – this is not very bright of him.

Ruby, on the other hand, goes on learning, quickly and obviously. Chaantallaimy and I drove her through Orton village; we had absolutely no problems of any kind. When only "I" give Ruby orders, ie when I'm driving alone, she is perfectly obedient, but when Chaantallaimy is with me she is more naughty. I deduced that Ruby was not sure what to do, or whom to obey, and so she got excited and danced about. So, I asked C if she would please not talk to Ruby except when she was on the ground, eg opening a gate or holding Ruby while I got into the cart; and lo and behold it worked like a charm, and we had no dancing about. Of course, it wasn't an absolutely perfect drive, because Ruby was in season (the down side of mare ownership) and she was thinking of alternative activities all through the drive – can we go down THAT road, or into THAT open gateway? and weaved about the road rather a lot. But on the whole, given the hormonal distractions, she was pretty good. The next day she was even better (I drove solo, because C had gone to school to get her GCSE exam results) and I took a route that included 2 cattle-grid gates to open. I'd forgotten that there are also 2 young entires in fields alongside that road, but Ruby behaved really very well. She only stepped out of line a tiny bit, once, at gate 1. She retreated when I growled at her, and was perfect at gate 2, even though it is a difficult gate only hung on one hinge, so needing to be lifted and carried. She is a very fair minded mare. She likes to be praised when she gets things right (very good practice for ME!!!), and doesn't mind being told if she does things wrong. She did a lot of trotting today and did her best to outpace a railway train that passed us alongside one stretch of road. She didn't manage it, but on the other hand, for a lass from the fells with no experience of trains, she did really very well not to bolt!

She's gone on losing fat off her sides, so I've managed to drop the tugs on the backband, and Danny the farrier has found me an old but sound 21" collar which my hames fit onto perfectly. The collar fits very snugly, works well and improves the draught line immensely. I fiddled with the hame straps until I got the draught as high as I could.

The only problem I've found with her in a neck collar is that going downhill, with her deep shoulder, once the draught slackens the collar can drift forward till it's halfway up her neck. She isn't ready to hold her head high enough to push the collar back into place. So today I put a fairly slack bungee cord from the top hame eye back to the crupper, and that was just enough to hold it back off her mane when we were going downhill. *Mater inventionis necessitas est...*

Ruby and T can go in the bigger field together now... the first time I went to bring them in from there, they were great; the second time, T decided he was Scared of Something that rattled in the breeze by the gate, and flew off across the field again taking Ruby with him. So now I know, I have to catch HIM first. I hope they have not been galloping about too often and leaving too many hoofprints (I spend quite a lot of time stomping down the edges of the bigger holes.) It has been so wet, the fields mark really easily. Several of the shows I would normally have gone to have been cancelled because of this. So maybe this was a good year to choose to change horses. Someone asked me if I was managing to enjoy my holiday, with no "horsey do's" to go to? Have to admit I AM!!!

Sue in the English Lakes

Intelligence is no defence against one's own stupidity

Getting Ruby's Goat, 5 Sept 2004

Okay. We've driven quite a few miles by now and we are tuning in to each other beautifully. After the 10 miles drive last week she had a day off (I needed to go and buy human food and do other boring things), but on Saturday we set off to do about 7 miles, up past the local racehorse training establishment and turn around at a farm, then come home. Ruby was a little restive on setting off – I had to put her back in place after I untied her, because she was for going without me! – but I was gentle with her, just very attentive, so she didn't have any excuses to try playing up. That's not to say she was trying to be naughty – just that she was feeling sharp and her thoughts were likely to turn into action quite quickly. I knew I needed to be on the same wavelength so as not to find myself in a field if the gate happened to be open as we passed it!

I kept her occupied with changes of pace, and concentrating on the long walk, and we reached our turning point relatively soon. I showed her the big black-wrapped silage bales on the farm lane, and she agreed they were not horse-eaters, and we set off home at a nice, brisk but balanced trot. Coming down the hill to New House, I asked her to steady, pointing out that the surface was "slippy", and she sat cleverly into the breeching, working well. Her quick brain said,"If I trot on the verge, I will get more grip", and I agreed, so she moved over a couple of points, and then! she saw them! a little paddock full of KILLER GOATS!

The term "bomb-proof" went out of the window immediately. We swerved, we snorted, we backed, we squiggled, we backed uphill and over humps and down again. Two motorcycles following us helpfully cut their engines and waited for developments. I had my hands full, but told them cheerfully: thanks, but they were not the cause of the problem, it was the goats! and that, if they would please go on, we would continue our argument once they had gone. I think they laughed – it's hard to tell under those full-face helmets – at NOT being the cause of a horse misbehaving for once.

Ruby by this time was 10 yards back from where she'd started fussing, and facing up a bank with the goats hidden behind her blinkers – puffing partly with fright and partly with the effort of backing in soft grass uphill. I knew I could rely on my vehicle's stability – it has always been excellent, but in addition, I carry a 4 stone potato weight buckled onto the back step, which is lower than the axle, so the centre of gravity is pretty low!! – so I had no hesitation in taking her gently round and down the hill past the goats once more. The owner kindly walked out and enticed the goats to walk to him at the other end of the fence, away from the direction we wanted to go.

Ruby snorted and fussed and tried to tie herself into a knot, but allowed herself to be steered past safely, and although she wanted to rush off once we had gone by, I didn't let her until some of the steam had died. Then we trotted home with no further incidents. (Although I admit her time along the "home stretch" was a record for her so far! and the goat owner said "By gum, once she got going she didn't half pick her feet up!")

I brought Ruby out this morning with a strategy in mind. I was going out with my endurance riding friend Rhonda and her Arab mare Hasty. Rhonda wanted to go up the fell and go some fast work with Hasty, but was willing to walk the first section with me and Ruby. We set off together from my yard about 8-30 am.

Both mares were soon quite hot, as the morning was warm and the air humid; they moved on freely but were not edgy. Ruby did a lot of throat-clearing when we trotted, so the walk across the fell was a good exercise, keeping her moving strongly without stressing her. We reached the road on the other side roughly an hour after we set off from home, and I took Ruby through the gate beside the cattle grid. She behaved very well, although she doesn't much like the noise of cars running over the bars of the grid beside the gate; she came with me quietly as I shoved the gate over the long grass, and sidestepped neatly round to let me close it again. Rhonda stayed on the other side and once I was settled in the cart again, she headed off for her gallop up the old Roman Road.

I took Ruby down the main road, which was going to lead her back to New House again. She jog-trotted freely down the long hill, balanced and sober, ears flicking as she surveyed the countryside. I put her onto the grass verge early so we had lots of sea-room in case she made any objections to getting near the goat paddock. And there, by prior arrangement, was David Trotter, her "friend" who started her in harness for me, standing between her and the goats and talking to her as she got near the "danger zone". She didn't quite know whether to make a fuss or not, but decided that after 4 miles and the walk over the fell on a warm morning, if David and I both said they were safe, she would go along with that. Provided they stayed on the other side of the paddock!

We took her past the paddock up the side road, and unyoked her. We fastened up all the trailing ends safely, put a lead rope on her headcollar, and then let her graze the young grass beside the paddock fence. She had a good look at the goats, and decided that they were not scary enough to stop her eating. David and I stood and talked to her, and to the goat owner and his sister, and with all the relaxed vibes around her she was soon quite calm. After about 30 minutes, we put her back in the carriage, and I drove her along by the paddock on the side road a couple of times; she looked at the goats, and pricked her ears, and didn't falter. So we did it a couple more times, and went quietly home.

The sun had broken through the low morning cloud by now; it was 10-30 am, the day was warm, the wet grass glistened in the sunlight and the families of lapwings practised aerobatics. The Howgill Fells lay brown and grey under the blue and white patched sky, with wisps of mist steaming up from their flanks as the air warmed above them. The sheep and cattle grazed peacefully, horses in fields were too preoccupied with eating to come galloping alongside, cars passed us peacefully and their occupants smiled at us, and Ruby trotted calmly homeward with some new knowledge in her head. It was a wonderful morning to be alive.

Sue in the English Lakes

Intelligence is no defence against one's own stupidity

Back on the Road with Ruby, 11 Oct 2004

I am glad to be able to report that Ruby is more or less recovered from her cough and is back on the road at weekends. She is now much slimmer overall and almost looking as though the 21" collar will soon be put away and swapped for the 20" one. But she's still huge compared to "little" Mr T – at 2 inches taller, her girth measurement is an easy 9 inches bigger than his and her hip bones are 4 inches wider! You could say she is well built... strong in the loin.

We are not doing any really serious work as she is now growing thick, harsh winter fur, a proper "brown Fell pony survival pelt". Mr T's coat is always rather velvety, but only Ruby's muzzle is soft; the rest is startlingly hard!

She's going fine in harness and just loves driving out to "have a good neb" at what everyone in the rest of the world is doing. Occasionally she'll try to sidestep onto a roadside verge in an attempt to stop and eat grass or a tasty looking bush, but needless to say she doesn't get anywhere with this feeble offer to be disobedient. It was a bit disconcerting on Sunday morning though, when she was trotting at 16 kph, to find her escalating a little flip of the head (due to sweaty ears) into a full-body shake; or turning her head at 90 degrees to our line of travel in order to peer through a gate as we passed. It's 17 years since we last had a mare on the yard – another Fell, though – so I suppose she's just reminding me that mares, like women, can multi-task.

Mr T has discovered that his "busty barmaid" girlfriend is perhaps not such a delight as he at first thought. He is distinctly making himself boss of the pair. "I was here first." He warned her off last week when she tried to come up too near the gate as I haltered him to go indoors one nasty stormy evening. Unfortunately, his snapping teeth made contact with ME just behind the elbow – OW! He's never EVER bitten any human deliberately... it was just my bad luck to be in his way when he meant to bite another horse. I let him know that it was not approved of. Ruby, perhaps not surprisingly, now lets his scowl drive her off the best hay. I wondered why she didn't retaliate, with that thick coat and superior size and female bossiness, but then remembered that she was brought up as a baby with T's former stablemate Boxer, who was HORRIBLE to other horses, so probably she believes that a mean face and flat ears on a little black Fell gelding really do threaten that she will be eaten along with the hay, unless she moves fast to somewhere else.

However, don't start thinking they spend all their lives competing with each other. I notice that since Ruby's arrival, T (previously an inveterate roller in mud, and frequently my despair on winter weekends because he was concreted all over in grey, clayey, hardened yack) has hardly rolled at all, and neither has Ruby. They have had every opportunity to plaster themselves, because the paddock is churned up as never before, but they are not rolling. Presumably, the roll is a solo back-scratch, and when you have a chum who will scratch your itchy bits, you don't need to roll.

Sue in the English Lakes

Intelligence is no defence against one's own stupidity

After the Storm, 26 Feb 2005

Winter has been strange this year, so I've just been lurking on the list and not driving. The North of England, and parts of Scotland, had tremendous storms in January with 140mph+ winds. We lost a lot of trees (plenty of firewood) but the horses were OK in their stone stables. No electricity for 36 hours, but we only have to re-roof half the hay shed and the outside loo, despite the hurricane force winds and the big tree branches flying about. The same weekend brought very severe floods to some areas; parts of Carlisle city centre were over 10 feet deep in water and livestock were washed away from fields near the River Eden. Again, we were lucky, as we live on a hill; if *we* were ever flooded, half of Britain would be underwater.

Then it turned milder, till last week when we had snow... or rather, areas around us had snow, and we just got an inch! I have shamelessly used the weather as an excuse for not driving, and got ploughed-on with writing the book... but *Hoofprints in Eden* has now gone to the publishers so I have no excuse not to get myself, as well as my horses, back in trim for driving.

The ponies have got used to a new regime of weekdays in the paddock (or the potato patch, by its looks) and the shelter, and weekends indoors where I can do things with them comfortably. Over the winter they have had several visitors from distant parts of Britain and from America. Ruby thinks this is no more than her due and T, at rising 18 years, is quite blasé by now. One of the visitors jokingly offered a whole Aberdeen Angus carcass in exchange for Ruby. My husband would have accepted... but she's still here. He has just made her a special trough on stilts so she can have her her own personal water supply outside the stable window... because she marmelises plastic buckets (her feed skip is recycled rubber, and needs to be). Mr T has never drawn this kind of attention from my husband; I suspect it's because of

Ruby's greater skill at batting her eyelashes. She is quite devastating when she decides to be charming.

We drove today, because the snow of last week had gone and we are planning to attend a carriage drive on Easter Monday so she needs to have done a little work. She is staying pretty fit charging round the ploughland of the paddock and kicking her heels in temper when T refuses to share his carrots at breakfast. However, I did think she needed to be reminded about "real" work, so off we went to get harnessed up. I am delighted to say that she now fits the 20" neck collar that only went halfway down her neck in August last year. She worked all autumn in a 21" but since the weather/winter/literary layoff, that one is now too long and the 20" is just perfect. (That tells you how much weight she has lost, and she is by no means thin even now. I have put her feed back up to maintenance level plus a tiddly bit for the work I am planning to do. On the other hand, I was so bundled up in coat and rug and dayglo/reflective yellow visibility waistcoat that I looked like Mr Pickwick.)

I have wondered for some time how Ruby would behave in company as I know she was very – ahem – *lively* – when shown as a youngster. Last time I drove out, we passed a field full of Warmblood show jumping/event horses who think a pony pulling a carriage is just the funniest thing they have seen all day. Ruby had not met them before and either stopped dead or produced an amazing suspended trot with her tail curled up Pekinese fashion, snorting like a whale all the time. She looked much more like a Hackney than a Fell pony. She didn't do anything really silly, but she did get a bit distracted. So it was very good for her today that when we went out, we met a neighbour who was going out for a ride with a friend who gives her lessons, both of them mounted on Icelandic horses, and going our way. Ruby was deeply interested, but made no real bones about going on ahead as we were asked to do (because the Icelandics had not really encountered ponies-with-wheels before and needed to keep an eye on them for reassurance). Ruby thought about them following her for some time and whinnied a good deal, but didn't argue with me, which was excellent. We passed the local Shetlands without comments, and the Warmbloods weren't out today because their owner Ian was cutting yet more fallen branches into firewood in their field, using a circular saw mounted on the back of his tractor. When he finally spotted Ruby he stopped cutting, but I don't think she was too bothered. Coming back, because of Ian's earmuffs and her unshod feet he can't have heard us at all, and Ruby never batted an eyelid at the noise; given half a chance I think she would have offered to give him a hand. Her family are like that: "bold as brass, wide awake and totally on the ball" as one Fell breeder puts it (and the other mare I had from that line was a bucket basher too <grin>). My main insistence was that she drove on the left of the road and went straight – she tends to drift to the right, which would be pretty dangerous on a busy road in the UK. But when traffic is about she clearly knows she really ought to be on the left and she moves over, preferably onto the grass verge if there is one! We did some nice steady trotting, and some faster, and some good walking. Coming back we overtook the Icelandics again, whose riders were just dismounting to walk the last few hundred yards home (and to get the circulation back in their feet!) and Ruby, though interested again, walked calmly and quietly past them and kept going while they followed and we humans all had a chat.

I don't know if this is actual progress on Ruby's part or just a continuing voyage of discovery on mine, but I do know that it felt good to be back in action and that she enjoyed herself as much as I did.

Oh and she thought the water-trough at the window was good fun and spent some time playing at making waves in it with her nose. My husband just looked ironic and said, "Can't you tell it's female!"

Sue in the English Lakes

Progress Day (Ruby again), 4 March 2005

This is not a wow-what-a-great-day post; just an ordinary Time and Miles one. I think Ruby is in the balance now between losing fat and gaining muscle. You wouldn't believe the difference between her shape when I got her and her new svelte silhouette. So of course I am now learning how much feed she needs to keep the energy levels up and the muscles building, without the fat reappearing.

I think I need to bump up the grain feed a little (she's currently getting 1.5 pounds a day of a mid-range molassed coarse-mix feed, and as much hay as she will eat) because today she started off a bit under-powered. She wasn't as keen to come out and work. But as the objective today was to meet traffic, particularly motorbikes, and just to put some steady miles in, this frame of mind was not a big problem.

We walk and trot steadily out from the farm at about 9:40 am, and up over the little piece of moorland called Whiteham. Ruby gives away her lack of energy by looking for side roads and gateways every time a hill appears. OK then, I will just insist that

Ruby drives my chosen route, but without stress, and I'll up the feed a little over the next week to see what happens. We drop down the sharp bank to the wooded riverside at Beckside Farm, and there we happen to meet my neighbour and her daughter riding out. Time for a check of the manners – we pass in opposite directions and the ponies all walk on obediently. So that's a plus. We also trot steadily past the lonely little red and white stallion who as always parades along his fence line. Another plus. Ruby hasn't so far shown in season this year... this might be something to watch for over the next few weeks.

We have to open a gate when we reach Scout Green; recently we've been through it with my neighbour who manages the gate without dismounting. Of course with a cart this is not possible so Ruby has to remember to stand still and behave nicely. I expect her to – but I am only partly successful and the longer new webbing handparts on the reins prove very useful at one point. So we wait a little longer than usual before moving off again (at least this is a forward impulse!)

No trains today (Sunday morning), so no learning either as we pass under the main West Coast railway line and trot away parallel to it. We trot up under the motorway and Ruby swings left on a voice command to take the Hay Banks road. As we ride up the slope, she begins to hear the traffic noise from the motorway northbound carriageway, and because she can't see it (even with her wide, racing half-cup blinkers) she gets quite forward going. I don't check her, nor do I drive her on, I just talk to her. A trot is all I want, and it's what I get; and when she starts to steady up I walk her again – she's done nearly a mile, all uphill, and the last half fuelled by adrenalin, so that's quite enough for one stretch. It's a mild morning with the sun just hazed by faint cloud building, and Ruby is sweating freely under the winter coat that's now shedding rapidly all over me! So we walk half a mile before she wants to pick up a trot again. All the while the traffic noise is getting fainter as the old road diverges steadily from the motorway. Soon she starts to whinny – *we are in new territory! Is anyone THEEERRREE???* A mile away on the other side of the motorway, there is a herd of black, brown and grey Fell ponies on the open fell, and a black Fell stallion in a field – but the wind is from them to us, and with the traffic hum in between us, there's no way he can hear Ruby's calls, and she doesn't appear to "spot the dots" on the fellside.

We meet the Shap to Orton road, and although there is no traffic I ask Ruby to wait at the junction. She doesn't see the point. I insist. Our halt is distinctly mobile for some moments before she gets the message. But I don't make her wait very long before moving off again. We march up the road and under the other half of the motorway. She is puzzled by the traffic noise passing above her, but takes it in her stride. We walk and trot on the tightly sheep-bitten grass alongside the road and she is content to go where I suggest without rushing or slacking. This is more like it. I am not rushing her; she is not rushing me. That's fine. This drive is not about speed but about learning a little more. Now where are those motorbikes? Aha! coming over the cattle grid ahead I see headlamps – two big road bikes coming at speed. Could be tricky – the quarry on our left is fenced tightly up to the roadside... but there is a big gateway ahead with a space in front of it, that offers us a buffer zone should we need it. I check Ruby's trot so we will be level with it as the bikers come up. They are good alert riders and slow down kindly, and wave and smile. I grin back and wag my head sideways at them, having my hands full, though Ruby does just a little sidestep and pricks her ears at the monsters. We don't need our buffer zone. THAT's a good girl. Not too scary after all. That's another objective ticked off for today.

We trot (quite actively but breeching for the downhill stretch) to the next cattle grid gate – mainly to get rid of the adrenalin from meeting the bikes. Ruby has a shake to ease the tickles from sweating and get some air under her bridle and her collar. How does she *do* that at a trot? She lets me get down and open the gate, and she stands still so she gets praise and a Polo mint. (<dummy me> I should have used them at the other gate.) I lead her through, give the gate a good shove backwards, then swing her round, to come back to shut the gate. There's a car coming so I pause with a steady hold on her headcollar, because I know this grid makes quite a zing as cars go over it. It does. She jumps a little, but nothing serious. Good girl – have another sweetie! I shut and latch the gate, get back in, swing her round again and walk her on down the hill.

There's not much traffic. We listen to the birds and watch the curlews planing down on curved wings, with their bubbling call that means Spring. Ruby sees the next hill and offers to take it on, so we trot up to the top and along the level – managing not to shy at the monster tree branch lying in the grass verge, though it merits a long hard stare. Obviously we haven't been along here since the big storm in January!

Down the sharp bank to New House, Ruby decides something is spooky. She can't quite remember what. I know full well that she's recalling the goats-are-monsters episode from August last year! I send her down the grass verge and she goes willingly enough but is still thinking about the goats! They are not there – they are still housed as yet. Their owner tells me they will be out in a week or two. I tell him Ruby will get used to them... So there's another objective for a few weeks' time.

We walk and trot to the junction for home. Ruby knows her ground now and is eager to go. We trot steadily for a mile and a half – and I know from the time she makes from landmark to landmark that we'd be right on target for 14kph if she were doing an event. It doesn't matter, but it's nice to know that she is comfortably doing that speed. We walk over the railway bridge and down the hill, the last mile towards home. Ruby's relaxing now – watching someone down in the village who is feeding sheep and trundling across the fields with a quad bike and trailer.

The air is hazy, and the sunlight is fading a little – looks like it will rain later. Suddenly Ruby leaps in the air, tightening the kicking strap, and comes down with the breeching up under her tail. There's a big four wheel drive (SUV) behind us that neither of us had heard. It overtakes, cautiously, while Ruby stands holding the cart on the breeching in what I think of as the "Stubbs position" – like on the famous painting of the two horses in harness, the breeching is firmly above the point of her buttocks rather than below. It doesn't seem to bother her though... and as she moves off again the straps gradually work their way down to the "right" place Hmmm ... another lesson learned? Or not? I think we were both not quite all there, to be so surprised at being overtaken....

We come back into the yard to the sound of Mr T's greeting whinnies (she never answers him!) and I get her unharnessed and brushed off. She's pretty sweaty, but the winter coat is coming out nicely so that should ease off in a few days (if the weather does not turn cold again!). Today isn't quite warm enough for a washing session. Ruby loves being brushed, so this is her real treat... though of course once she has cooled a little and had a drink, she's huffling at me for her feed...

Both ponies spent the day in the yard, teasing the dog, eating hay and nibbling at what grass they could pick among the trees. Mr T stayed up the top, away from Graham who was cutting up logs with the chainsaw in one of the sheds, but Ruby I am sure would have given a hand if she'd just been shown what to do.

By evening the rain clouds were hanging lower and lower and the wind was freshening – and the ponies were waiting to be let into the stables. Did someone say Fells were tough? Opportunists more like...

Ruby's first drive with another pony, 27 March 2005

Well, I just got back from Ruby's first drive with another pony pulling a carriage. I have found out (confirmed) what I already suspected – that outside of her relationship with Mr T, where he is the boss because he was here first and he's black and feisty like her very bossy previous stablemate – she wants to be in charge.

She WILL drive behind another pony, and since this was our first trip of any distance with another turnout, we took turns to lead. When we were behind, I insisted she kept a polite distance; but she definitely gets more wound up that way and my young groom, Christopher, needed several "wipe off the slobber" sessions as foam blew off her lips and back to us! Yet I wasn't holding her hard. (The need for that came later <vbg>).

When we were in front she delighted in zooming off at a fast trot and leaving the other pony behind. When we walked, she walked a little slower than usual and let him catch up. He has a good walk – and although hers is good, she wasn't really using it till we were on the homeward stretch :-). She behaved well, standing at gates, and on lay-bys for the cars we met, without fussing. However we did have a few whoopsies! She is not "boringly perfect" yet!

She objected to the noise of an overtaking tractor which was heavily laden with trailer and bale spike and several tons of silage bales and so was revving hard like a large motorbike. Her "objection" consists of a burst of canter, slamming into the collar then bouncing nearly on the spot. It takes very little stopping, but it makes a great impression on the passing car-driver because it is so spectacular, knees up, mane and feather flying, head tucked in and neck arched! We had another of these, of startling vigour, when passing the field of the Shetland ponies, who were trotting down to the fence in their usual twinkle-toes fashion to see the day's excitement go by. I checked her silliness and settled her into her trot again. Not long after, she thought she would slow down and I didn't let her, saying, "If you have energy to be silly you have energy to work, so get on." Christopher thought that was exactly what his teachers would say in class and then observed that we must be teaching Ruby to be good! He also said, "It's just as well she has shoes on or she would have worn her feet out by now!" – because when she is feeling a little stroppy she lifts her knees amazingly high and you can really hear a crash as her feet hit the ground.

When we got back to the yard it was beginning to rain, so I whisked off all the harness and loaded her into the horsebox to get her out of the cold wind. She thought that was fine, especially when I gave her a carrot. All good practice for tomorrow's drive 15 miles away. (Going into the horsebox, she thinks, is A Good Thing. On Saturday we had done an exercise in using the space within, involving a feed and some time standing in there with the gates shut; yesterday, she made two excellent attempts to get in by herself: once halfway through being harnessed, and again after the drive. So of course, once all the gear was off, I let her climb in and she got another feed. I don't think I shall have a lot of trouble with loading her tomorrow.)

Then I took her into the stable to brush her off and she really enjoyed that because she had got herself quite sweaty – mostly she wanted her jaw brushed underneath, between the branches where she can't scratch for herself. Her beard is still 6" long (startlingly black in contrast with her bright bay face). The coat is starting to shed but she is still pretty well insulated. I shall take a sheet to put over her tomorrow for the journey home, as I am sure she will be even more sweaty after a drive with MORE "ponies with wheels". More tomorrow – God willing, and if the horsebox starts!

Ruby driving in company, 28 March 2005

Today was a tale of learning – Ruby learning about driving in company, and me learning that I am getting OLD and starting to have serious Senior Moments. I mean, what silly C** drives away for a day out and leaves her favourite old pony tied up in the stable where he can't reach the water bucket? Yep, I did it. Fool that I am. I was so wound up about taking Ruby to her first proper drive, in the horsebox, that I clean forgot to go and untie Mr T after I'd taken Ruby out of the stable where they share the space in 2 side by side boxes. Fortunately my husband saw and let him loose ten minutes after I had gone.... slapped wrist for Sue.

However! Back to the big red girl. Ruby walked up the ramp into the horsebox like a trooper, no doubt thinking of feeds and perhaps associating the tail bandage with previous trips to the stallion :-). She had her little feed, then I shortened her tie rope and added a second at right angles, to stop her nibbling the harness hanging in the next partition and make her stand in the most stable position in the box. She is used to travelling facing forward in a cattle trailer, so the idea of standing diagonally in this almost-square space with her bottom facing forward has been hard for her to grasp. I know from experience that all my other horses have voluntarily stood this way in the same or similar horse box spaces, and once they get the hang of bracing their bottoms in the leading corner, you scarcely hear a thump from them the whole journey.

Ruby protested about the horsebox ramp being put up by starting to paw. We set off sounding like a marching band's Big Drum. She pawed for several miles, then it went quiet. I drive very carefully with horses (which had earned me brownie points when I passed my minibus test and the test sheet comment "very smooth drive" from the examiner) so I just thought she had got used to the idea that pawing would not get her out, and she had settled down. However, when we arrived and lowered the ramp, what she'd done was to get her foot over the rope, not once, but twice. She looked like an old lady studying her wool – knit one, purl one, drop one. She had her head at knee level and a distinctly chastened air. She was sweaty, but not panicked, and there wasn't even a rub where the cotton rope had been looped round her knee. We freed her and next minute she was pawing again and managed to get her foot on top of the OTHER rope this time. So, from now on both the ropes are going to be shorter (and they were, on the ride home – and no tangles.). Mr T was too easy – he just used to go patiently to sleep. Horses like him lull you into a false sense of security. I remembered, too late, that my old Rosie (Ruby's aunt) had also pawed, and got her feet caught in things, and never panicked....

We were early for the drive. Always a good thing with a pony who needs time to learn what's going on. We left Ruby in the box with the ramp down while we watched other people arriving on the field. One van had to be towed in by tractor as it couldn't get a grip on the damp muddy grass. (We were OK with our double-wheeled back axle.) Ruby neighed at all the new horses but went back frequently to her haynet – probably as a displacement of the excitement. But it worked. Several people commented on her colour and thought she was a Dales because bay is now relatively unusual in Fells (unless, like Rosie and Ruby, you are from Sleddale stock which has been bay and brown for generations beyond memory).

The weather was better than we'd expected; we'd had some heavy rain overnight, but although it was not a sunny day, it wasn't windy or really cold or wet, and so it was ideal driving weather for ponies still in their winter woollies. The grass is just starting to grow, the sheep are lambing, but the trees and hedges are still bare. The views up to the Pennines are spectacular. The lanes around Appleby (our venue) are wide enough for cars to pass a convoy – with care!

I unloaded Ruby once she had had time to take in the scene, and we harnessed her up but without putting on her bridle. I rolled the trap out of the horsebox and she pricked her ears but didn't flinch as it bounced down the final 8" from the ramp. Then we let her pull at her haynet again while we had a look round a cone course that had been set out. Some people had put to and were trotting about by then, which made Ruby snort with excitement – I could hear her from 200 yards away! I walked the course (a futile exercise as it turned out – more later!) and then we put Ruby to. She had got over her whale snorts very quickly, and was calm again. I took care to get the kicking strap just right. Ruby HAS kicked out exactly once (2 days ago when restrained from passing a comrade being ridden). The strap worked as it was supposed to! She did no damage to self or cart, and yesterday's drive which was more exciting produced no kicks at all; but I certainly wasn't going to do this VERY exciting drive without it.

We got in the cart as soon as we had put to, and I drove quietly round the outskirts of the activities. Ann, my "groom" for the day, is a neighbour who rides out with us on her Connemara, and she was thoroughly enjoying herself (she has a Shetland whom she drives at home, but Bracken can't keep up the pace of the big horses for mile after mile). I kept Ruby moving quietly along. She wanted to jog and express her excitement, but the ground had a bit of cut in it and she had to work to pull us, so she quickly settled down. An old horseman who is a friend of both Ann and myself always says, "When you take a young one anywhere, don't let it stand still. Keep it on the move and it'll be all right." We had the room to do this, and Ruby worked calmly for me. By then, most of the drivers had put to, so we worked our way quietly to the gate and followed a mare of similar size and speed onto the road: Tara is a Welsh cross cob, fast but sensible, and I was happy to ride behind her. Her owner Amanda set her off at a good walk, and Ruby dropped in behind, pulling a little and wanting to jog, but taking my restraint well. She doesn't drag at the bit but she does get strong, so I worked with her, holding her only so long as she was jogging, then letting her relax when she walked. All this was repeated over and over as we walked along! Not long after, some of the others who had followed us came up at a trot, and the rhythm of their feet in the tarmac set Ruby wanting to trot also, so we did have a little tussle, but nothing major. A difficulty is that when excited and being restrained, Ruby curls up to the left and throws her right shoulder out; so I know that once the ground dries up a bit, we're going to have to do lots of steady schooling to straighten her up (though I think this excitable "curl" is probably going to be difficult to cure.) We met quite a few cars but the steering proved sound and we didn't hit any :-)

Anyway, after a while we got going into trot, and that suited Her Majesty much better. She still wanted to go faster though and we had several bursts of canter and attempts to drift right to overtake! However, there was nothing bad happening in her head and when, after a couple more miles, I asked Amanda if she minded us going in front, Ruby sprang forward and went into power mode the moment I told her to go. When we came back to walk, Tara caught her up. I thought Ruby could "walk" but Tara is 15 hands to Ruby's 13.3 and she really strides on!

By this time we were onto quieter roads heading out towards Long Marton and Dufton, and beginning to hit the hills. I think Ruby began to get the message at this point that fighting the bit to go faster was not such a good idea, because she found her energy was really needed for the work. She didn't give up on me but she did come back a little more easily! We had one "scuttle" when we met a noisy train going over a bridge just as we approached it, but all was well.

Ruby and Tara changed places for lead every so often and the rest of the drive followed a good 300 yards behind – in fact for much of the afternoon we hardly saw them. Some of those big hills really made the horses work. Ruby dropped her backside and powered up them like a hero with huge swinging strides. (I'm sitting here now with the same big grin on my face as I had this afternoon.) This is some horse, even though she IS only a pony. She just loves her driving.

Towards the end of the drive, a big black and white gipsy cob joined us – terrific bone and feather. The driver kept him behind us. I was quite glad of this because when we got back it turned out the cob was a stallion! What a distraction THAT would have been for Ruby, who had thought anyway that travelling in the horsebox meant we were going to stud!

After taking a long steep slippery downgrade relatively sedately (for Ruby) we met two helpers on the roadside who asked if we wanted to take "the water crossing option". Staying on the road avoided this. I wanted Ruby to do the crossing as we have only driven into water once so far. Amanda however wanted someone to give Tara a lead as she doesn't like water! So Ruby went ahead. I asked Ann to shout back to Amanda to keep Tara back in case Ruby had to stop and think about it! We trotted along a narrow grassy and muddy track cut into the side of the river bank, and there under the trees was Trout Beck, running quite full from the night's rain. It has sandy banks and a stony bottom. Ruby understands stony from her life on the fell, but SAND? What's SAND? She had to dither a bit and have a good look before she trusted the strange stuff and would put a hoof on it. After that, she popped into the water and trundled straight across; and the same on the return loop. The water was about 2 feet deep in the deepest part. I heard later that Tara had tried to jump the whole beck, all 20 feet of it … But we were having too much fun to look behind.

By this time we'd been out about an hour and fifteen minutes, and were nearing the end of the drive. I looked on the map tonight and I think it must have measured about 8 miles. Ruby had been sweaty before we started, due to her argument with the tie rope, but she wasn't any wetter when we got back than when we set off (except for the legs and belly from the river!) and she was still keen to trot as we came down the lane to the field.

When we arrived back, we could see people attempting the cones course that had been laid out. I kept Ruby quietly walking till it was our turn. Some people get very competitive and rush their horses, but I didn't want Ruby to start getting hot about something that is essentially a test of accuracy. We have driven briefly through pairs of cones at home, but not much, because the ground is still very wet on the farm and I get told off for cutting it up! So a quiet drive through was all I wanted for today. I've already said I'd walked the course, haven't I? Second senior moment of the day coming up: I drove through pair 9 backwards immediately after going through the start! However, everybody just laughed at me, and Ruby didn't know any different, so we just went back and did it properly second time around. I think we hit one cone. What I really wanted was what I got – smooth, calm forward movement, listening to me, getting the idea of driving straight for the middle of the gap. We weren't there to win... In any case the prize was just half a dozen farm eggs! (I told everybody that I'd driven through 9 deliberately in order to go Hors Concours.) Tara won with a time of 48 seconds and Ruby was fifth in 1 minute 18, which was perfectly satisfactory. For comparison, Mr T did HIS first ever cones round in about 2 minutes 30, the stickiest I have ever seen, because he stopped to look for dragons behind every pair of cones, but he now adores the game and does it well, so Ruby's much smoother introduction to it was very pleasing.

We unharnessed and rubbed her down, and then she had a nice relaxing walk about with a thick denim sheet over her back, nibbled the grass and had occasional mouthfuls of water (just to please us I think – she was much more focused on the grass). Then once all the gear was reloaded, she went back onto the horsebox, and travelled home quietly, only pawing a couple of times and NOT getting tangled up. When we turned up the road home she started whinnying. How did she know? There are no windows in the box.

She and Mr T were allowed to nibble grass in the yard after that. They ended up in the garden because part of the fence has been taken down, but T has been my lawnmower for years, so I wasn't too bothered. But I did have to go rescuing crunched daffodils afterwards.

I bet Ruby is now telling T huge tales in the dark of the stable. "And I had to walk through a river, can you imagine? but I beat them all, I showed them how to do it. I'm the fastest. I put them all in their place. Yes I did, I'm the best." And Mr T will just yawn. "Yeah, yeah, whatever. Been there, done that... If you've got to talk, just step back from that haynet will you, so I can eat it for you!"

Collars: What's THIS? 5 April 2005

I do not have personal experience of using a French/Austrian collar (I dislike the term "brollar" even more than "brunch", as to me it sounds like "brolly", the English nickname for an umbrella) – HOWEVER a friend has been using a French collar almost exclusively for a couple of years on her ageing Fell pony and I have observed a few things. One is that his neck has changed shape!! His neck collars no longer fit him because he has put so much muscle on the top of his neck and shoulders. This is not due to fat or maturity – he was 19 when the collar was bought and he hasn't put weight on. I have observed also that he moves more freely in the French collar. He extends more willingly than he did in breast collar or neck collar.

Now I am not saying that there isn't a potential heat problem with the large area of horse that this collar covers. For this pony in the British climate it isn't a terrifically big issue as he isn't asked to work hard and fast.

However, to my eye it doesn't pull from the required point of least motion in the shoulder-blade either. It is really no more than a breast collar with a stiffened neck strap – an improvement but not really a huge one. My daughter has had experience of using them with commercial carriages and I will ask her for more info on how they stood up to work – I have a vague memory of rubs on the horses and tears in the collars from bad handling but can't be specific. (More when I find out. The more we know, the better the judgements we can make on the equipment for our horses.)

Neither am I saying that this Fell pony's evidence makes the French collar a better piece of equipment than a neck collar, because (looking at the whole once more) I am also aware that the patent faced neck collar my friend used, apparently sturdy and delightful-looking though it was, was a "bent" or "swept back" show collar, not a working straight-profiled collar, and it just plain annoyed that pony – and mine, come to think of it! I borrowed it on 2 occasions and both times, my ponies – two different ones – spent a lot of time stretching their heads down to their knees as though to ease something at the withers. Her pony did this a lot too and she always put it down to him having an itchy nose that he wanted to scratch on his knees. Until I borrowed that collar, I believed her! But I didn't like it and I don't think the ponies did either, so it would not be hard for the French collar to have been an improvement on THAT collar for this pony.

The adjustable quality of the French collar is one of its main attractions – and I think that the pony I'm talking about needed that adjustability during his change of shape. Compared to having several neck collars, it is cheap to buy just the one. (I have six neck collars, and I only have 2 ponies). The French collar is a numb thing to actually put on the horse though – surprisingly heavy, and more clumsy than a collar with hames and tugs.

As a separate observation, is there ANYTHING more numb to handle than a pair of hames that are off the collar but still joined by the bottom hame strap??? I swear at mine regularly when cleaning for shows and always have to take them apart completely for the sake of sanity.

More about French collars, 5 April 2005

Well, I called daughter and we've had a good discussion on the French collars. She said "I don't like them!" very emphatically.

She said her big horses worked better in a breast collar (despite a heavy load of driver and 4 adults in a 4 wheeler carriage) than in a French collar. She has never had the option of traditional neck collars at her workplace, unfortunately. I am not sure who made her collar so some of her comments that follow may be less of a problem with different makers, but I don't know about that for certain.

Although a breast collar inevitably "narrows" in draught, it does spread the pressure somewhat over the horse's chest (and her Zilco breast collar has up to 1" of padding).

She said that the French collar seemed to suit only the smaller narrower horses, not the big chunky ones. It wraps around the neck and shoulders, and seems to press on the front/lower end of the shoulder blades. Horses got sweat marks there, though they did not get sores or white marks.

The top/cap is round, not pointed, and there's a possibility of pressure on top of the neck.

The inside is flat, with only half an inch of flat padding, so the trace buckles pull inwards onto the shoulder where on a neck collar they are held out by the hames and the thickness and rigidity of the traditional collar. I think this is possibly the reason that there seems to be pressure on the top of the neck from the French collar – with weight on the traces the oval round the neck will be widened, and therefore shortened. I'd have to watch one in action during a whole drive to be sure of that, but Jen said her collars were floppy, not nearly as rigid as neck collar and hames.

She too has observed the muscle thickening of the top of the neck and withers in all the horses that were driven regularly in a French collar – so much so that their saddle pads had to be fitted further back or else they rolled back in use. Riding saddles also needed changing to a wider tree, or girthing up further back – and if a horse was at all one sided, the muscling developed in such a way that the saddle rolled to the opposite side. If he was naturally bent left, the saddle rolled to the right.

She said her favourite driving horse hated the French collar. If she was told to use it, she used it only in the morning and changed to the breast collar for the afternoon – like changing your boots for another pair on a long walk. He would rush in the F collar instead of being calm, and would wear his ears back in a grumpy way if made to work in it (nuff said, really!). Her opinion was that the increased muscling over the neck was a defence against the pressure on the shoulders – that the horses carried themselves differently in self defence.

So, the jury's still out but the evidence I hear makes me think the French collar does not have much to recommend it – even though it was a better choice for my acquaintance's pony than her "showy" bent-back neck collar.

Bridle shaping, 7 April 2005

I drove Ruby today after her increased feeds (and a day in the stable because of horrid wet and cold and VERY windy weather), and yes, she is back on form, full of bounce and curiosity and keen to show off her 16 kph extended trot at the least excuse. Very nice... sweetly on the bit and listening, but flying, with huge suspension between the downstrokes. This is why I drive!

But when I took her bridle off at home afterwards I saw that she has a bald, nearly raw spot at the junction of the headpiece and top cheek buckle. I have recently had to adjust the bridle to move the blinker rim off a prominent brow bone for the same reason. She does not throw her head or show any sign of discomfort, but obviously I want to deal with it before it gets to that stage.

It isn't the blinker that is causing the rub this time but the turn of the leather at the top of the blinker/cheek piece, round the buckle. I know this precisely, because the the skin that came off was stuck there! Browband is not too short – if anything it is a little long, to accommodate the Fell forelock. The leather is smooth and doesn't have sharp edges. It's just that the bridle runs over prominent bones on her face!

I may have to wire the winker stays to push the blinkers out at a wider angle. It won't be pretty but it will be possible.

I have never had a Fell with such thin facial skin and sharply prominent brow bones. If I can't solve this with my current range of bridles, I am seriously thinking that I shall have to drive her, as I did with my first Fell Rosie, in a riding bridle. I will test this of course before I do so – test the fit of the riding bridle, buckle positions, strap positions, and remind her of pulling stuff like a log or a tyre, before I even think of putting her in a vehicle – and I then will have help and the yard gates will be closed. (I don't believe Ruby will have a problem with that; she was broken in with an open bridle and Rosie, who was Ruby's close relative and had many similar character traits, certainly did not worry about turning wheel-spokes at any time in our 5 years of driving *sans* blinkers.)

But if the riding bridle runs over the same bones, and causes the same problems, I am no further on! Have any of you come across this problem and if so how did you solve it?

Barb Lee replied:

Sue, I have a clicker die that produces a shaped crown. The crown is 24" from end to end. The billets will actually rest lower on the face than a conventional straight cut bridle crown. ... This would perhaps drop the bridle behind the bony ridges. I know it worked for a draft horse friend, whose Percheron always came in with a rub about that same spot. I cut special shaped crowns for the boys' bridles, and the cheek then fell well below the critical spot. No more rubs. They also give lots of nice ear relief.

I would be happy to "click" you a crown blank, which you could then finish to your own requirements. I believe I have a piece of nice English bridle leather on hand. Also a piece of American harness leather, but it is excessively heavy.

Let me know if you would like to have a go with this idea!

Ruby and the Septic tank, 23 April 2005

I am in the middle of a strange weekend here. The weather is fine and drying winds are firming up the ground – the ponies may even get out onto the grass in a few days ;-)

Husband Graham has therefore decided this is the weekend to renew the septic tank (do not read further if you are eating). We are planning to turn our old stone barn next door into a house and the current plumbing arrangements – though perfectly adequate over the past 23 years w/o even any need to empty – are not up to statutory criteria, so we need to plant "a plastic onion" flask- shaped new tank. Hence, a mini digger and dumper truck have been pootling about in the field all day today digging out and removing tons of wet black earth, brick, stone, gravel and concrete, and will probably do the same tomorrow. At least this means that some of the wet field gateways will get filled with the spoil. (Tomorrow I must collect up the tadpoles from the puddle that is rapidly drying in the hayfield gateway and dump them in the ditch instead!)

Mr T does not like large machines much but as he was parked in the paddock round the back, that didn't matter. Ruby on the other hand considers herself Investigator-in-Chief to anything new. This afternoon she not only drove out through a narrow space between the dumper and the barn end without even looking at them, but she wanted to go in the field and watch the digger walloping its way with a jack-hammer through the concrete base of the old tank. Graham said it would be OK so tomorrow I might just let her do that. I love this line of ponies – Rosie was just the same. Would help you dig a hole, and would march through parked machinery demanding its removal Out Of Her Way.

Ruby is casting her winter coat still and the remaining undercoat is much darker bay – quite a dark brown in fact. It will be interesting to see whether it brightens as summer comes in and we get some more sunshine. The other nice thing is that after losing all the podge she brought with her last August, and having looked for some time (from the rear) a bit too wide at the top of the hip and narrow at the stifle, she is suddenly rounding out. The hip doesn't look nearly so prominent and the stifle area is becoming broader than the top, just like Mr T's muscly little behind. :-) Yeah, I know – my garage man tells me it is not normal to find any enjoyment in "sitting on a plank on wheels and staring at a horse's backside." But another friend reminds me that schooling horses is an art form, akin to animated sculpture. When you get it right it looks lovely. And it seems to stay that way. Mr T has done no serious work for about 18 months and he still looks like a little work horse (of course, he has Ruby barging about to keep him on his toes!). One of my neighbours wants to drive him occasionally, so she is bringing her exercise cart here to have its tyres inflated and the bodywork checked over, then we can go out as a little cavalcade. :-) Ruby and T together.

We are hoping to take Ruby to a little gathering of drivers on 15th May which involves a 5 mile trot, 4 hazards and a cones course, so Ruby is having to go out a bit more often to develop the stamina. Last night was the first night it has been both light and dry enough to consider driving after I came home from work, and Ruby thought my change of timetable was NOT amusing. She expected her evening feed and hay, so a tiny feed and work were not something she approved of. She was miffed, and consequently mischievous all the way round the drive. While one startle was excusable as we drove over the railway with an express train going full belt underneath, the ones that she claimed were due to the Shetland ponies or the Warmbloods trotting alongside their fence, were just pretences and a wonderful "reason" to prance along at an elastic trot, uttering huge trumpeting snorts, neck curved like a dragon and ears as stiff as horns. But she has a lovely mouth and no inclination to shy or spin round, so the "go forward" ethic didn't have to suffer at all!

I am testing a new crown piece on Ruby's bridle. Barb Lee VERY kindly cut it for me and sent it as a blank. I finished it earlier in the week and exchanged it for the older one that has been allowing the blinkers to rub on Ruby's sharp face bones above the eye. We have driven out a couple of times so far and everything seems fine – though time will tell of course! If you're reading the List – Thanks Barb!

Dalemain, May 2005

Every year in May we mad carriage drivers gather in the East Park of a beautiful Georgian-fronted country house called Dalemain. Our " fun event" always follows the Fell Pony Stallion Show held on the Saturday at the same venue, and we drive an established route which used to be part of the show drive for the stallions at this show. The drive is followed by hazards (usually simple ones) and a cones course.

The event is always a magnificent one, through the greening countryside under the budding trees. Every year I am amazed afresh by the myriad shades that green can be. I take photograph after photograph and drink in the electric brilliance of the new leaves, everything from grass to the topmost branches of the wild cherries and lime trees. The lambs are sturdy and frisky, the cattle are turned out and gallop alongside us as we pass their fences, and the hawthorn, apple and cherry trees are bursting with delicate white and pink blossom. Under the hedges the wild arums are still tightly furled and the spring convoys of tourist walkers are bunched up on the grassy banks eating sandwiches.

I would have loved to take Ruby to show her off on the Saturday but – no surprise – the driving class at the stallion show is only for the boys. Mr T has strutted his stuff there twice and been second twice, but sweet though he is, he isn't the horse that Ruby is. However, I had quite a task on for this weekend as my duties were as follows:

Saturday: do an interview for BBC Radio 4 about Fell ponies and trotting races of the past; help organise the marathon and hazards for the Sunday, check the distances and learn the hazards for myself; talk to the owner of Dalemain about some exhibits I have been given for their Fell Pony Museum... take photos of the Fell pony stallion driving class (very poorly attended – just ONE entry with an exercise cart, and the pony's forelock tied in a bunch with baler twine.)

Sunday: transport Ruby, cart, harness, horse "feed", water, rug/sheet and waterproof sheet (in case of rain), young "first timer" groom Christopher, lunch and event paperwork all safely to Dalemain, get the hazard judges organised and briefed, brief any competitors who hadn't driven there before, give the starter her list of runners and times, give the cones course builder/judge his list of entries and work out the max. time from his measurement of the course; and then start getting Ruby sorted out to actually drive ourselves!

Luckily we had lots of helpers and, apart from the very new secretary who was having "canary fits" helping her husband to prepare their pony to drive, everything went off very calmly; with the experienced hazard stewards teaching the less experienced and several people saying "I hardly feel I've done anything to help." Which is wonderful, and how it should be... nobody should feel stressed or shouted-at, which would make anyone decide not to help ever again. OK we didn't have a huge number of drivers, but next year it will be packed, because word will go round that it went well this year.

The really nice thing was that Ruby was much more settled than she was at the Easter Drive. It's so good to see a horse using its wits, and Ruby was quite cool about travelling (no sweating or stamping and no getting wound up in her leadrope) and also about standing around tied to the horsebox while I dealt with people. I suspect she would have quite liked to organise it herself and thought all the visitors were only her rightful due. She is an artist at leadrope stretching in order to eat grass (no matter that the grass was all of one inch long) and it wasn't until my very pregnant daughter shortened the rope to about 8 inches that Ruby stopped munching, or trying to.

Our marathon was 8km in length, all one stage at any pace, with a fairly easy max time and 4 hazards. Ruby was wound up as we began to walk around the Park before our start, and used the whizz of motorbikes racing down the main road as an excuse to semi-startle and break into trot, but she took my calming orders in good part and carried on walking until it was our turn to start. She'd seen other turnouts setting off and was curious about where they'd gone to so once our 6 minute gap had elapsed, she was off at top speed to find out! We clattered through the cobbled entrance to the courtyard and under the carriage arch, then out along the stony track towards Dacre Castle. Chris, on the back step, spent a lot of time in mid-air as the bumps and rocks flung him upwards and I was never quite sure if the squeaks and exclamations were pleasure or horror, but "the pace was too good to inquire".

Ruby performed magnificently, keen but biddable, and with her huge "I have ambitions to be a Dales" trot, we almost caught up the young Welsh Sec C who'd gone off in front of us. My daughter took some lovely photos of her thoroughly enjoying her first go at "hazard diving" (the missing R is entirely appropriate). I thought she might hang a little as she tired, but I gave her big smooth turns and she swung sweetly either left or right, ears pricked and full of running. My problem was that the obstacles were very mathematical and despite my drawings and studying overnight I got marked with Error of Course in 3 out of 4 of them (they were pretty horrible to remember). Most of the time I didn't know I'd gone wrong so I just told Ruby how brilliant she was, and she preened herself and surged onward!

The cones course was not a novice pony's course, though it could very easily have been, had not so many of the pairs of cones been offset from the natural angle of approach. We had 35cm clearance and with those twisty approaches, I once again revealed my true vocation as a Grannie Driver – hit 2 cones AND got time faults. But again, Ruby did not mind; she wasn't sure if she had to drive between or past the cones, so we wobbled a lot, but the sound of a couple of cones going BUMP didn't phase her. (I used to drive a little Sec C cob who would dither between the cones saying "OOOh, I'm going to hit it, panic panic, BUMP, oops now

77

look what we've done, panic panic" – thank heavens Ruby doesn't do that!)

Both at the end of the marathon and after her cones round, she hustled back to the horsebox at a trot... though as we passed the gate into the courtyard, she veered that way, as if to go round again!

Chris had a good time too. He was shyly pleased that his Mum and Dad had come to watch and take photos. At one point I had to tick him off, because while he was holding Ruby he unfastened a rein from the bit when she was still harnessed to the cart. I felt really bad about telling him off with his parents standing there. He's never got anything wrong on our yard! But that was too big a safety fail to let him off, and then he bucked his ideas up and made Ruby stand still too – previously she'd been walking all over him! Happily, his parents are both teachers who fully understood that a big risk must never be taken if it can be avoided. They didn't stay till the prize giving; I think Chris was tired out, as much by excitement and expectation the night before, as by his actual job on the back step! So, once I got home I unearthed a nice Driving Club rosette for him and took it round to his house. He was hugely impressed with it (it was twice as big as the one we actually won so he was doubly chuffed!) and I gathered it was going to have pride of place on his bedroom wall.

Ruby was immensely pleased with herself the whole day, unashamedly soaking up all the admiration and interest she gained by being my first new pony for 13 years!

She would have come in on time from her marathon had it not been for aforesaid Grannie Driver getting things wrong. As it was, we were only half a minute over time despite rambling around the outside of three hazards saying, "well gate E must be here somewhere, all the gates go inwards!" . She stood untied in her "loosebox" in the back of the horsebox and "nebbed" with great interest at everything happening around us, over the back gates.

I'm sure she believes that she supervised the scoring and the prize giving. (I was tempted to offer her the pencil and calculator.)

It is SO nice to have a pony whom you can see behaving better each time. She was nowhere near as excited on this trip as on the last, and much more interested in what was happening. I have posted some pics ... not the one of us in full flight through gate C in the wrong direction though.

I'm sorry to have to tell you that here in Cumbria we have had six dry days in succession with drying winds and the turf was thoroughly dry and just great for driving. NO frog stranglers here... for once!

The Line from bit to hand, 7 June 2005

This is a topic that is more complex in driving than it is in riding.

In English traditional road vehicles (as opposed to farming and working vehicles where the driver may well have been walking, using levers on implements, and opening and shutting gates) the driver sat high. This is particularly obvious with tandem and coaching vehicles. Why? So he could see where the leaders were going! The angles of the reins therefore came sharply down over his forefinger, and at the terrets they made another sharp angle forwards. The lines of the reins never were really straight from hand to mouth. You didn't want to carry all that length of leather, nor to have it rest on the horse's mouth at the other end. You carried the part from hand to terret, and the horse carried the part from hame ring to bit. Rein directions of course added to this weight, as necessary.

Achenbach style helps you to use your arms, wrists and hands flexibly, which is what the riding edict is really about: feel. It helps to make rein lengthening and shortening quicker and more effective, whether with two reins or four. This is more important in driving than in riding as your position, or distance, re the horse's mouth varies with the terrain, as well as with his activity.

Also, those angles at hand and terret gave you some friction to hold the reins. I believe that this is one reason why the high-seated English style uses reins running OVER the fingers, and the American style with much lower seating often uses a style with reins running UNDER the fingers, as in riding. You need the change of direction to help you "get a grip". (I know this is not universally the case as some drivers run the reins over the top of their fingers even in lower vehicles, though not necessarily in Achenbach / English coachman style.)

Achenbach / English coachman style is very much the more comfortable style for a tall vehicle. You don't need to hold your arms nearly as high as in a lower American vehicle; you can drive with your arms in a natural and relaxed, yet instantly "available" position. "Hands at the third waistcoat button" ... or as a middle aged lady instructor I know says to other middle aged lady drivers, "hands at tit-height!" But in a low vehicle this may mean the reins run onto the horse's backside.

However, I'd rather see a driver being sensitive to the action of the bit, and looking where s/he is going, than getting the rein angles or rein holds "absolutely perfectly right". I once judged a mixed driving class at a show in south Cumbria and one lady driver was so focussed on showing me how she could drive with one hand (and this is not what Achenbach / coachman style means) that she drove her pony into a show jump.

(BTW Yes, you spelt Achenbach correctly. In England we often call it "coachman style" – Benno von Achenbach learnt it here <VBG>)

Despooking, motorbikes (1), 18 July 2005

Well, it's raining here, that fine soft misty Cumbrian rain that makes you wet even though it doesn't appear much. The weather forecaster promised us a "damp sandwich" of a day – dry start, wet middle, dry end!

For various reasons that i won't bore you with I've decided to drive out this evening or afternoon, so this morning has been the first of the motorbike despooking sessions with the two Fell ponies.

I downloaded six or seven different and really scary motorbike sounds (some I didn't have a codec for, but most played fine.) I shoved them into a sound editor and pushed up the volume as high as it would go, then copied and pasted the sequence so I had all the noises in one track, in turn, two or three times over. It made a big file but it gave me about 8 minutes of sheer hell on wheels! Then I copied it to CD and tested it on the boom-box – a sequence of really NASTY loud noises resulted. Perfect.

Well, being dopey this morning I forgot to take the boom-box out to the stable at feeding time!

Anyway, I left the mucking out till quite late and the ponies had eaten their first slice of hay by the time I went out so they heard me and started whickering. While they were asking for food, I plugged in the boom-box on the socket in the empty stable and I turned the CD motorbike track on at half volume.

Both ponies were surprised, but they weren't seriously frightened. Mr T stood rigid for a moment and then began to circle his box at a walk. After thinking about it, Ruby did the same. (The two boxes are side by side inside a stone cow byre, with chest height partitions so they can see each other.) I went in to them and produced Polo mints from my pocket, and the two impostors instantly forgot the noises, turned to me and began competing for treats. So each time the next noise started up, and they were still, I fed them a mint saying "NICE motorbikes". Mr T was still nervous – you could tell by the way he couldn't quite remember how to nibble a mint; he was "all thumbs"; but he was relaxed enough to think about it and to take it from me. Ruby was more interested in chasing him off so she could have all the treats!

We got to the end of the mints, and into a Fell to Fell argument about who deserved the treats more, well before we got to the end of the track, so then I brought them each a tiny bit of feed, and pushed the volume up a notch while they ate from their bowls. They were relatively quiet even when they'd finished the feed – and the horrible noises were still going on. So I fetched them some hay and began tidying the beds and went on with my normal routines. Mr T was still pricking his ears every now and again towards the boom-box location, but by then Ruby wasn't really all that bothered!

Tonight I'll go through the feeding routine by playing the bike track as I come to the stable with the feed, and it can play through again while they eat. I'll keep using the phrase "NICE motorbikes" as the cue to accompany relaxation – whether reinforced by mints or feed... There was a distinct improvement in the anxiety levels just in the one session, so I'm hoping to make a permanent dent in them over time. Just am not sure how long it will take.... loose in stable first, then tied outdoors, then standing in harness, maybe walking about on long reins in harness, then in carriage in yard, then (maybe – if it seems necessary) going down the road. Each time starting with moderate volume and turning it up as they settle.

I can only say that so far (fingers crossed) I'm satisfied with the results of Step One.

Penrith Show, 24 July 2005

Today Ruby got it right.

With many tribulations we got her and the cart to the show. Borrowed a horsebox, and she hated the slippery wooden floor and slippery straw bedding and stomped all the way there and all the way back as she kept sliding about on corners (and I don't do fast cornering with a horse in the back. Or even without.) She'll be happier when my own box is put onto its new chassis and she is back to a stoutly rubber matted floor and a few shavings.

We spent quite a while just letting her take in the sights and sounds of the big show field. We were parked in the edge of the car park field, away from the worst noise, but she jumped about a bit while tied to the box, mainly at loudspeaker sounds. My groom led her about and she trotted a fast circle and gave a huge buck and fly kick. However, with that out of the way, she settled down! We eventually harnessed up 15 mins before our class and did a small warm up in an area of the car parking field, sharing it with a very up-and-down actioned Friesian stallion (did I mention she was coming into season?) She took no notice of him though!

The show runs its 3 harness classes all together as it rarely has enough entries to make separate classes worth while. Today there were 10 turnouts in all (better than in other years). The pattern is, preliminary judging with individual show, then road drive, then come in to the main arena for final judging. It was all a bit cock-eyed today though as we kept getting conflicting information about where the prelim ring was to be – empty area at side of car parking, or Ring 4 on main show field? I think we had at least 6 changes of plan through the morning. Eventually we filtered over to the main show field and were judged there. Ruby did not take any notice of the bouncy castles, rattling balloons, generators, smells of frying food, large animals (like Shires with a dray), people with baby buggies or dogs, wandering spectators failing to see or hear that they needed to get out of the way, other horses (show jumping warm up ring next door with practice jump alongside our ring ropes), flapping flags, show photographers running into the horses' path etc. And the loudspeakers that had been making her jump during the morning were totally ignored. What a girl!

We trotted round on the left rein, then on the right. She still has the left-bend on the right rein when she gets showy, but it's not as pronounced as it was. No fireworks this time; no leaps into canter when we met a corner of the ring. It was all much more sober, though not less active than our last attempt at showing! We lined up along one side of the ring. The judge gave us a specific show to do: one figure of eight, with a trot extension "on the long side" – now, as she's an old acquaintance, I knew that she meant "extend as you change the rein", but would anybody else know what the "long side" of a figure eight is? – walk to her, halt for ten seconds, rein back three strides. Ruby stood very peacefully while the rest of the line did their stuff. Some did it well, most lost rhythm, one pair (no – truthfully, it was two Dales ponies alternately pulling their cart side by side) were not working as a pair and the driver's reins were in deep sloppy loops that could even have caught on the pole head. Frighteningly inept... Ruby stepped out willingly when it was our turn, did her best to maintain her bend (not perfect but much better than on other occasions) and rhythm (ditto), and offered me, well, a little more speed on the change of rein. I can't say it was the sizzling extension we had at Tebay, but it was a try, and more importantly, the rest of the show was calm! She halted and stood and reined back, although too far – she's nothing if not generous :-). She stood in line quietly after that and still ignored the stallion screaming at the world, even though he was right next to us.

I had wondered if I should put Ruby at the back of the road drive so she could see any of the carriages that might rattle or make other odd noises. However, she was so calm and cool, that when the stewards were discussing who should lead, I just said we would. I know the route from other years, which only one or two others did. It proved a very good decision as she drove extremely well, calmly, actively, obediently and yet with real enthusiasm. She adores exploring and I think I must do more visiting once the horsebox is on its new chassis – just going out to new places, not only shows. Her clever mind deserves fun, not boredom.

When we came back to the showfield, however, there was more disorganisation evident. Due to a judge starting very late in the Mountain and Moorland classes, the ring we were to have gone into originally was still full of champion ponies and horses, and a junior equitation class. We were told we could have the main ring when the dog agility display cleared it; in twenty minutes' time. So we had to stand in a horse alley with people walking past and among the horses, and with other ponies and horses walking by, for at least half an hour. It was not an ideal situation for inexperienced carriage horses, especially with the stallion in our midst, though I have to say he remained a gentleman. Ruby appeared to think that all the passers-by were coming to admire her, and stood very nicely, with my groom sometimes holding her and sometimes not. I was asked whether she was a Highland or a Fell... I replied, given our location in Cumbria, which did the lady consider more likely? She appeared dumbstruck by this response. But her husband knew enough to nod when I pointed out that although bay is a rare Fell colour, it's the "right colour" for a pony born in Shap; Sleddale ponies are known to be frequently brown or bay.

Eventually we were allowed into the ring, where the dog display team were clearing fire-frames, jumps, and other strange paraphernalia. Ruby just tucked in her nose and went into show off mode. And we were called in first!

For the record, despite there being a photographer hopping about among the class in the prelim ring, while he managed to get five or six of every other horse, there were none of Ruby at all. You win some, you lose some.

One thing we have learnt ??? 24 July 2005

Something I find I have repeatedly mentioned to my young helpers this year is probably worth mentioning here. In my observation, the most dangerous time at any gathering of horse people is AFTER the competition or drive or ride is over. I have seen more accidents happen in that time than at any other. Lots of factors are at work – human tiredness, relaxation of earlier anxiety, adrenalin running down. People do silly things that they would never normally do. My daughter once started to remove a bridle from my Welsh cob before I had even stepped down from the carriage (something I have seen done by others – and witnessed runaways in consequence); Chris had also unfastened a rein when Ruby was still in the carriage. So, coming in from the drive yesterday at Penrith Show, I had cautioned my groom to be alert because we'd have to be standing, possibly for a long time, among people and strange horses. It's so easy to lose concentration after an intense high like a good fast drive or a competitive event.

Stay alert. Even tired horses are quick.

Insights in Neck Collars in use, 31 July 2005

My daughter came to visit today (to use our washing machine – a long visit!) She is very pregnant, so doing no riding or driving. Body "on hold" but eyes and brain fine! So after we did the usual catching up natter, I thought I'd drive each of the ponies in the field so she could give me feedback on how they were going.

The problem I have to solve is that I have lent my show harness to a friend for the Lowther show class on Saturday. Ruby is not ready for such a big show in an arena that has a natural grandstand, draws large crowds, and proves somewhat exciting for the horses. This loan, however, means that Ruby's good plain leather collar, and the "fits everything" set of hames that must go with it, are out of my use till Saturday night. So I wanted feedback on the other collar/s I thought I might use on both Mr T and Ruby this week.

I drove T first. He's unfit, so all I wanted was to do some quiet walking and trotting to warm his shoulders a little. We're preparing to take him as a lesson pony to a beginners' "taster day of driving" later in August, so he needs a few short gentle drives to get his brain back into working mode and his shoulders toughened to pulling after his long semi-retirement, before we do anything longer or more demanding. The collar I tested is an old, once-smart English one, 19.5", straight in profile and a touch narrow. It's the next size down from the nice show collar which is a bare 20" but slightly wider at the top of the neck; that show collar is too big for Mr T when he's in normal condition so he has seldom worn it. The only hames that will go anywhere near it, other than the ones I've lent out, are the ones that came off a small-ish 19" collar. But, on the bigger collar the draught point is of course lower than it should be; perhaps 1.5" lower. I wanted to find out if my daughter could see any effect on the ponies' way of going.

Mr T is a trooper and walked willingly as I drove him round the clumps of thistles (next holiday job – cutting down the thistles!). He also took up a trot happily, but was stiffer on the right rein; no big deal since he has been laid off for nearly 2 years. I only drove him for about 15 minutes. Jen said he looked as though he was trying to shift the collar up his shoulders by moving down through it! When he managed to do this (the collar is a touch long for him) he got the draught into the sweet spot and was happy and engaged and tracking up. But she said if he slackened off and the collar (and draught line) dropped again, "he fell apart and looked horrible!" So, I have a choice: either drive him in his smaller, barely-19" collar with the same hames, which should lift the hame pull into about the right place, or return to the heavy 3" wide padded breast collar for a week. OK, I now need to drive him in the smaller collar and observe again, in order to decide. Tomorrow maybe.

We then drove back to the yard, put T in the little paddock out of the way, and put the 19.5" collar on Ruby. It's a much closer fit on her; she is deeper in the neck and shoulder. It fits well for length but for her, this collar is really a little bit narrow at the top so there's no room to shift the collar at all. She too worked kindly, but pulling faces; and oddly her normal slight left-handed bend had turned into a right-handed bend. Jen said Ruby gave the impression that she was doing the work to please me, despite being uncomfortable. So this collar is out as far as Ruby is concerned. I have no others that will fit her, they are all too small, and the hames that fit her previous "fat fit" 21" collar are the ones out on loan. So for Ruby, there's no option: it's a week in the breast collar for her.

I should have taken pics, but we were too engrossed in looking at the problems!

What I need to do some time in the near future is to draw a pattern of the show collar and the hames, and get a combination ordered that I can use for daily work. That will mean that the good collar can be kept nice for show use and if I do lend it to someone, my ponies, particularly Ruby, will still be comfortable.

FOOTNOTE

I drove Ruby in the breast collar while her good hames were out on loan. Everything went well until we reached the village and had to turn uphill. She took a few strides and then stopped and turned to look at me with the most disgusted expression. "How do you expect me to pull you up a hill in THIS THING!"

She obeyed when I insisted, but I've never driven her in a breast collar since. She knows which equipment makes her job easiest.

Taster day for new drivers, 22 August 2005

I'm whacked! Our driving club ran a taster day for new drivers yesterday and I was on the go, talking and teaching, from morning till teatime. But it was very good fun and everyone went home looking enthusiastic! I was very pleased with the turnout of people. We knew at least 22 "beginners and improvers" were due to come, and we got more, some from 60 or 70 miles away in the next county. It was great that we had people coming as families, so we had a lot of children there between 6 and 18 years as well as young adult couples and of course the older couples who were thinking of what to do with horses now they were getting a bit too stiff to ride a lot.

Mr T was our patient "model" pony for harnessing up, along with another Fell, Rob, and a Shetland, Bracken (who just gave carriage rides to the children and smaller adults). We were able to make a good deal of progress in explaining neck collars vs breast collars, SBB saddles, breeching fit, order of harnessing up, putting-to, and getting into the carriage safely with someone as helper with the horse.

Everybody who wanted to ride in a carriage got to do so before lunch. I made a point of demonstrating how body position as well as seat position could influence the balance and ride of the carriage. Mr T was very tolerant of all the trotting about in his own little arena and thoroughly enjoyed being the centre of attention. He was as fit as a flea despite his long "lay off" and never broke into a sweat despite the very hot sunshine. Obviously grazing out with Ruby has kept him up to the mark physically (yesterday in our practice run at home he behaved like a half broken three year old but at least on the day his innate common sense prevailed!) Christopher put my spare reins on and practised driving Mr T.

After lunch we got a bit more technical (those who were real beginners mostly went home before then, after reading the timetable on the noticeboard!) We talked about lines of draught, high and low swingletrees etc. We had three different modern vehicles to fit the two Fells; two that were too small, but interesting due to smaller wheels and fixed balance (or lack of it!); and four different sets of harness. EVEN the British Driving Society Area Commissioner said she'd learnt something when she phoned later in the evening! I said, "What was that then?" and she said, "Lines of draught – I knew you should pull from the axle but I didn't know WHY!" I asked everyone to handle the five vehicles, pull them about by the shafts and judge how easy they thought they would be to pull. Some even got their partners to climb in the carriages while they held the shafts, so they could judge how much the balance changed during getting in and out, and when the driver was on the seat. You could tell by the expressions of surprise that people were really taking in all the dynamic information they were getting through their hands and bodies!! (You could also tell which drivers didn't quite trust their spouses to hold those shafts steady when they were up on the seat! We kept an eye on them just in case anyone felt puckish!)

I got one of my "familiars" who doesn't mind being a guinea pig in front of strangers, to pull a vehicle with small diameter wheels over a 4" block of wood, then do the same with a vehicle with larger wheels. Everyone could see how much easier it was with the bigger wheels (although he claimed that the effort had made him a "member of the National Trussed"). Then we talked about balanced draught, which nobody had ever heard of but which was easy to demonstrate with a coloured rope held taut from pony shoulder to axle/swingletree. We had a carriage with axle draught and also one with a high swingletree at shaft height (the height familiar to many of our USA list members I expect). So between our two Fells and their neck and breast collar harnesses, we had all the combinations and could show how different setups were correct with different types of harnessing. I did explain why the neck collar and axle draught is our best option IF we can afford the collar, and the hames, and the spare collar for when our equine changes shape...

Finally we let people have a proper drive with our "dual control" system (spare reins for the owner driver just in case of confused beginner steering!) They could also drive through a cones course, set nice and wide. Mr T thought this was his chance, and kept wanting to swoop off into a canter. Eventually when everyone had had their turn at driving (and some of them tried English coachman/Achenbach style too) I offered Christopher another drive, but by this time he felt shy of all the other strangers and refused, although he was happy to come with me as passenger when I let Mr T rip through the cones course! T had an absolute blast, cantering almost the whole course. This has always been his treat after schooling, just before going home and unharnessing, so when someone else asked if they could have a drive, I am afraid I said no, we had finished. But they didn't seem to mind as they knew they'd been a bit slow at coming forward! Everyone seemed to go home happy and with smiles on their faces, and full of enthusiasm. I've had lots of nice thank you phone calls, and we got several new members for the driving club.

It was really interesting to see, too, how intently Ruby and Mr T exchanged information at the end of the day when they were reunited. After all the long distance field-to-yard whinnying, they both pricked their ears sharply, arched their necks, and sniffed deeply at each other's noses for several minutes. I wish I knew what they were passing on to each other (other than, "have you had anything better to eat than I have!") Then Ruby squealed and Mr T did a VTO and they both hurtled off round the paddock, bucking and kicking. Looks as though HE'd be willing to do it all again, even though I feel stiff as a board!

Crosby Show, 25 August 2005

Sort of a progress day, but one I could have done without :-)

I took Ruby to a small local show today. I had entered her in the traditional vehicle class but had difficulty getting a groom since it is a serious holiday week, so chose to turn out with the XC vehicle which I find less intimidating in solo situations because it's much easier to get in and out of. I knew this would put me down the line, but I looked on it as a training day, so that didn't matter too much.

I showed Ruby in-hand in 2 classes for Fell ponies, and she took a third in the Mares class despite jogging sideways several times down one side of the ring. She did not like the chug chugging display of "stationary engines" working in the Vintage exhibits, which she wanted to run away from but could not because I had her by the bridle. However, by the end of the second class in which she was unplaced, she'd decided she *could* walk in a ladylike fashion without having to turn sideways to keep an eye on the chug-chugging, since it hadn't hurt her. However, she was not too happy about the fairground organ (calliope, which I kept calling carousel for some reason) that was playing for much of the day. The owner was willing to stop it if requested by stewards in the horse ring, so it wasn't a big issue. I rather enjoyed the sound, and was whistling along with the tunes, but Ruby wasn't too enamoured.

A young horsewoman who came by stopped to admire Ruby (and got collared to act as groom!) and we did our show class. Ruby by now was getting into tank mode because we were in the same ring as before with the stationary engines going and the organ pumping away, and for the second time this summer we had a judge who didn't ask the horses to change direction so we kept on going round and round on the right rein until the poor animals were nearly screwed into the ground. It does help literally to unwind them if the judge just asks for a change across the diagonal ...

The first competitor's own choice of show demonstrated how the pony could do tiny circles pivoting on one wheel, to compensate for the fact that it doesn't back at all. So we all did the same exercise so we could prove we too could do it, as well as extend quite prettily AND reverse back. Pivoting just happened to the be first exercise Ruby learnt so it came as no surprise to her at all!

We were 3rd (or last, as you care to look at it). Fine. We then expected to have twenty minutes or so while the exercise cart class was judged, before the cones course was set up. So, I substituted another young lady who wanted to have a drive with me, and I didn't take Ruby out of the cart. Mistake. Of course it took much longer than twenty minutes to get an empty ring AND some cones. We kept walking about, which for a while was good because there was a great deal of space, and Ruby got to pass the cattle in pens, flapping signage, piles of jump stands lurking in the grass, a Clydesdale pulling a farm cart with passengers hopping on and off, and that silly Shetland chariot thing we discussed here a few weeks ago (ask me if I like it any better having seen it – later!) etc etc. Well, Ruby kept on walking but was getting bored. She started to invent places to go and trying to make unilateral decisions. I kept thinking that we'd be going into the ring shortly, so the time she spent in harness got longer, and longer, and while she didn't do anything remotely naughty, she must (I now know) have been getting cross. And an hour and a half's worth of cross is too much :-)

Eventually a simple course was set up and at the judge's invitation I drove into the collecting area. Same ring as the previous three classes; same fairground organ and stationary engines. As Ruby drove through the gate, I mentioned the fairground organ to the steward who went off to ask for it to be stopped, but while we walked about and waited to be asked to drive the course, Ruby's temper finally went up in smoke. "What, this ring AGAIN! And that nasty noisy music! I have HAD IT." She picked up her front feet and shook her head and generally gave everyone to understand that she was completely pissed off. She didn't rear totally, just did levades. I can guarantee I didn't hold onto her with the reins, nor smack her, but for what seemed a very long minute she did not listen to my voice telling her to go forward. People began to converge on the action, in that helpful manner that drivers do, but thank heavens, the fairground organ stopped and she settled down!

I asked the judge if I could drive my cones first and leave, and as he's an old friend – and a sensible chap – he of course said yes. So I set Ruby going and she settled down to her job nicely once she knew she had something to do and was not distracted by the noise of the organ "as well as" being bored. She has got the idea of "hit the centre of the space between the cones" and so she drove quite a tidy round though she had never seen a slalom before.

I took her quietly away from the ring as soon as we finished, and I unharnessed her and gave her all the little attentions she clearly felt I had been withholding – like mints, and water, and access to grass. I went back on foot to line up with the other competitors, and she'd been placed fourth, which was fine given the earlier excitement. Several people, however, asked where was my horse! Obviously they had not understood what had been going on in Ruby's head!

Lesson 1 – if there is a delay, get Ruby out of the shafts and give her off duty time, including that essential for Fell pony sanity, grazing. Lesson 2 – I still need a groom who's competent. The girl I had with me for the cones course was a complete novice in driving terms although she helps and rides from a yard where driving is done. Lesson 3 – make sure the previous ingredients are in place if a fairground organ is likely! Time for another despooking CD???

Champion at Dufton, 28 August 2005

Ruby has got over her boring day at Crosby Show. Yesterday I took her to her last "proper agricultural show" of the year at Dufton, which is known as "The Fellside Royal" – a little, quiet, slightly idiosyncratic show below the slopes of the Pennines, where, instead of every second person leading a dog or a family of small children, they seem to be leading or riding a pony. The health and safety people would have a fit but it seems to work so nobody worries. As in many horse-oriented establishments, the "industrial" (domestic) entries were not so well supported! <vbg>

Dufton is one of my favourite small shows although it is a pig to get to, and the only reason I haven't gone in recent years is because I have usually been working in the preceding weeks. I hadn't entered Ruby in any Fell in-hand show classes this time. I still planned to arrive early but I thought I'd maybe walk her about then bring her back to the horsebox and let her just stand and eat hay instead of being taken to do anything disciplined, while I took my time over cleaning the brass on the harness. There were far fewer scary noises at Dufton; no carousel organ, no vintage engines, just the occasional generator lurking in the grass behind a tent, and a big bouncy-castle-cum-children's-slide in the shape of the upturned stern of the Titanic.

An old friend, Christine Morton, and her daughter Alison, were getting ready to drive their mare Tilly, who is by a Hanoverian x B&W cob colt out of a Fell (she is a tall, clean legged black and white!). Tilly was another who appeared to have been disturbed by the fairground organ at Crosby. Since we were parked next to each other at Dufton and were both on the field really early (about 4 hours before the show class was scheduled, if it started on time, which is always rare at any agricultural show), Christine suggested going for a drive out before getting ready for the show driving. I thought that was a very good idea, making a complete change from going round in circles in the show ring, and with just the two of us it would freshen up Ruby's mind nicely. Christine said she actually wanted to wear her mare out! but we just did a steady couple of miles together, out and back. Ruby led and had a wonderful time exploring. She had been to Dufton earlier in the year, on our Easter drive. This time she wanted to follow the tanker collecting milk from the farm on the outskirts of the village, and she was quite unbothered by the gathering show traffic on the single track roads, or by tractors or vans, or having to wait on laybys to allow rattling builders' trailers to pass. It was a nice way to start the day; it relaxed all of us and it certainly put Ruby in a good frame of mind. She likes to lead and it seemed as though she took charge of Tilly who was following.

Christine and Alison both get a bit nervous about showing in the driving classes. They have not been driving very long (about 18 months). They said their ambition was just to get round the ring without Tilly doing one of her U turns and leaving! But I was feeling fairly calm so I told them to think positive, as we were both going to win!

Ruby decided several weeks ago that Winter is on its way in the North of England (and today's weather proves she is no slouch at meteorology!) She has been casting her summer coat and putting up a layer of white grease that is hard to wipe off the inside of the harness. So cleaning that off was the first thing that had to be done following our drive out. Ruby spent the day munching hay and watching the world go by, while we driving competitors parked cosily in one end of the stubble field and chatted and cleaned our harness and vehicles.

Did I mention that Dufton Show has its own idiosyncrasies? One of them is a difficulty in defining its show driving classes. I simply could not make head or tail of the show schedule (one class was for "any vehicle" and the other for "traditional or exercise vehicle") so I wrote when I paid my entry, explained my non-comprehension, and said, "Put me in whichever class you think is right, because I am bringing an exercise cart". How did they solve that? I ended up with two entries, one in each class! Also, I was in the catalogue under number 88, but was given number 89 because the competitors' list had got mixed up so "that one is the right one". I didn't bother to even try to understand. Alan, the regular steward for the driving, is a local man who trains and breeds driving horses. He knows all the Cumbrian drivers and most of the National ones personally. Should we be in the ribbons, I knew he wasn't going to mistake "me" for the sylph-like young lady whose name appeared against number 89 on the class list :-)

Once again the driving classes were delayed. It's the need to amalgamate two rings to make room for us that is the trouble. But Julie the commentator (wife of Alan) regularly gave out the time lag over the loudspeakers, so at least we knew how long we were likely to have to wait. I harnessed Ruby up, but unlike our day at Crosby, I didn't put her in the carriage. I sat in the horsebox talking to Chris and to his Mum while Ruby dozed in the cool, but welcome sunshine. We were given clear warning by Julie of when the class before the driving was about to start, so it was only then that I put-to to go and walk Ruby round to the show ring entrance and study the generator and bouncy castle/slide. And the show officials did in fact move the Veteran Horse classes to another ring to give the Driving two rings that adjoined, so we were treated well really!!

The grassy ground was perfect underfoot, the ring(s) not huge, but big enough. I had planned to be first in, and start off on the left rein " just out of badness" because although the traditional direction on entry is the right rein, Ruby gets more het-up on that rein.... And bless the steward, I didn't need to make any special effort because he TOLD us to take the left rein. That of course made Ruby very happy and she strode on willingly. It was a day when she was great to drive, really swinging her backside and powering onward. There wasn't room to overtake anyone but she was obedient and collected when we were held up, she didn't fret when I kept her collected to let the slower horses get away, and then when she had enough room to go she took full advantage of it. She stood quietly in line with Chris at her head and then did a neat, obedient, vigorous individual show, with every indication of enjoyment. (My daughter looks at the bent back ears on the show photos and reads "resistance" but to me they say "I am listening and being obedient, tell me what to do and I will do it.")

Ruby was pulled in first in the exercise cart class.

The steward (who I suspect was enjoying a great deal of discussion of the classes with the judge) said to me with deep approval as he indicated Ruby's place to stand, "THAT is a REAL driving horse. Hang on for the championship, you'll see..." and gave me a conspiratorial wink. "Real" is a terrific compliment up here; "it's a real 'un" is a horse you are proud to own, a good sort, something near perfect. It's almost the equivalent of the Spanish "real" meaning "royal". Appropriate for Dufton.

The judge chose Tilly for her "traditional" carriage winner (the power of thinking positive?), but even in her cross-country carriage, Ruby was the champion. And of course, she just loved being able to lead the rest of the class in her lap of honour!

It must have been the weight of the brass horse-and-carriage "Moonstroller Trophy" and the class winners' cup and all the rosettes that made the horsebox clutch give way 16 miles from home... so that Ruby had to be taken home in a friend's horsebox, and I got towed back about 9:00 pm!!

Sue

British Driving Society proficiency tests, 31 August 2005

I'd like to comment and to correct some misconceptions in previous RED list discussions about BDS proficiency testing:

On 31 Aug 2005 at 1:23,
RecreationalEquineDriving@yahoogroups.com wrote:

> *I also like the idea of having different levels of instructors available such as I think the BDS program tries to do.*

That's not what the various levels are intended for. The proficiency tests are tests that drivers take for their OWN benefit and improvement, and that of their horses. They are not instructors' tests. They just evaluate proficiency in driving, road safety and horse management. They check that you know the safe ways to do things and, sometimes, that you know the reasons behind the traditional ways to do things.

The only differences between Light Harness Horse Instructors are which optional units they took in their Level 2 (en route to Advanced and LHHI), eg: "horse driving trials; private driving; pleasure driving; driving for the disabled. There is a unit for pair driving which at level 2 is optional but becomes compulsory for those wishing to progress to the Advanced Certificate."

You either ARE an LHHI or you are not. There are no grades, such as there are for ridden instructors (Assistant Instructor, Intermediate Instructor, Fellow of BHS and so on).

BDS however do list people in their Year Book as capable of instruction if they have passed Advanced level test and First Aid and the teaching test. (More on this below.)

> *However, in backwoods areas (like my own) where people are few and far between – regulations like that are either going to be completely ignored or even protested.*

These are NOT "regulations", even here in Britain. Nobody HAS to take them, neither driver nor instructor. BDS are simply offering them to give a standard for people to aim at. There is much discussion at present as to whether it is worthwhile insisting on standards, for example on drives out should people wear hat, gloves, and apron? I believe the proficiency tests serve a useful purpose in maintaining standards and therefore helping horses. Nobody else does it for us drivers, so we have made the tests up ourselves. SOME of the principles enshrined in them are now part of Government policy for the licensing of commercial driving businesses.

Of course if you pass "Advanced (2 reins)" and/or "Advanced (4 reins)" and the teaching test and First Aid test, and if you further become an LHHI, you can teach with some authority. You are "probably" better at teaching than someone who has not undergone the training-and-testing. However, I agree that there are some people who would remain poor teachers despite it, and others who are brilliant teachers without it.

But: in Britain people may, can and do teach driving with no qualification at all behind them other than their own experience, and people may, can and do drive a horse with bog-all knowledge, skill or intelligence.

Winter Projects, 29 October 2005

It's probably tempting fate to start thinking I will have spare time over winter, but here goes:

I got a bargain at Clitheroe Auction sales a fortnight ago, when both I and Derrick, a friend, wanted a pair of old beat-up cheap 22 inch hames to renovate and use on our Fell ponies' work collars. There was just one lot listed in the catalogue, with no measurements. It was for 2 pairs of hames; no details of size or condition. Plenty of collars were listed, of all ages, and a few with hames on them, but we both have collars, so we just needed hames – besides, we are both mean. Derrick said he'd pay up to £25 for a pair and that was about my top limit too.

The sale room was closed once the sale began (so as to prevent items vanishing unexpectedly – you all know what I mean) so because the lot in question hadn't arrived before that closing time I couldn't measure the hames before I bid. I just had to hope I'd see what size they were when they came under the hammer.

I bought a few bits and bobs just to get my eye in; 10 brass buckles, a pony bridle for a friend's Shetland. (That meant the auctioneer knew I was a bidder and saw my bidding number clearly!) Bidding was pretty mean so most things went quite cheaply, though quality made its money, as it ought: full sets of used black patent gig harness – two pleasant sets – sold around £750 and a good pair of driving lamps £250. Asian harnesses were going for £90 (I thought that expensive! especially given the typical quality), but oddments made almost nothing and I bought a part set of "Shires" English harness, around 20 years old, for £95 which I thought a much better deal.

When eventually the hames came up, the auctioneer tried them at £5. They were rusty and tatty and the hame billets looked very sad, but one pair had both its trace buckles and the other was an old trade set with a ring instead of a buckle to connect the traces. The auctioneer offered £5 again. I looked away and listened, and when he had to drop the opening figure to £3, and even started to say "Looks like nobody wants..." I lifted my number card and bid. Someone else tentatively offered £4 so I raised it to £5. And there wasn't another bid.

I collected all my purchases later in the morning and took the two *very* dirty pairs of hames to the car where I could put the measuring tape on them and lo and behold, both pairs were 22"!

When I got them home, I laid them on Ruby's work collar and both sets match it for shape. Keeping one set and doing it up will save me having to try to keep her brass plated show hames smart and unscuffed. I've been scrubbing the acquisitions with the wire-brush drill attachment today, and the set I've decided to keep, though of a relatively heavy "delivery" design, look as though they were once silver plated. I think I have a strip of leather, and buckles, to make a couple of hame straps, but the hame pulls will be webbing... I used webbing pulls years ago with Rosie, Ruby's great aunt, to pull some seriously large logs with this collar (before I had the better-quality hames sandblasted and brass plated and fitted them with proper leather pulls and brass buckles). I know I can trust the webbing so I will use some again.

Tomorrow's job is to paint that clean bright steel with Hammerite – gold or bronze to go with the browny-green leather of the work collar and its fawn wool lining. Might have to ask daughter to go and buy gold or bronze paint for me ... yes they're only work hames, but why not make a nice picture while I'm at it? I'll be looking at them every working day after all! and doesn't "Big Red" Ruby deserve to look delicious?

Then there's the repainting of some chips in the black enamel on the show lamps (last done-over about 20 years ago, so not a big deal) and of the lamp brackets, and of the spacers on the show gig that widened the shafts at splinter bar and shaft tail, and of the renovated swingletree to replace the original show one that is FAR too narrow for Ruby's big ribcage ... roll on, rainy winter weekends.

Ruby has a cheeky Christmas, 27 Dec 2005

I managed to find time out from the kitchen yesterday to go and drive. Ruby didn't mind. She prefers "out" to "in" any day, and work is "Out" so it's OK.

We wandered quietly down into the village, and I had my instant reward (quite apart from going driving) in the shape of a kingfisher who'd been perching in one of the bare alder trees by the river, who flashed away upstream in a streak of brilliant turquoise light.

Ruby set off to trot up the hill but decided halfway that she really wasn't that fit, so we walked the rest. She'd been indoors quite a bit so I wasn't going to press her. She was sneaky on the way out, finding grassy verges where she suggested we might turn round and go for home! Cheeky mare. I kept her going at "walk-March", watching the new/refurbished hames carefully; they work fine, as I thought they would, being the same size and fitting as the "good" pair I want to keep nice for showing. We did about a mile and a half, crossing the noisy motorway bridges just as an exercise to remind her about traffic, of which we see very little at the farm.

When I turned her for home she got a bit strong – typical Fell! She wanted to canter all the way home. When I checked her she bucked before going back into her 10-mile-an-hour power trot. We sailed home, she thinking very naughty thoughts, and I taking care not to disturb matters. Once she slackened speed I told her to keep right on going, which she did, with a little less fizz! At one point when she slackened I shook the whip to make a slight noise, and she gave another buck, cheeky woman, and shook her head at me. So I scolded her verbally and told her to get on, and she settled down and went on working... She's clever enough to try your control yet give in as soon as she knows you're still in charge. She so rarely shows any temper, and her head shake is so funny with her huge black mane and forelock flying, I can't get mad at her. I know it's just freshness, because nothing has changed since her last drive out except being stabled a good deal, AND she behaved with great decorum last time we were out, and that's just as well, because we had a BBC radio 4 presenter recording in the passenger seat!

She is going back into her kicking strap for the next few drives out though!

Sue

Training day at George Bowman's

I went to the NWDC "do" on showing your horse in harness, at George B's, on Sunday last. We'd all thought George would be running it. Not so. George told my daughter Jen (the secretary) on the preceding Tuesday that "that woman from Greenholme who used to be chairman" was going to organise it.

"You mean my mother?" said Jen.

"Aye, that would be right," said George. "I'm off to a birthday party for our Robert."

So Woman from Greenholme had to hurriedly print off handouts and round up photographs and harness, while Jen arranged for someone to come with a horse and carriage and give a "how not to do it" demo. We got the lads to put down a line of straw bales to display the harness, handouts, magazines and photographs and Jen brought a table for my laptop which had a photo show going. We set out George's motley crew of chairs behind the bales, and left the rest of the arena for the horse and carriage.

George did come and answer questions from us for about 45 minutes before he went to Robert's party. He discussed proper whip length and use, and how a lady or gent would handle it while giving a salute to a judge, and also showed us some of the different bits he has in his tackroom – one was a version of the Sam Marsh pelham, with a broad, flat, swivelling mouthpiece that always lies flat across tongue and bars, no matter whether the driver has the reins set at curb or cheek.

Alison, who although young is the current Chairman of the club, brought her black and white mare Tilly, who is by a Hanoverian x B&W cob colt out of a Fell. Tilly's about 15.2 and often inclined to mess about, going backwards, but perhaps because Ali and her mum Christine were trying to show us "how not to do it", she entered into the spirit of the day and was only naughty when told to be! Ali came in wearing dirty leggings, no hat or gloves, with her harness all wrongly set up, and she and Christine had loud conversations about Going Too Fast (with Tilly cantering and being tapped on the rump with the whip to make her buck), then Christine tried to grab the reins off Ali and then, when things slowed down, she put her feet up on the dashboard, while spectators, as part of the game, offered Ali a cigarette and had conversations with her from the "ringside".

George spent some time adjusting the "wrong" harness on the mare, which was interesting because Ali had set the traces a hole too long, but George thought they were better that way because the mare was further from the dashboard of the cart (which was a vehicle made for a 14 hand pony and was on the point of being too small for her). On one side, the shaft tug hung behind the pad; on the other it didn't. There were lots of possible reasons for this – one trace longer than the other, the removable shafts being set up slightly differently, or even the mare bending more one way than the other. It took 15 minutes of discussion to settle on the trace length. It certainly gave weight to my comment later in the session about "never buy a new set of harness and fit it for the first time at a show".

After George went off to his family party, I carried on with a discussion of what the judge is looking for in a horse shown in harness; making the point that the horse is mainly what is being judged, and all the other accoutrements are just add-on goodies. I didn't go into the specifications of the "perfect horse" – merely saying that every single person in the audience KNEW they had the perfect horse in their stable. Christine and Ali recalled an incident late last year when a Welsh cob, in an exercise cart with dirty webbing harness, wiped the floor with several smarter turnouts. It drove really well and behaved impeccably, while all the others were either idle or naughty.

The day went well, despite the short time we'd had to organise it. There were lots of questions and plenty of discussion. The non members coughed up a fiver each; a couple of people who had not previously shown their ponies in harness found the session very helpful in planning their summer outings to shows; and we even got a few new members joining the Club.

Rein Handling?

>*Regarding whip use: what do you mean by drive an "apparatus"?* *Do you mean we should practice our reinsmanship using a rein-board before actually driving our horses?*

It would certainly help you to spot any inconsistencies in your rein handling, eg when using the whip. And, if you end up wanting to learn to drive English coachman / Achenbach / German style, you can profit a great deal from using a rein board to practise turns of differing severity. (PS – this is an ENGLISH style that just happens to have been popularised by Benno von Achenbach, who learnt it in England; and therefore it may SEEM to be German from its name, but it wasn't originally.)

>*How do you drivers – the ones who always keep the whip in hand when driving – hold your reins?*

THIS IS THE NO-FRILLS, NO-FLUFFIES EXPLANATION .... IF YOU NEED SMILES, IMAGINE THEM PLEASE.

Starting at the shoulders: I sit up straight as though riding. I let my upper arm hang vertically to the elbow. My forearms point inward at roughly 45 degrees to my upper arms, more or less parallel with the ground (so a touch more than 90 degrees of angle between upper arm and forearm).

The backs of my hands follow the same angle as my forearms and my thumbs are uppermost, knuckles pointing forward and nails facing my lower chest/stomach. (Does this sound familiar from riding???) They're about 6 inches from my middle.

The left rein comes to my hand over the top of my left forefinger and down through my palm. The right rein comes into my hand between ring finger and middle finger and down through my palm. I keep an even pressure on the reins by slightly squeezing the edges with my lower 3 fingers (I use a 1 inch heavy ribbed cotton webbing rein that narrows in use to about 7/8ths). The slack of the reins falls down my left outer shin.

I create a basic hold, as above, that gives even contact on either side of the bit. By turning my hand nails-up I can incline the horse to the right – it gives the left side of the bit, and takes the right equally. (Read your palm, turn RIGHT.) By turning the back of my hand up, the reverse occurs. (Look at your watch, turn LEFT.) NB contact with a driving horse can often feel heavy to a rider – but don't forget, the driving horse is only carrying the weight of the rein from the neck terret to his mouth, which is less than the hand-to-bit distance when riding; while you are carrying the weight of the rein from pad terret to your hand, which is much longer. So what YOU may feel is rather heavy, the horse often barely notices.

I carry my right hand forward and place the middle 2 fingers between the reins, which enables me to adjust the length of either rein without letting go of my basic hold in the left hand. My right hand is always there, barring I need to use it for signalling, whip use, blowing my nose, waving to friends, insulting idiots, etc. When I do that, I leave the whip under my left thumb.

English driving uses both hands, not the left only. For sharper turns: You form a loop in the rein, by taking a rein in your right hand, that you can tuck under forefinger or thumb then let slide back to "basic position" as the turn is completed. You can also adjust both reins with the right hand, eg let them slip through the left, or feed them back with the right. Don't forget to give with the opposite rein as well as take with the "turning" rein. Don't put your left hand in front of your right.

The whip is ALWAYS in my right hand, held by balance not by grip. Every whip balances differently and you need to find one that suits you and your strength. You hold it just below the point of balance, not by gripping the end of the handle. This enables it to lie in your hand ready for use, but it doesn't stop you adjusting the reins, because the holds (above) allow the whip to lie independently of your fingers. The whip, held in this manner, will lie at 45 degrees from everything (if you are a math person, 45 degrees from the x, y and z axes!) not upright or horizontal or leaning on the person sitting next to you. You need a long enough whip to be able to touch the horse on the shoulder or pad or girth without you reaching forward bodily and losing contact with the reins. A long-ish stock and a decent thong are required to enable this. Those little smackers used by the trotter and pacer men will not suffice :)

You also need to be sitting high enough in your vehicle to see over your horse. You can't drive comfortably for any distance if you have to hold your arms up at shoulder level just to keep the reins off his arse.

As for getting the whip caught up in bushes, just move it temporarily to the vertical or horizontal (as required) when passing bushes. (I drive on the left and sit on the right, so if you are in a country that has to drive on the right, this may be more difficult for you because you may be sitting on the left of your vehicle.)

I thank you. Pay at the desk please.

More than we bargained for (bridles and Shetlands), 10 September 2006

I arranged with my friend Ann to go driving this morning – another fine September day, too warm for a jacket. Along with the growing winter coats, the warmth makes for dozy ponies. Dozy drivers too but that's another matter. We had thought of inviting a neighbour to drive with us as groom but evidently she couldn't make it because when she arrived Ann was on her own and so was I. We were both wearing our hard hats and our reflective waistcoats. Ruby and Ann's Shetland pony, Little Black, sniffed noses when we met on the green, and the meeting was gentle and friendly. That turned out to be important for what came later!

We set off at a walk, then trotted up the hill out of Greenholme, having agreed we were setting our course for Orton, which 5 year old Black has not yet visited. This seemed a nice training goal for her; a leisurely drive in some new territory.

We walked and trotted (gently, with respect for Black's short legs and somewhat unfit condition) and were thoroughly enjoying ourselves, chatting about this and that. We were walking when suddenly Ann's voice from behind me said, "SUE! SUE!" on a very agitated note. I looked around and there was little Black following us with her bridle hanging round her chest! "WHAT DO I DO!"

"Keep talking, keep hold of the reins and tell her to whoa." I thought of putting Ruby across the road, but it was too wide at that point for my turnout to stop her. Black was picking up on Ann's anxiety, and ignoring the Whoas she came trotting past me and down the slope to the guidepost, with Ann trying hard to stop her with reins as well as Whoas. Black trotted out of the junction and across the Orton-Shap road. We were just lucky no traffic came. And then, bless her, she turned a circle and started up the road to her home farm. I didn't follow with Ruby at the fast trot which she could easily have done, or try to overtake Black, because I didn't want to do anything to add speed to the situation. A Shetland trotting steadily is one thing, and not all that fast – but one in a flat out gallop with a panicking driver would be quite another.

Black headed up the hill at a trot and then, feeling the gradient, began to slow down – Great! I thought. Let her get her head in that grass on the verge and we've got her. But Ann had decided to get out of the cart, and before I could say DON'T, she stepped down and loosed the pressure on the reins and Black started forward. The wheel caught Ann's leg and she fell flat, hitting her head on the road. She rolled and lay still and Black started forward again with the bit and bridle down by her knees.

I could hear something with a heavy diesel engine coming over the brow of the hill – and evidently Black heard it too, because she turned round and came trotting back towards us. I quickly put Ruby across the road with her nose at the grass verge. Black carefully trotted round Ann who was still on the floor, walked down to us and put her nose to Ruby's. Needless to say I was out of the carriage in a flash and had grabbed the little one by her headcollar. Ann sat up, groaning. Her helmet had saved her head from any serious damage, though I think she had been "out" for a minute. She dragged herself to her feet and told me there was a tractor and silage trailer coming up the road from the next farm. "Tell it to stop!" I said urgently, "it must stop!" There was no way I'd be able to flag down the driver with a pony in each hand – one with no bridle on – and still control them and their carts while that large vehicle drove past us. In any case, I'd effectively blocked the road! Ann limped up the brow to wave her arms at the driver. Ruby stood like a good'un (eating grass) but I kept hold of her reins while I unfastened the throatlash and noseband of Black's bridle and popped it back on Black's head. I pinched a strap off my carriage (the kicking strap loops have been hanging there on the shafts just-in-case since about July) and fastened it through

Black's too-large throatlash to the headcollar and to the bridle noseband, so her bridle couldn't be shaken off again. Thank goodness the silage trailer had stopped. By then there was a milk tanker behind it, but at the sight of Ruby and her carriage standing across the road and Ann in her reflective waistcoat, obviously hurt, waving them down, both drivers sensibly just waited!

Suddenly it was all under control again. The traffic was stopped. Ann was up and walking and talking sensibly, though in pain from a scraped elbow and twisted knee. Ruby and little Black were calm, and the harness was all in order and the bridle unlikely to come off again. So we signalled thanks to the drivers of the tanker and tractor, Ann got back into her cart, and we quickly moved the ponies out of the way so the men could get on with their day's work; and then we abandoned our plan to drive through the village and instead set off to walk quietly home.

Ann is OK, though she'll be stiff and sore for some days and will need to use hot-and-cold treatment on her swollen left knee; when you're over 60, falling on a hard road even from an easy entry Shetland cart is nasty. Ruby and I were in accord and she had never put a foot wrong. Black was amazingly unbothered by the whole thing.

What have we to blame for this accident, and to thank for this escape?

What lessons have we learnt, or what actions have we found right or wrong?

Well, first of all, we ought to have had an active, knowledgeable person with us who could have got out of Ann's cart and grabbed Black. You all know, and I know and Ann knows, that this is a rule we ought not to have broken. That I break it very nearly every time I drive doesn't make it OK.

Ann ought to have made sure that Black's bridle fitted properly. That said, as any harnessmaker knows, a little head with little ears and lots of mane equals "shake your head and off it goes!" I have now shown Ann how to use a small strap (eg a dog collar) as a gullet strap – and to include the headcollar throatlash for good measure when putting it on. It wouldn't hurt, either, to put a spare hole in the bridle cheekpiece, in between the holes that are there; they're too far apart to use the next hole that's available at present, because that would tighten up the bridle fit rather too much.

The things that saved us were: two calm ponies, both trained to harness *in an open bridle*. David Trotter had done this for Black, as he always does when training a new pony, and so Black stayed calm and took no notice of the cart behind her simply because she had seen it all before. She didn't panic. She was trying hard to make sense of Ann's commands and of the pressure on her chest from the bit! She had recognised Ruby as a friend, so she stood with her and remained calm while I sorted out her bridle. And, of course, she had that headcollar on so I was able to grab her easily.

She shook her head a good deal on the way home. That's probably how the bridle came off in the first place, because she was hot round the ears and sweaty, and there were flies about that bothered her. But going home the bridle stayed where it was supposed to be, on her head, with the bit in her mouth. Ann kept her behind me; Black was totally serene, ears flicking to and fro, neck relaxed, mouth relaxed, and behaving as though nothing much had happened (which for her, I suppose it hadn't, since the cart remained upright the whole time).

Once we'd done most of the way home at walk I suggested we have a trot (agreeing the start and end places beforehand) and then that Ann should take Black in front for a few hundred yards, as much for Ann's confidence as for Black's. We did this and Black was suitably stodgy about going in front, so that Ann had to drive her rather than hold her back – excellent!

Then I led again, and I went home with Ann to help her to unyoke and unharness Black.

I made sure Ann was OK and everything done for Black before she went out in the field. After we'd had a quick cup of coffee, which Ann insisted on as she said she needed it, I harnessed Ruby again and went home. I was very proud of her. I hadn't had to think about her while the emergency was taking place. She just did everything she was told to do.

As I drove along the lane to our house I heard the roar of fighter jets, and there, flying low, nearly on the same level as us, were the Royal Air Force Red Arrows Display Team, scarlet-painted and glittering in the sun, going south through the gorge in two tight formations of five. What a strange end to a very unusual drive!

Drive one, 1 hour 45 mins, 5 miles; and drive two, home, 10 mins, 1.5 miles (1:55 and 6.5 miles total)

Sue in the English Lakes

and "Matron" Ruby.

Peace of mind, 7 October 2006

It's a blustery, rain-spitting day here with the sun hidden behind increasing banks of cloud – the sort of day that you know will get worse, and if you go out driving it's on the edge of being drivable for pleasure.

I get itchy to do things at weekends, because so many days of the week are a waste of time (any day is wasted that you don't do things with your horse!). So as the wind is from a quarter which means most of our yard is sheltered, though the pine tree branches are tossing and roaring, I tied up a haynet for Ruby in the yard, and got her out and groomed her. What could I do that would be worthwhile but not take us out of the yard? Well, it's been a long time since Ruby saw the cart behind her without her blinkers on. She'd been started with an open bridle and had shown no sign of any tension, but that had been two years ago. Considering Ann's accident with Black, I thought maybe a little quiet reminder of life without blinkers might be useful future-proofing.

I put the dog away and shut the yard gate. I harnessed up with all the usual gear but with an open bridle. Ruby chomped on the unfamiliar bit for a minute, but it was the same shape as her usual driving bit, a stainless steel mullen mouth, so she soon returned to the haynet. Funnily enough I think the racing half cup blinkers actually enhance her head; they appear to broaden her face and now it was odd to see her without them; she looked a different animal.

She took absolutely no notice of the carriage being brought up and put in place, so I went on with yoking up. She looked at me a few times but no more than usual, and concentrated on the haynet. Graham was around on the yard too, so I left her standing tied there while I mucked out. She went on looking relaxed (bored, even) but was clearly making the most of being allowed to eat while in the shafts.

I came back and untied her, and got into the carriage. She went on eating and looking bored (she looks SO like her mother when she wears her ears at that angle). I moved the whip about so she saw it both sides. She went on eating and looking bored. I spoke to her and we went for a walk round the yard, turning both ways so she saw the following wheels from both sides. We moved around for about 10 minutes in all, walking, turning and standing. I even asked her for a little trot up the yard. She could not have been less bothered. Probably she wondered, "what the devil is Mother on with now? This is Old Hat." ... I let her eat the rest of the haynet while I unharnessed her, gave her a taste of coarse mix as she demanded ("I have been Working, Feed Me!") and now she is wandering up and down the yard grazing all the little corners that have grown grass during the summer.

She obviously didn't need any refreshers about unblinkered work, but maybe I did, just for my own peace of mind.

Ann, BTW, is back to riding out; I saw her go by riding Rampy (her 30-year old grey Connemara gelding) during the week. So that story had a much happier ending than it might have had.

Challenge time? 10 minutes!

Sue in the English Lakes

Intelligence is no defence against one's own stupidity

but it helps me to think up better excuses.

Two Lovely Black Eyes

Distance today only about 2 miles, as I was fitting our "good" harness to the exercise cart ready for a show next weekend, and although the harness and cart have been used together before, the shafts are new this year, so I needed to do some trials to get the fitting right.

We met a gang of motorbikers. Ruby paddled her feet a bit (they were a noisy lot) but didn't try to swerve or run away. We rarely have any trouble with the bikers but I do wish they would signal which way they are going at junctions. I had to ask them, so I could avoid blocking their way!

I do have a pair of lovely black eyes though, having reached out to brush Ruby's long forelock without first putting a hand on her headcollar. She often has forelock hairs stuck to the "sleep" in the corners of her eyes, and on this occasion when I brushed her she pulled her face away, hit the wall, and rebounded smack across the bridge of my nose. And this is the mare who was hiding behind me this afternoon to avoid grand-daughter Naomi washing her legs and tummy (which are all Naomi can reach). Just shows you, even the sweetest, kindest horse can do you damage in a moment.

To Tie or not to Tie

> *To tie or not to tie is a subject that most people have strong opinions about...*

I drive solo most of the time. I know I ought not to, but that's just how it is. If the law said, *no helper, no driving,* then I probably would only drive three times a year, other than at shows, which I wouldn't go to because the mare would not be fit. Anyway, I like driving solo, just me and the pony. I don't always want human company!

At home and when working alone I too always tie while hitching. I leave the halter on under the bridle and take a lead rope with me in case I need to tie up to deal with anything while out. This can range from adjusting harness to rescuing a sheep or lamb from a wire fence. My mare is good about not pulling on her halter rope – my little granddaughter aged not quite 3 can lead her about safely. I won't claim she's perfect – that would be tempting fate! – but she's pretty trustworthy.

At a show I will tie only while harnessing, with a nose-buckle halter under the bridle, then I have my helper/groom hold the mare by the lead rope while I hitch. (She actually fidgets less if she's tied up as she is at home, but I go by our Club rule book when at a show.) When we're ready to mount the cart, we release the nose buckle and the crown buckle of the halter and it comes off from under the bridle. I do not undo ANY parts of the bridle to achieve this. I carry a spare halter and lead rope in the show spares box.

I know hitching while tied is really only practicable with a single, but then, driving a pair/tandem or more with no help is foolish if not impossible. (That's why I drive single. I'd love to put Mr T in the lead of Ruby and drive them tandem, but I don't have the help.)

I sometimes attend clinics given by George Bowman. His common-sense advice for harnessing AND hitching: "train it to stand still, but if it won't stand still, tie it up!"

Fell & Dales Show, May 2008

Someone sent me one of those round-robin "get to know your friends better" e mails the other day, and one of the questions was, "What's your favourite day of the year?" I answered that 31 May and 31 October were my favourites because good things seemed to happen on those days. Today certainly was a nice day :)

Ruby and I went to the Fell and Dales Pony show today to do the driving class. I am not certain yet whether I can climb into my show "vehicle" following my surgeries (and thank you Linda for beating me to the Latin translation involving *Veho*, good on you girl!) so I took the cross country cart that I use every day. It's done a lot of miles in its 15 years, and needs careful tarting up for a show outing, but it got that, and I polished the nice leather harness, and washed Ruby, and oiled her feet. I tarted-up me, too, with apron and good gloves and smart jacket, but I decided to drive wearing my helmet, rather than a soft hat. It does seem ridiculous to drive in a helmet all week then remove it for the far more exciting surroundings of a show. So I put my money where my mouth is, and wore the protective stuff.

I expected a road drive of about 3 miles, but Ruby's feet are standing up well to the work we're doing at home and by using her Easyboots during the week beforehand I was sure she'd have more than enough foot to handle it.

The weather was splendid – warm and sunny with just enough breeze to keep things bearable. My daughter Jen brought Naomi to watch (she's not quite 3), and little'un tootled about with baby wipes, "helping" Grannie to wipe the wheels and shafts, and asking if it was OK wipe the wheels, "are they dry?", because she'd seen me painting the rims on Friday. I think she nearly likes driving more than swimming. (I'm working on it.) She was sufficiently engrossed not to practise using her new word, "Why?" ... well, not much, anyway.

I lunged Ruby before the class, getting her to canter out some of her excitable bucks. She bucked so enthusiastically, she actually lost her footing on the young grass and slid over on her side – which surprised but clearly didn't hurt her.

I was amused that people kept coming up and looking at Ruby and asking, "Is that the horse you were driving on that TV program?" (Dales Diary) – even the judge asked!

I must give this show full marks for timekeeping – the driving class started on time, which is something that is becoming rare. The organiser had set up relatively big rings, so that we only had to wait for one to be empty; that is, we didn't have to wait for two small rings to be empty so they could be combined.

We expected four entries in the Fell and Dales class, but only two were forward, and despite the common view that "Fells and Dales are black", both entries were dark bay mares!! One young Dales mare, and Ruby. They were so similar we could easily have made them into a pair or a tandem. Ruby took exception to the Dales mare's triple hanger of bells – when she heard the rattle of the cart and the jingle of the bells behind her, we got some remarkable floaty extensions and a couple of mild explosions – but luckily the judge wasn't looking when we had those, and the brakes and steering remained usable :-) Anyway, I asked the Dales driver to go in front on the drive out, and Ruby soon settled once she could see the object that was making the noises. In fact, we later overtook the young mare, who flagged after about half the drive, and Ruby didn't mind the jingles after that.

One funny episode occurred as we passed a farm that had eight or nine llamas in a small paddock by the roadside. The horses couldn't really see much, other than their heads over the stone wall, and we walked past them, but the llamas still got very excited and trotted about with their heads and tails up, snorting loudly and possibly spitting too, but I can't be sure as I was concentrating on driving Ruby, who thought it was a horsey shock-horror run-away signal. I convinced her otherwise, and she behaved very sensibly on the rest of the drive.

And the judge, although he noticed our absence of steel shoes, wasn't bothered about it.

After the class, Naomi had to be held back from rushing into the ring to ride as groom – "It's MY turn now!" – but she did have a nice quiet ride back to the horsebox, and then helped to wipe everything down, and give Ruby a drink. There were baby wipes all over the place by the time we'd finished. (I did tidy up after her!)

It was nice to win the class, even though there were only the two of us in it, but it was just as nice to have a day out in the sunshine and a drive with two good horses.

Sue

Bretherdale Drive, June 2008

Yesterday was a "hurry" day: taking Ruby the Fell pony to a show. That meant taking all the impedimenta and et-caetera that make up the detail of a carriage driving turn-out. It was worth it, as it happens, because we won; but it was very hard work and some of my joints are now telling me they are too old for it. Today, it's time to relax the mind, and enjoy the day outside before the weather breaks.

Graham, my husband, calls Ruby's road boots her Pink Wellies, though they're actually boring black. Pink Wellie Girl knows she normally has a day off after strutting her stuff in the ring, and she's not really in any hurry to go out. A drive round home is very small beer, after being a show-stopper, but once we're in harness and moving she rather enjoys exploring.

We drive down from Daw Bank into Bretherdale, where the quiet single track road leads over open grazing land and we have gates to open and shut. Ruby doesn't mind waiting by the Millennium sheepfold; as soon as I get down to open the gate her teeth are in the grass. Not for her the pleasure of lining up the eye on that exact division in Goldsworthy's stonework. She doesn't care about the calendar break between December 1999 and January 2000. Her only interest is the edibility of the lush roadside vegetation. Fragrant flowers and shrubs abound: clouds of wild garlic fill the damp hedge bottoms with their medicinal pungency, under lemon-scented tea-leaved willow and creamy heads of rowan blossom. The purity of the hawthorn is pink-tinged, and nearly over. Yesterday we wondered, "What's hitting us? is it rain?" as its cool petals scattered over us on the wind. Today there is no breeze. The air is still and crystal clear. Sound carries with the peculiar immediacy of an impending storm and Ruby's Pink Wellies seem as loud as metal shoes on the gravelly road.

I need to be in the right mood to visit Bretherdale, because all the gates we have to open can be a pain. But for a chill-out drive, where the focus is relaxation, each gate is just another and different way of enjoying the day. Ruby swings along at a comfortable walk, turning her head intelligently to observe the countryside. The dale is narrow and twists deeply into the fells like the road to a secret shrine or a holy retreat. Once it lay in the possession of Byland Abbey, and was valuable for its sheep and cattle pastures. Though the Abbey has long gone, there are still relics to be found; a few years ago a doctor, out walking, came across a seven-pound piece of lead built into a stone wall. It turned out to be a shield-shaped wool-weight, hundreds of years old, yet only the second one known of its type.

Although farming is precarious in these urbanised, supermarket-controlled times, sheep and cattle still remain. At present they are grazing the rougher pastures or the open fell. The flat meadows at the top of the dale are closed to the stock, so the grass can be cut later for hay that will feed the beasts through the winter. James, who farms Midwath, cuts his fields late to enable wildflowers to set seed, and just now they are full of colour: the pale green of flowering grasses, brilliant yellow of buttercup and catsear, purple of wild geranium, rusty red of sorrel. Although the air is so still, the frail stemmed meadow plants ripple like multicoloured water.

We cross and recross Bretherdale Beck, over tiny bridges that, despite the narrowness of the road, have been strengthened to carry 44 tonnes. One tiny tributary flows over a cobbled ford, a "wath". Midwath is at the next bridge; the third ford must be upstream from there. I daresay James could tell me where it is, if I just remembered to ask. His family have farmed this dale for centuries.

Higher up, past Midwath, the road runs parallel to the beck which runs steeper and noisier, the peat-brown water occasionally breaking into white cascades round small rocky islands. We make steady progress up the streamside. Ducks rise in alarm as we pass. Ruby takes no notice

Here on these wet pastures are some of the rarer plants of the hills; lilac-pink bird's-eye primrose, lousewort, deep purple butterwort, sundew and later in the year the delicate white buttercups of grass of parnassus. Blue speedwells dot the turf alongside white daisies with intense crimson-edged petals widely-opened to the sun; in shadier places blue-purple bugle lifts stately spikes, four-cornered and straight like little towers. And everywhere is the white froth of Queen Anne's Lace, and the wiry little pignut whose tuberous root, if you can bear to dig up such slender beauty, tastes like water chestnut.

Ruby's appreciation of botany is based entirely on its food value. Her ears and head position tell me that she would like to pull onto the grass verge and feast on the short sweet turf. When we rest at the top of the dale, down goes her head to the grass, and I sit with slack reins, under the shade of the alder trees, and listen to the beck.

There were once other farms higher than Dale Head: that elusive third ford is probably the one next to Green Head. The road to Parrocks is only a rough track. The houses are ruined, and their tumbling boundary walls let the sheep wander from the rocky fields to the open fell. These lands are now merely extensions of another farm.

All the way up the dale Ruby and I have passed houses created from redundant barns; even our own barn is in the process of transformation. It is a sad commentary on the state of English hill farming. Nevertheless, converting barns to housing is better than the alternative I see from any window of my home: the farms of High Whin Howe, Parrocks, Green Head and Daniel Hill are roofless tumbledown shells, while the barns at Nichol Hill and beside Bretherdale Beck are merely unnamed outlines in the grass.

That's quite enough thinking. I remind Ruby that we should go home, and she agrees. I'm sure she remembers that there are gates to be opened on the way back, where the grass was longer and juicier.

She is relaxed and moving freely, and there's an added eagerness now she's facing home so we trot cheerfully down the narrow road, black mane flying, gravel crunching under the Pink Wellies with never a false stride. A strayed sheep scuttles for the safety of the beck-edge. As we pass she turns to watch, a nervy, ragged-fleeced mother with her fat twin lambs clinging close. In human terms she would be a chainsmoking thirty-something in a supermarket checkout, with brats called Jade and Wayne. Here, she's just "one o' So-And-So's dam' Jumping Swardles."

Facing outward from the dale, the views unfold again and its secrecy recedes. We turn the dog-leg up from the valley bottom and the meadows, we rise over a shoulder of land, and see the Pennines lying in blue distance under mottled cloudshadows, with the Lune Valley lying lush between. All round us are the signs of summer. The hedges are in full leaf, the dark conifer wood is putting out pale green candles of growth. Birds flash in and out of the hazels and willows: blue-tits, great-tits, finches, Little Brown Jobs gone before they are identifiable, pied wagtails dipping and fluttering, swallows and martins twittering as they chase each other in brilliant swoops and turns. Bigger birds pop out from the hedges too, pigeons with their startling wing-clatter, pheasants that scuttle and make Ruby shy, and once a heron who lifts off the bleached stones at the beck-edge, tucks back his neck, aligns his long legs, and floats away in slow-motion on too-big, hand-me-down wings.

At the Bretherdale Hall cattle grid, a local forester is just getting into his pickup and does the gate for us, which disappoints the grass-focused Ruby but is helpful to me. I move the carriage off the road for him to pass us by, before we descend the sharp little gradient of Nichol Hill and turn, at last, for home.

Ruby wants to trot the flat stretch across the meadows. It's a proper Fell trot, a 12 mile an hour celebration of her own power and vigour, that carries her over Dolly Bridge and all the way up the hill to home. We breast the rise of Daw Bank, and slow, and turn into the yard. All round the house, as though lying in wait on the still air, is the powerful, seductive scent of honeysuckle, the scent of my home in June. And as we unharness, the sun bows out and the soft summer rain begins to fall.

Balanced Draught: Harnessing for comfort and efficiency

NB – where comments have been made that may appear critical of the turnout in a photograph, the drivers' faces have been obscured to save embarrassment!

No matter what type of carriage driving we do, harness is something we've all got to have, or our carriage is completely useless. Throughout the nineteenth century, harnessing became increasingly efficient because driven horses provided our fastest means of transporting large numbers of people and goods.

Today, it is only our sporting interests that demand equine speed, whether for cross country work, long distance, showing or just leisure – and I wonder if we still know whether our horses are harnessed in the best and most comfortable way.

Efficiency isn't just making sure that the straps and equipment don't cause injury. Modern harnesses, like modern carriages, have moved toward lightness, with many leisure and competition products based on synthetic strapping. Toughness, cheapness and ease of cleaning are all very well, but the horse and his mechanics, and the laws of physics, have not changed. Has the new technology obscured some basic facts which we still ought to take into account?

Let's look at the principles of draught. We want the horse's forward motion to be transferred to the carriage behind him. For convenience we say he "pulls" it, but in fact he *pushes* into a padded piece of harness. Now, how should we decide where we put this pressure on the horse?

Let's imagine for a moment that it is not a horse that is going to pull the object, but a human. Suppose we have a stack of of hay bales on a sledge and we are going to pull the sledge using a rope tied from the two front corners, making a big loop. If we hold this loop of rope in front of our shoulders and walk forward, our movement is indeed transferred to the sledge; but it will be very hard work. It will choke us, and we'll feel we are being pulled over backwards.

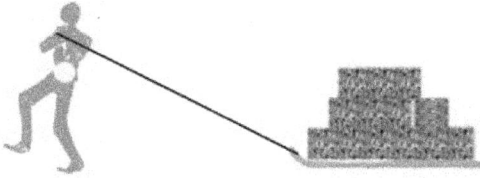

Diagram 1: Pulling from too high a point will choke us, and we'll feel we are being pulled over backwards.

If on the other hand we put the rope around our shins and walk forward, the movement might just move the sledge, but it will be very *very* hard work. It will be painful, because shins move a lot and have very little fleshy padding; worst of all we will tend to fall forwards over the rope.

Diagram 2: pulling from too low a point, we will tend to fall forwards over the rope

There is a wide range of places where we might test the draught, between head and feet, but it's only when we hold the rope at our centre of gravity that we can move the load comfortably and efficiently.

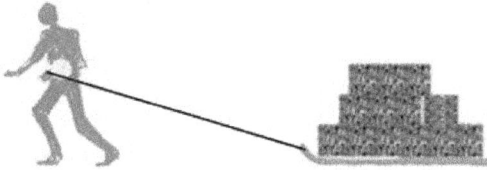

Diagram 3: it's only when we hold the rope at our centre of gravity that we can move the load comfortably and efficiently.

We have to draw the weight of the load through our own centre of gravity, so that we remain in balance.

Unfortunately, the horse's body is parallel to the ground, not vertical like ours. There is only a limited range of places where we can apply equipment for pulling.

The breast collar around the chest is widely used.

Breast collar

The rigid, padded neck collar has various forms.

Neck collar

The traditional English collar is leather stuffed with rye straw and has alloy or steel hames cased in brass, while the Scandinavian collar has padded wooden or steel hames. I

n the past there were sprung collars, elastic collars, even inflatable collars, and zinc-coated steel split collars were used by the Victorian fire services. Lately there have been further developments with V shaped "empathy" or "sweetheart" breast collars of varying depth, plus the combined breast and neck-collar "brollar" or French collar.

Swedish style collar and logging harness

Without going into the merits and otherwise of all these pieces of equipment, let's put our knowledge of the ideal draught point on a human into studying harness draught lines on a horse.

To keep his own body in balance he should draw the weight of the load through his own centre of gravity: the horse's centre of gravity is roughly half-way up his girth and one third of the way along his barrel.

Photo 4: 1 – draught point for full collar. 2: Draught point for breast collar. 3: centre of gravity. TH = Trace Hook position. Line 2 – 3: draught line for breast collar. Line 1 – 3: draught line for neck collar. (Dales X gelding belonging to Charlie Parker's Working Dales Pony Centre)

"Balanced draught" lines on the horse

A breast collar can't be fitted higher than the junction of the windpipe, because we don't want to choke the horse; or lower than the point of the shoulder where there's a sharp point of bone that moves a lot. From the breast collar our balanced draught line, through the horse's centre will run out roughly parallel to the ground. (Line 2 – 3) The trace hook position (TH) will ideally be high.

From a neck collar, which places the pull over the part of the shoulder blade that moves least, our balanced draught line through the horse's centre slopes towards his hocks. (Line 1 – 3). The trace hook position will ideally be low.

I'm not saying that either of these lines is better than the other. I'd just like you to look at the different lines of draught for the horse wearing the breast collar and the full collar, applying the principle of "balanced draught".

So far though, we haven't looked at the other end of the business, the position of the trace hook on the vehicle. This will also have a bearing on the type of collar that you should use.

High trace hooks

On a two wheeler the balanced draught line may be quite high, in line with the shafts. Assuming that the cart fits the horse, the trace line produced by using a breast collar will match the balanced draught line, that promotes comfort and efficiency.

Photo 5: a basic exercise cart with high trace hooks, and breast collar harness – the trace line matches the balanced draught line.

The horse can push into the breast collar and his full weight is aligned with the draught line of the load. Some horses do object to the squeezing action of a breast collar, but most should work well and happily in this setup. You **must** provide a swingletree to accommodate his shoulder movement if you use a breast collar.

Photo 6: neck collar with high trace attachment; trace line goes above the natural balanced draught line (yellow). This is less common in British turnouts than in those where the draught line is normally high, such as buggies in North America.

A full neck collar on a horse working with a vehicle with high trace hooks is not going to be very comfortable; the draught line will be too high and like the human who was being pulled over backwards in Figure 1, the horse can't get his body centrally into the load. The problem is compounded when a horse has a very sloped shoulder and high action.

Compare this to the high cart in photo 7: which has the same trace hook position and neck collar, but the horse has a straight shoulder. The cart is also higher than the gig in photo 6. The trace line matches the balanced draught line.

Photo 7: Light high cart of about 1908, with high trace hooks, and a neck collar on straight shouldered horse. The trace line correctly matches the balanced draught line, although the neck collar looks tight.

Low trace hooks

On the other hand, if the vehicle is a two wheeler with a low trace attachment, such as chain draught to the axle, or if it is a four wheeler, then a breast collar set-up is not going to work nearly so well. Often the trace line is much too low and does not go anywhere near the natural balanced draught line.

This draught line runs too low, so like the human with the rope around the shins, this horse would be "falling over" the pull of the load. Although the shafts look right, the cart is too small, which makes the problem worse.

This pony was in training, just being accustomed to the shafts, and was supervised. **You should never tie and leave a horse alone in a carriage.**

The solution is to use a neck collar with the draught point over the "sweet spot" of the shoulder blade. My own ponies work in neck collars, but that is because the vehicles I use now all have "axle draught", which means the swingletree pulls via a pair of chains directly to the axle.

Photo 9: neck collar and axle draught; the trace line matches the balanced draught line (traces are slack here as the pony is going down hill).

Horses working hard in forestry or agriculture, pulling heavy logs or implements with trace attachments near ground level, will normally be wearing a full collar. It is the only efficient way to harness for this kind of work.

Photo 10: plough team at National Ploughing Championships; neck collars enable the draught line to run correctly through the centre of gravity and down to the plough. When pulling, this pair will be much further from the plough.

Pairs harness is even more definite about the trace line coinciding with the balanced draught line, requiring the pair tug buckles to be fractionally lower than the centre of gravity, so that they rise and remove all pressure from the pad when the horses are in draught. On a four wheeler the draught line should not go directly to the front axle or it would try to lift the fore part of the carriage. The draught line needs to run somewhere between the front and rear axles, in order to pull the vehicle along rather than upwards.

Photo 11: the trace line coinciding with the balanced draught line.

Many competition turnouts' trace lines, with breast collars, diverge from this principle; they "break" at the neck strap and change direction downwards, putting a painful drag on the withers, where there should be no pressure. It's particularly obvious with 4-wheelers that have a low trace attachment, sending the draught line down to the front axle so that the horse has nearly to lift the front of the carriage in order to pull weight that lies over the rear axle. There are too many of those to choose from as potential illustrations.

The coach horses, photo 12, are harnessed in accord with the principles of balanced draught. If they were not, they would find it very difficult to handle the weight of a fully laden coach.

Photo 12: The coach horses are harnessed in accord with the principles of balanced draught.

Not re-inventing the wheel

Balanced draught is not a new idea by any means. It was described in the nineteenth century by Dwyer and by Youatt, and more recently by Barb Lee (see the reading list at the end). However, it is something we too often forget when setting up our horses for driving.

I'm not exclusively recommending breast collars, nor exclusively neck collars. Nor am I saying that the old timers always got it right or the modern competitive drivers get it wrong; there are saints and sinners in both worlds!

By using the principles of *balanced draught* you can suit the harness to the carriage and its trace attachment point. This is going to make life easier for your horse no matter what discipline you're working in. A horse who is feeling an inequality in the draught is going to be distracted to a greater or lesser degree, so if you can remove that distraction you are going to have better communication and be safer when driving. Consider also the effect of savings in efficiency. The effort "saved" by good harnessing might allow a horse to win a competition, instead of only being placed.

Look through all the driving photos you can find, armed with the points I have made here. You can judge for yourself. Decide whether the horses you see in the photos are working *in balance,* to their *best efficiency.* Identify the trace hook, and hold a ruler over the picture to help visualise the line that goes from there through the horse's centre of gravity. Does the line meet the collar at its point of draught, or miss it completely? The answer will often surprise you.

Practise on other people's photos and then look at a picture of your own horse, side view, harnessed to your own carriage. Once you've "got your eye in", checking with the guidelines here, you can confirm whether your own harnessing is the best it can be. If it is, all is well! If it isn't, then by making a few carefully judged alterations, you can make life a lot easier for your horse. When you see how much more happily he can work, you will know you've done the right thing. And if your harnessing does indeed conform to balanced draught, you'll know a bit more about *why* it works.

Further Reading

Hobbs, S, 2000: *Draught testing of a work horse*, Draught Animal News, Number 33, December 2000. Centre for Tropical Veterinary Medicine, University of Edinburgh.

Lee, B, 2004: *Understanding Harness.* Self Published.

Youatt, W, 1832: *The Horse, with a Treatise on Draught.* Longman & Co.

25 hands high, 16 July 2008

I booked the scrap man to come and help clear a building today and he brought "staff" in the form of two youths.

In a lull in the proceedings one of them asked where my horse was.

I said, "She's in the stable next door."

So they peeped in at Ruby through the window, and said, "What kind of horse is she?"

"She's a Fell pony."

"Oh. Isn't she little!"

I explained about the ground outside, where we were, being higher while Ruby was standing in the old muck channel, which was lower, so she looked smaller than she really is.

"How tall is she then?"

"She's thirteen hands three inches."

One of them said airly, "*We've* got a horse that's 25 hands tall."

"Amazing," I said, "it must be in the Guinness Book of Records."

"We just got it at Appleby Fair," he said. "It's one of those that they used to use to pull things, you know, in olden days, it's got feet this big around." (Demonstrating dinner plate circle with hands). "We had to have the trailer modified to get it in, it's so tall."

"So what are you going to do with him? I assume it's a him."

"Yeah, it's a gelding, we're not doing anything with it really cos we're going to get a foal out of it."

Give that boy a coconut.

August 2008 – The Fell Pony Society Breed Show

I've missed going to a couple of driving events while Ruby has been suffering from some eye ailment. I think she had been scratching her head due to midge bites, and had scraped her eye in the process. I had previously entered her for our Fell Pony Breed show, but I was not totally committed to going, not until the night before, when she took me for a five mile drive and came home in cheeky spirits wanting more.

So we went.

Ruby was on VERY good form, possibly on account of it being Fell Pony Weather – ie, p***ing down with rain. In fact even though it faired up at the end of the day we still had to be towed off the field, because my horsebox, good though it is in heavy conditions, just sat and spun on the 3 inches of mud on the roadway out.

The day turned fine in time for the driving class so I did at least get out of the waterproofs and didn't need the plastic bag under my too-well-ventilated helmet! Before the class began I took Ruby up the hill to Brougham Hall and past the Church in the Barn and "the Llama Farm", perhaps a mile and a half away, and then came back to the showfield. Ruby was going nicely, sharp when we trotted and relaxed but ongoing in walk. In the ring she didn't put a foot wrong – I managed without a groom as my usual helper lady was away – and Ruby really showed herself well. She didn't give me the "floaty snorty trot" (she'd used that up before we got in, when a riding class went by at canter going splosh-splosh through the mud) but she was really using herself and having fun. We were placed second out of five. The winner cantered a lot of his show – perhaps excusable with the ground being so wet and the dray weighing nearly half a ton – but Ruby DID manage to control her exuberance. Until we got to the cones course ... remember how sweet and light I said she was earlier in the week, when we had grand-daughter Naomi in the cart? Forget that. All she wanted to do was tank! Preferably through her OWN choice of cones! Was I glad I'd decided to use the everyday reins with the webbing handparts! After the slalom halfway through the course, I had to stop her galloping "for the finish", so out of frustration she did her bounce on the spot and wasted about ten seconds. She stormed through the last 3 cones and galloped out. (We were third. It was a tight course and we hit one but I think EVERYBODY hit at least one.)

So I think we can say she is better! I know the skin round her eyes will peel off after being swollen and itchy, but it all looks normal again underneath and she is not showing any signs of pain in her eyes. The driver of the winning turnout remarked that he had successfully given a horse Piriton (chlorphenamine maleate) for a similar allergy a few years back.

Sue in the English "it's only liquid sunshine" Lakes

Be seen, be safe

Published by Carriage Driving Magazine in 2008

Darker nights are coming. I have to say the weather this summer (2008) has been so appalling that many daylight hours have been pretty murky too. While out driving my car today I was startled not only by the increased number of Bank Holiday cyclists on the road but by the difficulty of spotting them when they weren't wearing high visibility clothing or displaying lamps. On major roads, when traffic is travelling up to the 60 mph speed limit, it seems crazy not to give cars as much notice of your existence as possible. Anything that makes you, as a vulnerable road user, more visible, will help to keep you alive. The further ahead car drivers can see you, the more easily they can slow down and give you room as they pass. This doesn't just apply to cyclists. You as a carriage driver are highly vulnerable, and your horse even more so.

I know that traditionally the appearance of the gentleman's private carriage was quiet, almost understated. But think about it; when we're out exercising today do we use our good holly whip, our show harness, our glossily painted and patent-leathered gig and our candle powered lamps? No, we drive battle wagons and exercise carts, for practicality not tradition. We share the roads now with cars and heavy goods vehicles, not to mention tractors and farm implements, and they all travel much faster than we do and are very much more likely to hurt us than we are to hurt them. We need to make our working carts and carriages as visible as possible, and reserve our sober traditional turnout for ceremonial occasions.

Adding visibility is not difficult. A visit to any cycling web site will give you lots of tips. For a start, the driver (or cyclist) who wears a high visibility waistcoat, fluorescent yellow with reflective strips, will be seen from a greater distance than one who blends into the landscape in grey, dark green or brown as many of us do

149

in winter waterproofs. My coat's pillar box red but I still put a waistcoat over it, and that only cost me £3.

You're lucky if you have a grey or a piebald or skewbald horse, whose white coat will be readily seen out on the road. For those of us with darker coloured animals, reflective leg bands for the horse will be highly visible on account of their rapid movement, while a reflective noseband or browband sleeve should make it obvious where the front of your turnout is!

Many carts and carriages are painted very soberly in green, black, maroon or dark blue, which again blend too easily into their surroundings. My everyday cart has a black body but I've redone the wheels and shafts in Hammerite scarlet. Yes, it's loud, but black and scarlet is quite a traditional combination, and it gets seen. Cost, about £7. Tip: avoid blue, which is a "receding colour", in other words less visible than the red end of the spectrum.

Down narrow country lanes, a fluorescent flag displayed above hedge height may well be useful to warn oncoming traffic of your presence, and there's no harm either in hanging a fluorescent banner of some kind, possibly with a warning triangle on it, from the back of the carriage. However, legal minds in America have sometimes advised against also displaying messages or advice, such as "Caution Young Horse" or "Please Pass Wide and Slow" reasoning that in the aftermath of an accident (which God forbid) these might be construed as an admission that you were not in control. Concentrate on being visible.

Does your vehicle carry lamps, or reflectors? In the Road Vehicles Lighting Regulations 1989 most of the attention is focused on the lamps and reflectors of motorised vehicles, while the poor old carriage horse is pretty well ignored. However, we're told that "Nothing in these Regulations shall require any lamp or reflector to be fitted between sunrise and sunset to – (e) a horse-drawn vehicle". It doesn't say you *can't* carry working lamps in daylight though, and it certainly helps your visibility to do so.

I'm not supposing you intend to drive on the roads in darkness, though having once been overtaken by twilight when hacking back from a show in the 1980s, I can say it was a very pleasant experience to drive a trap with the lamps lit – but only so long as the roads were quiet! You probably wouldn't want to use your good carriage lamps for everyday work, and even the best traditional candle powered lamp only gives 25% of the minimum required light (4 candelas) legally required for use on the roads at night.

Cycle lamps, however, are not expensive, and they come with mountings that adapt very kindly to the metal frames of modern carriages. They don't require any drilling and they don't damage paintwork; the most complicated tool you'll need is a screwdriver. I carry a red lamp on the rear of the cart, and a white on the front. Two would probably be even better. Bike lights using LEDs are surprisingly powerful, and by using rechargeable batteries – about £8 for a set of 4 AA NiMH – you don't have to keep on forking out for fresh ones. They last pretty well; I've only recharged mine twice this year, and I drove for over 50 hours between May and the end of August. A pair of cycle lamps, a front white and a rear red, will set you back anything from about £12 to whatever you feel like paying (some are very expensive). They stand up to weather and cross country work without complaint, and they do get you noticed. Neighbours who see me regularly on our rural roads tell me they spot the pony and me from much further off when we're carrying lit lamps, even though we've always got the red wheels and the yellow waistcoat.

Up to 2005, flashing lights were reserved for the emergency services because of their high visibility, but cyclists may now ride with flashing lamps provided that the "light shown by the lamp when flashing shall be displayed not less than 60 nor more than 240 equal times per minute and the intervals between each display of light shall be constant." So now you know. Flashing lights are particularly noticeable when the light sequence is "chaser" mode. This rapid sequence is very different from the binary flash of the emergency services, but it's highly visible and motorists certainly associate such LEDs with a vulnerable road user. Flashing lights are not discussed in the Statutory Instrument as a mode of lighting for carriages, but I often flash when I'm out driving, and I haven't been told off by a policeman yet!

NB I make these observations as a regular carriage driver, NOT a lawyer.

Statutory Instrument 1989 No. 1796, Part I, The Road Vehicles Lighting Regulations 1989

Statutory Instrument 2005 No. 2559, The Road Vehicles Lighting (Amendment) Regulations 2005

A Question About Bits

Bits are such a "can of worms"! It's hard to know where to stop!

I used a single-jointed snaffle for a lot of years, and found it was OK for riding with a trek of steady ponies (it stopped them leaning on your hands) but it was no good with a hot headed driving pony. I changed to a straight bar loose cheek Liverpool which gave me the option of several curb settings, and gradually I've migrated to a mullen-mouth Liverpool with loose cheeks, or a mullen-mouth "Spanish jumping snaffle" or Kimblewick (and as it's named after an English village that's the way I will always spell it even if every bit catalogue in the rest of the world spells it Kimberwicke!) The mullen is such a kind mouthpiece for horses with big fat tongues; it can't poke a low palate nor pinch the tongue against the bars or the teeth.

I do use cheek rubbers inside the loose cheek Liverpool, because those cheeks can nip. I bought a bit that was a quarter inch wider than the ponies needed, to accommodate the rubber disks. That also shifts the upper eye of the bit away from the molar teeth. That turn of leather on the bridle can be a tight fit on ponies with small muzzles and wide cheeks – something perhaps not thought of by owners used to "horse" anatomy.

Curb chain settings are one of my bugbears as a judge. I've seen them so tight I wonder how on earth the groom or driver managed to hook them up. All you end up with is a horse you can't stop because no matter what he does he is never rewarded with a relaxation of pressure. I've also seen curb chains hanging so low that they caught under the horse's chin. If a horse doesn't need a curb then take the chain off or replace it with a light elastic or leather strap.

An interesting thought is that a curb bit doesn't have to be harsher than a snaffle. It can be gentler because (so long as your chain is not already tight) when you take up or change rein contact, the bit rotates, it rises a little in the mouth and it presses a little on the poll, before any other action happens. That's like touching a friend on the shoulder to warn him you need his attention. Quite different from the plain snaffle which pokes him in the ribs and immediately says, "Oi, get on with it."

Something to watch with a long-cheeked Liverpool (one with three slots in the cheeks) is that it doesn't get caught up on things. I saw a long cheeked Liverpool in use at a show last week where, when the driver asked the horse to reverse, the horse overbent and the cheeks caught in the bottom hame strap of the collar – luckily not permanently. If a driver is at all heavy handed or the horse overbends, it might be better to get a shorter cheeked bit or trim off the lower part of the cheeks.

The loose cheek Liverpool was designed for going straight down the road with a single horse, and not for the many bends and turns of competition or for pairs work. The Military elbow bit or the Buxton work better for that, because there is no half-circle of metal in front of the mouthpiece that can press into the horse's face when the rein is drawn sideways.

And of course no bit can be better than the hands behind it.

Trouble comes in threes

I took my Fell mare Ruby out for a drive this afternoon. The weather was just too good to waste!

She's had her hooves trimmed by the blacksmith in the past few days, so I fit her road boots – Easyboot Epics on the front and Easyboot Gloves on the back – to prevent her getting sore. Said boots all go on very easily (which should really have been a warning to me). Harness up, yoke up, and away we go.

I am planning to do 6 miles, going round Orton and back. The outward leg of the journey is lovely. Just enough wind to keep us cool, lots of sunshine, and spectacular huge spikes of bright purple Northern Marsh Orchids coming into bloom in damp spots along the roadsides. Ruby settles into the work and goes past the event horses at Selsmire without any spookiness. Her bugbear, the extremely-white grey one, hasn't got his green rug on, so this time she recognises him as a horse and not a walking collection of garden chairs, or whatever she imagined he was last time they met.

She isn't bothered by going down the middle of Orton village between all the parked cars. She isn't very bothered either by the Water Board men cleaning out drains at the junction opposite Hall Farm, until one of them retrieves a ten foot length of drainage rod, wipes it and throws it down beside its mates with a noise like a whipcrack. She jumps sideways about six feet. And the bloke shouts, "Hey – you've lost a shoe!" which is much more polite than what I am thinking!

Ruby isn't keen on standing still, but I tell her – fairly mildly – not to be such a fool. She takes her cue from the tone of my voice as much as anything else. The bloke retrieves her boot and trots obligingly after us, off the main road. He tosses it (he obviously has a habit of throwing stuff) and it misses the carriage and lands between Ruby's feet. I move her on a few yards so he can pick it up, and this time he manages to deposit it on the floor. "I'm not used to horses," he says. I say, "Not to worry," and thank him, and we walk along the lane past the school, then I stop in the Methodist chapel car park where I tie Ruby to the fence, and while she reaches over for grass, I reinstate the boot.

It goes all right after that, for a while. I meet a friend and have a chat, and Ruby is perfectly happy to wait for us. Then we set off to trot home.

Back past the eventers and the stands of marsh orchids. Suddenly there's a rhythmic clanking and I see that the yachting quick-release shackle on the end of one of the traces has quick released itself and the trace is swinging free. This doesn't seem to worry Ruby, but it worries me. I suspect the wind blew Ruby's long tail onto the webbing pull-tab and that was enough to flip the shackle open. Fortunately the trace-carrier loop does its job so the trace isn't tangling round her feet. We pull up and turn onto the grass verge, where with moderate swearing I re-fasten the shackle, and off we go again.

Ruby's got into her stride by now and as we trot down into Greenholme I can feel her bunching herself to canter up the brow to the farm.

And the bloody boot flies off again.

This time I say, "Sod it!" and let her canter on home. Unyoke, unharness, give her a small feed and leave her munching, still with three boots on, while I whizz back in the car to pick up the boot, before anyone can run over it and wreck it.

When I'm taking off Ruby's remaining boots it occurs to me to try the much-too-keen-to-fly hind boot (the Glove) on her front hoof, for which it used to be too small. And it fits. So now I am wondering – have *all* her hooves got smaller over the time she's been working unshod? That seems very strange, but it's possible. Or maybe the boots ease a bit with use? Measuring and re-fitting will have to be done before I can be sure. I may have to get a smaller pair of Gloves for her hind feet and move the current ones to her front feet.

I turn Ruby out into the paddock, which is what she's really been wanting since before we went for our drive.

Last of all, I dismantle both the quick-release shackles, take out the helical retaining springs, decompress them by stretching them quite a lot, and re-fit them. It will now take a much stronger pull to flip them open, and if necessary I will shorten the pull tabs, or do without them altogether.

So, although things went wrong, we coped. And that's the main thing.

I conclude, though, that I must be in a time warp, because this is the kind of day that usually happens to me when we go back into work after winter. I can only assume it's very mild for January.

PS – I happen to have Ruby's foot measurements from 2007 which was when we went barefoot/booted. While assessing the actual figures is a bit mind boggling, charting them makes it very clear that her hooves have got BIGGER over the intervening years. The lines indicating length and width for each newly trimmed hoof make a significant upward leap from 2007 to this year's measurements.

Therefore – it's imperative that I clean the boots and her hooves of the oil I use to protect feather! I must away to the shops for some cheapo toothpaste!

Sue's books can be found at her web site, Jackdaw E Books, http://www.jackdawebooks.co.uk/

2012

Ruby's not done much because I've been busy, so she has probably had too much opportunity to graze spring grass. She's lost a lot of her winter coat and has come up nice and glossy despite a heavy coating of mud.

We went out for a drive just after lunch and immediately met one of the big timber-wagons that are coming past us for the felling of the wood in Bretherdale. I now know that the Bennington is shorter overall than the Quayside gigs because when we turned to get out of the way it went round on a sixpence in our "narrows" between the stone walls of the garden and the field opposite. Ruby stood in the yard while the monster went by, and we started the drive over again.

It all went OK, including having our photos taken at the railway bridge, until we reached Selsmire where the event horses were all out at grass in their heavy rugs. Ruby knows that the first 4 in the field on the left are not really interested in her any more, though they look up and stare; but once again, when we reached the next field she spotted "that grey horse" and ground to a halt. She considered trying the spin-and-run that she caught me with a couple of months ago, but I talked her out of that and she just stood there, assessing. This is most unlike her because she is normally such a bold mare! She has even met this grey horse a couple of times, out on the road. So why the sight of a grey in a green rug is so scary, I can't really work out, unless she can only see the legs and head and not the rug in between. Talking to her, twitching the rein and outright smacking her with the whip all produced only one or two steps forward so once I'd got her to the side of the road enabling cars to get by (if necessary) I was prepared to sit it out. Eventually after about 5 minutes a van came from the opposite direction and at that point she appeared to come out of her "trance" and walked on! I think I need to get her a supplement with magnesium in it, to counteract the grass.

I took her another mile or so, then turned and came back. She behaved fine coming past the horses this time (the grey was further away and behind a couple of other horses). We met the timber wagon again but I had spotted him coming from over a mile away as I came down the hill, and I found a gate open into a little garth, where we stood out of his way and exchanged waves with the driver before continuing on our merry way.

Ruby was hardly damp at all when we got in – combination of shedding winter woollies, and a quite cold wind.

Poor Micky Wippitt was furiously jealous that I had done things with Ruby without taking him into the game – biting the wire of his kennel run and yelping – but I can't let him run free with me because it's lambing time and he is far too keen on chasing after leaping lambies! Plus, I once lost a dog who was running free, when he ran across the road in front of a car, and I'd need more hands than I currently have, to manage him on a leash in the carrriage.

Historical Fiction

I've joined several forums for historical novelists recently while I've been completing COACHMAN. Reading some of their book previews on Amazon it has dawned on me that although historical novelists seem interested in being authentic about costume and weaponry, I've only met two who have any direct knowledge about horses, and only one who understands carriages.

Given that until the start of Victoria's reign (or William IV if you are a Northerner – look up the Liverpool and Manchester railway) the fastest means of transport anywhere was either a well bred horse or a well-horsed carriage, this seems rather strange. It's a bit like writing about modern London and not knowing that you can get your character across the city far more easily by Tube than by Ferrari.

Allow me to make some helpful information available!

Horses

Even for late medieval knights, war-horses were not huge beasts. The modern Shire horse of 17 hands or more was developed for agricultural use, well after gunpowder put an end to the mounted armoured knight. Ann Hyland proposes that the 15th C knight's "destrier" was likely to have been a sturdy cob type of about 15-2 hands. This type of horse was a "square gaited" or "hard trotting" animal who walked, trotted, cantered or galloped.

Horses for general riding were probably not taller than 15 hands, often smaller, and frequently they were "lateral gaited" or "soft gaited", which means they walked and cantered but their in-between gait was a pace, rack or amble, rather than a trot. All these were more comfortable than a trot. The pace is similar to that of a fast moving camel or giraffe, with the legs on each side moving at the same time (watch videos of harness-racing pacers).

The amble was a rapid, level, shuffling movement. Over good going the rack, like the pace, could be quite fast. Horses that moved in this comfortable way were amblers or palfreys, popular mounts for both ladies and gentlemen.

Horses for racing or hunting were "coursers", ie running horses, who moved "square" like the knight's destrier; they trotted when not galloping. Even the racehorses were not large. Many early thoroughbreds were under 14 hands high.

A useful type from Shakespeare's time onward was the Galloway, originally a type from south-west Scotland. Later the term became a generic one (like Hoover for vacuum cleaner) for any sturdy, sensible small cob of 13 to 14-2 hands. They probably looked much like a Highland, Dales or Fell pony, though for practical reasons they probably weren't bred to carry anywhere near as much hair on neck, tail or fetlocks ("foot locks") as their modern counterparts do.

Women travelling would have a choice of riding pillion behind husband or brother; rich ladies could ride side-saddle, being led by a servant; or ride in a litter, which was a covered seat carried on 2 long poles, suspended either side of a horse before and behind.

Distances

Modern endurance horses ridden intelligently at suitable paces for the terrain can cover anything from 25 to 50 or even 100 miles in a day. This isn't just the racy Arabian types; I know a Fell pony that has completed a 100 miler in less than 18 hours. Bear in mind that the riders don't flog on at full gallop, which being anaerobic activity would rapidly exhaust the horses' energy; they go at the pace that suits the country they have to cover, and much of that is aerobic, steady trotting or cantering, with intervals of walk to allow the horse to have a breather.

Military dispatch riders galloped, of course, and covered short distances of 3 or 4 miles in a quarter of an hour (12 to 16 MPH);

but ridden horses for civilian travellers over longer distances would average no more than 6 MPH, so a day's journey was probably no more than sixty miles and often much less if roads were bad. Working horses in a city were often forced to walk because of other traffic, and there were few highway regulations to ease their passage.

Unlike cars, horses do need recuperation time before they can reasonably be expected to make another journey. This involves them being groomed, fed with grain and hay, and given water to drink and a stall under shelter in which they can stand quietly and perhaps sleep – though horses can sleep standing up and tend only to lie down for short periods.

Next: travelling by carriage and coach.

Coaches: Tudor

In the TV series "The Tudors" 19th century carriages were shown conveying certain grand personages about on behalf of Henry VIII. WRONG. This was the point at which I began to shout at the screen. Coaches were not in use even by Royalty until his daughter Elizabeth I's reign, and they were uncomfortable, jolting unsprung things suspended on leather braces. Elizabeth complained of being badly bruised from being thrown about in a coach that had been driven too fast, and she was a fairly hardy lady. There was no glass in the windows at this time (guess why) and wheels were shod with iron rims.

17th Century

Lots of authors forget that in a city, it was often convenient to travel in a sedan chair. Of course it didn't allow of company unless on foot, on horseback or in another sedan chair, but it had a lot of advantages over a horsedrawn carriage in the city. It was narrow and manoeuvrable so it could take you to places many carriages could not go, and the motive power understood speech! Also, in London and other cities based on a major river, watermen provided a taxi service up, down or across the water. John Taylor the "Water Poet" complained in "The World Runs On

Wheels" that hackney carriages were taking away the ferrymen's business.

Steel springs made an appearance in the 1660s, and Sam Pepys remarked on them on a coach in London. He bought himself a private 4 seater carriage and two black horses, and probably employed a man to drive; and he seems to have been happy with his purchase, despite having to pay £2 to replace the glass in a window.

Commercial coaches were starting to appear on the roads. These were "stage" coaches which changed horses at inns along the road. One "stage" of its journey would be anything from 8 to 15 miles depending on the nature of the terrain. In winter, warmth for the passengers' feet was provided by filling the floor with straw – it works, but could be infested with livestock ranging from woodlice to fleas and even mice, depending on the diligence of the stable staff in providing clean straw.

18th Century

By 1688, stage coaches ran from London to 88 different towns and by 1705 this increased to 180. However, Mail coaches were not seen until after the Post Office adopted John Palmer's suggestion to convey letters by coach instead of on horseback, following a successful experimental run from Bristol to London in 1784.

Smart light two wheeled vehicles for private use, such as gigs and dog carts, became popular from the 1800s onward. Four wheelers such as the various forms of phaeton were common. But for independence and access to open country, to make your own way to a destination, you rode – and were liked all the better for your active character, as opposed to being carried lazily about by carriage.

As for the curricle, that vehicle so beloved of the romance author, like a tandem of horses driven to a gig it was racy and showy and difficult and inherently unsafe... so beware which of your gentlemen you put at the reins. It was an owner-driven carriage. (I mean, you don't buy a Ferrari and let a chauffeur drive.) And don't forget that with a pair or team your whip, no matter how skilful, needs a groom behind him. Why? Common sense and safety... and the blasted curricle wouldn't balance without him.

Manpower and brakes

A gentleman driving his own carriage and four would have had one man, and more likely two, to see to tangles or mishaps with the horses. In Regency Buck, the hero tells off the heroine for driving her four-in-hand with no groom to help her, because her passenger has an injured arm. Georgette Heyer knew her stuff.

Not even an exceptional "whip" – male or female – would ever have driven a heavy carriage without a servant, because early coaches and carriages had no brakes. Down gentle inclines the horses could hold the carriage back with the harness, but on steeper ones the footman or guard got down and fitted an iron drag shoe under the gutter-side hind wheel. At the bottom of the hill, he got down again, the whip backed the team so the carriage wheel rolled off the shoe, and the guard picked it up by its chain and hung it on the hook again – not touching it, because it was hot from the friction! The guard or groom had to deal with broken harness, kicking horses and so on... or just to hold the horses when the driver and passengers got down at their destination.

19th Century

Hand or foot operated brakes were late Victorian inventions which eased the work because the coach did not have to stop for them to be applied. They could still only slow the coach downhill; when loaded it weighed between 3 and 4 tons and the wooden brake shoes only operated on a 6 inch by 2 inch area of each wheel rim, so brakes couldn't stop it completely. Equally, rubber tyres for wheels were not invented till the 19th century, and they were solid, not pneumatic. Vehicles with rubber tyres tended not to have brake-blocks because they pulled the rubber off the wheels. The idea of a "parking" brake didn't arrive until the advent of the internal combustion engine... a carriage you could turn off when you stopped.

There are contemporary stories of coach teams being left unattended at inns, and taking fright or assuming a noise behind meant they were to start, galloping off with the coach with no driver at the reins. Horses require manpower, time and knowledge, and constant attention. Therefore – pretty please, authors – your characters driving a carriage can NOT abandon it at the roadside like a car, unless you want to plot a horrendous accident. You always need someone to take charge of the horses.

Terminology

If you've got to describe a carriage drive or even a ride, it probably pays not to be too clever. Even simple things are very easily got wrong! For instance, you all know reins are for steering. You may possibly know that traces run back from the horses' neck-collars to pull the carriage. The difference between the two purposes may seem obvious, but I've seen a mainstream published novel confuse the two.

Coachmen and good drivers held the reins in their left hand in an understated, workmanlike English coaching style and steered by turning the wrist, or by helping with their right hand which also carried the whip. They wouldn't drive with a rein (or two reins) in each hand; not unless you want to set them up to be ridiculed by their fellow drivers. For sheer style, watch any video of a British Royal parade with coachman driven carriages... a Royal wedding, or Trooping the Colour.

There is a big difference between sporty owner-driven carriages like phaetons (yes, and gigs and curricles), and sober coachman-driven carriages like barouches. It's very easy to get lost in their subtleties. For instance: pole chains. They were used to steer and stop commercial coaches, carriages and coachman driven vehicles, while pole straps denoted owner driven private vehicles... Probably best not to go into it too deeply unless you are prepared to read specialist books. Even the sainted Ms Heyer occasionally got things wrong.

Phew – I'd better leave waggons and farm carts and commercial trade carts for another day.

Sex

There, that got your attention, didn't it? I saved the racy bits for the end.

Don't forget we have three genders in horses who are used as transport. There's the intact adult male, the stallion; the female, the mare; and the gelding, who is an equine eunuch and was probably "attended to" fairly brutally at the age of 18 months or so. Most working horses were geldings, whose lack of sexual interest made them easy to manage even for inexperienced staff.

Mares are the natural leaders in a herd situation – so they can be bossy. If they aren't in foal they come into "season" every three weeks from early spring to late summer, which means they may be distracted as well. Stallions have a sex-drive that rises and falls with time of year – up in early spring and throughout the summer, down again as autumn comes. To deal with either stallions or mares successfully takes tact and good horsemanship. So please don't have your heroine ride a stallion, unless you can also write about how she manages him in the company of strange mares, who will flirt by peeing at him if they're in season and try to kick his teeth in if they aren't. (Don't you love how horses can be upfront and obvious? My two favourite Fell ponies have been mares.)

In *Black Beauty* Anna Sewell tactfully fails to mention such matters, so generations of readers may well have assumed that Beauty's lack of sexual commentary simply meant that he had excellent manners, and that he was capable of retiring to stud and begetting. This is, sadly, very unlikely.

One final note

A horse in war, in a carriage, hunting or doing any other kind of work will NOT neigh or whinny when in a stressful situation – eg, battle or accident. You may hear a snort of fright, or a grunt of pain or effort, but mostly the sound of hooves galloping rapidly away. Unlike movie heroines, horses rarely scream.

The Single-Jointed Snaffle Bit, 2013
The effect of rein angles, auxiliary reins and nosebands

© Sue Millard 2013

> *Do not believe in anything simply because you have heard it. Do not believe in anything simply because it is spoken and rumoured by many. Do not believe in anything simply because it is found written in your religious books. Do not believe in anything merely on the authority of your teachers and elders. Do not believe in traditions because they have been handed down for many generations. But after observation and analysis, when you find that anything agrees with reason and is conducive to the good and benefit of one and all, then accept it and live up to it.*
>
> *Buddha*
> *Kalama Sutta*

The Horse's Mouth

Have you ever bitten your tongue, or your cheek? What about that moment when you misjudge the night time tooth cleaning routine and knock your gums or your palate with the back of the brush? Hurts, doesn't it?

You may possess equine books with drawings showing the theory of how your bits work, but forget them for the moment. Let's think about actually putting the bridle on your pony. Think about his mouth.

Lift the bridle up and prepare to put it on. Feel the velvety hair on the pony's muzzle, the smoothness of the leather and the metal of the bit. Hear the noise of the bit joints, and the "tlock" sound as your pony opens his mouth. Wait a minute – a sound as he opens his mouth? Yes... Hadn't you noticed that? To make it with your own mouth you would have pull your tongue away quickly from the palate so air rushes in. And that's exactly the sound you are hearing from the horse – he is unsticking his tongue from his palate to let you put the bit in. There is not normally a space between the pony's palate and his tongue.

Whatever we put between the pony's tongue and his palate is going to touch both of them.

Do some more exploring. Put your finger and thumb around the outside of the pony's lower jaw. That jaw is NARROW. It is nowhere near as wide as you think it is (nor anywhere near as wide as most horse book diagrams, either). You could wrap your thumb and finger around it, if it wasn't for his lips and tongue. In a native pony, his tongue often bulges out between the incisors, tusk and cheek teeth. And his lips make a soft fold in front of his molars.

You will have to slide your finger quite a long way into his mouth, under his tongue, to find the narrow, sharp-edged slippery hardness of the bars – the toothless, skin-covered bone at the gap between incisors and molars. The bars aren't directly in contact with the metal of a bit. Although the bars do "support" the bit, it is cushioned by the mouth, the tongue and the lips. That's why when a horse gets its tongue over the bit we immediately get "wooden" resistance and lose much of our control. The horse carries the bit with its tongue and its lips, not the bars of its mouth.

Here's a Fell pony head with a headpiece and throatlash only (over a headcollar, pushed well back just to keep the picture simple). The snaffle bit is correctly fitted with a wrinkle at the corner of the lips.

Fell Pony Head And Snaffle Bridle

Where is the bit lying in relation to the teeth and the upper and lower jaw?

Here's a Fell pony skull superimposed on that same picture.

Fell Pony Head With Female Fell Skull Imposed

This is a mouth designed to chew tough fibrous plants. Notice how short the distance is from the bit to the cheek teeth, even though the bit in the previous picture only just wrinkles the corners of the lips. The rings of the bit partly overlap the cheek teeth.

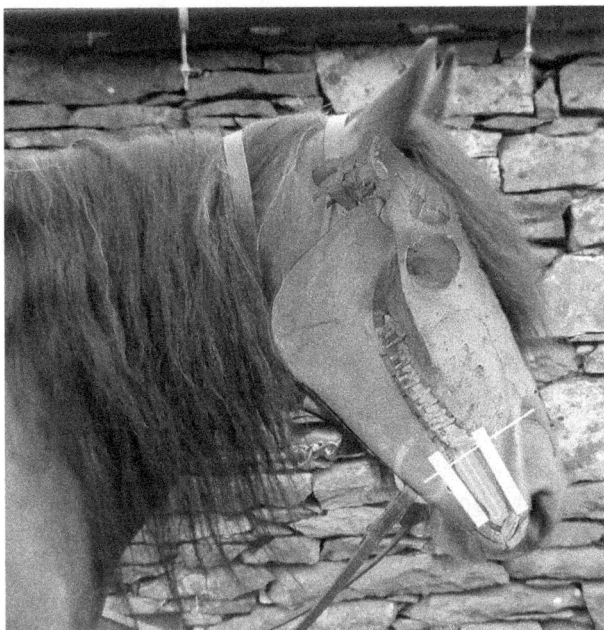

Fell Pony Head With Bars, Palate And Cheek Teeth Marked

This is all the space that is available to carry the bit. In a gelding or stallion (and some mares) this space is further complicated by the tusks, partway down the jaw towards the incisor teeth.

The Snaffle

I won't have space to look at curb bits or gags in this article. Whole books, and many of them, are devoted to the many varieties of metal things to put in our horses' mouths. Annual issues of bit catalogues list the new fashions alongside the old.

I'm focusing on the snaffle here because novice riders and novice ponies are expected to use a snaffle. We're always advised to use one for a new pony before trying anything else. In fact, for many competitive events such as dressage, at lower levels the snaffle is the only bit permitted. So: what is a snaffle?

Classically, a snaffle bit is one that acts directly on the horse's mouth. It doesn't work through leverage like a curb, nor by lifting, like a gag. A snaffle is just a straight pull. With a plain round ring, the rein will pull at one side and the bit mouthpiece will slide round on the ring until it's pretty much opposite that pull. It's as simple as that. And simple is kind, right? Surely that's why it's recommended, even mandated, for novice riders and novice horses?

Well, yes and no.

The Single Jointed Snaffle

The single-jointed mouthpiece is often the only kind of snaffle that is readily available. When I was 20, every pony on the yard where I worked was ridden in a single-jointed snaffle. I never thought about why, but it must have been because it was common and it was cheap. It still is. That means it is used a lot by people starting out with horses.

I did the same, after all, when I bought my first pony. I bought a jointed snaffle and I made a special effort to find her a jointed driving bit, the Wilson or Hungarian snaffle. Now, for most of the time I rode and drove with only a light contact, so the bits caused no trouble, until I drove her in company at a show. When the excitement got to both of us, she wanted to go faster, my contact became heavier, and her response was to stick her nose out and run like a racehorse! The judge advised me to: "Put another bit in its mouth. I would – honestly."

I had to have a rethink then, and I'm still doing it.

Let's look at how a single-jointed bit actually behaves with different angles of rein pressure. Incidentally, I am not making any of this up. The skull is a photo of a real Fell pony skull, sized to the photo of the real Fell pony head, and not manipulated. The bit angles can be checked against fluoroscope photos taken by Dr Hilary Clayton – see the references at the end. I mention this just in case you don't believe what these diagrams will show you.

First is our Fell pony head, with the jointed snaffle on a completely loose rein. The bit hangs from the headpiece and lies over the lips and tongue. It droops a little in the centre – ie, the joint points towards the nostrils. It's neutral. It doesn't do anything to the tongue or the sides of the lips. This a resting position.

Next, the single jointed snaffle takes up its "working position" when the rider's or driver's hand takes the "dip" out of the rein. Remember – in a snaffle the rein acts directly, so when you take contact on the rein on one side of the ring, the mouthpiece will rise in the mouth to a point roughly opposite on the ring. That means the mouthpiece of the bit is pointing in the opposite direction to the rein. Direct. It's only prevented from straightening out completely by its position on top of the tongue, supported by the lower jaw at the bars. It also presses on the lips in front of the cheek teeth.

As the bit draws backwards over these areas, the angle between the two halves of the bit (the cannons) gets smaller. Also – remember what I said earlier about the pony's tongue and palate usually touching each other?

When the rein draws the snaffle ring to its working contact, it makes a small gap between the tongue and the palate. Any bit will do this. The slight space together with the movement of the jaw produces bubbly saliva, that we call a moist mouth, which we take as a sign of relaxed acceptance of the bit.

The sides of a single jointed snaffle, however, move inwards as well as backwards.

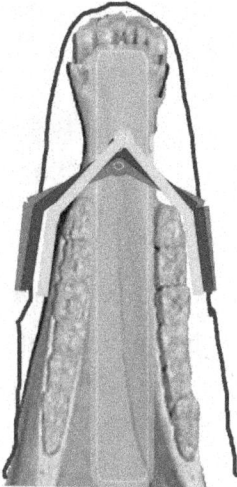

View Of The Jaw From Above

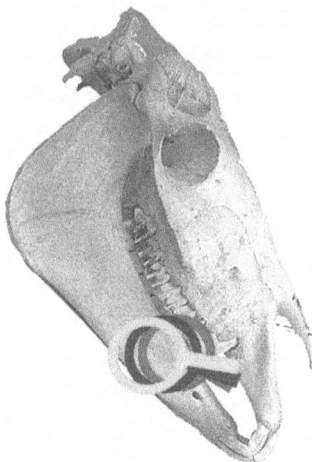

And From The Side

The ring position furthest to the right → in the diagram is the resting bit position.

The middle is working contact.

The left-most position equates to a hard pull – for instance, the rider pulling to ademand a stop, the horse pulling to go faster.

Again, this isn't manipulated. The parts of the bit are all the same size – all I've changed are their positions.

Any pressure on the reins has a pinching effect on the tongue and lips. They are pressed in, towards the cheek teeth – and remember – there isn't much space there in a pony's mouth.

The middle of the bit moves forwards at the same time and if the pull is increased, the joint hits the palate.

Arguments For The Jointed Mouthpiece

If the pony has been taught in early training that "giving to pressure is a good idea", then he will bring his chin in and change the angle between his mouth and the rein. We want him to do this – to relax and let his head hang from the poll, and put his face nearer the vertical.

Provided the rider has good balance and good hands and tact, he will then permit the pressure to ease a little, and the bit will reward the pony by coming back to a resting position.

When the pony accepts the bit and the head moves towards vertical, the bit returns close to resting position

My problem with the jointed snaffle is that it is recommended for beginner riders who – because they are beginners – do NOT have good balance or good hands or tact. The pony may not get his reward for compliance. He may instead get the pressure prolonged, or even increased.

A pony in a single jointed snaffle will often open its mouth when a beginner rider takes contact.

A frequent statement is that a jointed bit offers "independent side action, wherein one side of the bit moves without the other"

(Myler web site). I've never understood the physics behind this assertion. The statement seems to imply that because the two sides of a bit are hinged, only one side of the mouth will receive a signal from a single rein aid – up, down or backwards. The general practice of using an "open rein" to assist in steering a novice horse demonstrates that this is untrue. Horse people are given to making big statements in order to get a point home, and maybe what is meant is that a jointed bit can give a signal that is stronger on one side than the other. But I can do that with an unbroken bit, too. In any case, movement of one side of a jointed mouthpiece must affect the other side of the mouth because the cannons of the bit are joined together.

"An unbroken mouthpiece can have a painful effect on the opposite side of the mouth." I suggest that people who say this are thinking too much about "pulling" instead of "elastic contact." It doesn't matter whether your bit is a jointed or unjointed one, or whether you pull hard or softly. The "both sides" effect is still there. What you do with either rein affects both sides of a pony's mouth.

Resistances

The ideal, restful bit angle is only steady if the pony's head is steady, and if your hand at the other end of the rein is steady. If you fix your hand low because you aren't in balance, or if you haven't been taught how much or how little rein contact to use, or if the pony isn't yet capable of keeping its head still while it changes from one gait to another, or if it wants to go faster, or if it tosses its head at a fly – well, you get the idea.

It's all made even more complicated if the bit is old and the joints have worn slack (they can even wear right through, though stainless steel takes a lot longer than the old nickel bits used to.) At any rate: a change of position at either the bit or the hand end of the rein WILL change the angle of the jointed mouthpiece.

What if the pony, instead of "giving" to your hands and dropping his face to the vertical, resists you? What if he opens his mouth? Or throws his head up?

What if he d[...] Have you ever wondered why [...] ve, when the bit clearly crushes tl[...] eth?

When the pon[...] with his head in a *normal* positi[...] inst his palate. If he is clever he [...] lly high or bore downward – we[...] bit and the rein closer to the res[...] ay stick out his

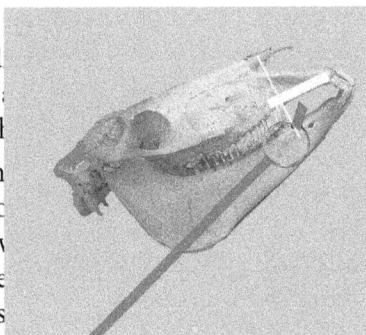

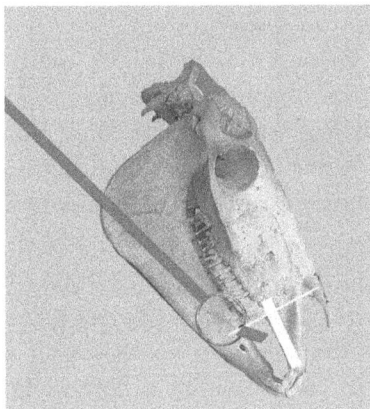

neck and take off like a racehorse, the way my first pony did. Anything to stop it poking the roof of his mouth! You won't need be told that this is dangerous! Did you know that at least one American equine dental practice is collecting data about the damage done by single jointed snaffles to horses' palates?

Auxiliary Nosebands

Every saddlery catalogue will offer drop, flash or grackle nosebands to strap a horse's mouth shut and discourage evasions of the bit. Of course they would like you to buy some leatherwork. Or possibly a more complicated bit.

Let's assume you just buy a noseband – flashes are fashionable at the moment, though the drop noseband has lost popularity. Now, if your noseband is meant to stop him opening his mouth, we want it tight, don't we? Well, no. Look again at the pony's skull. When his mouth is shut, his teeth are already together, and the tongue and the palate are touching. The recommended tightness of a noseband is "enough for the pony to still be able to take a treat off your hand and chew it." He has to be able to separate the top and bottom jaw, and to move his tongue inside to achieve the "wet" mouth we want to see.

But how often is that forbidden by nosebands that are too tight?

A noseband isn't necessarily going to convince the pony to put his head where you want it to be. It's more likely that he'll continue to resist your hands. His tongue and cheeks will still be pinched by the bit. And where is that central joint of the bit going to go if he can't now open his mouth? A tight noseband is only going to force the pony to endure the bit poking into his palate.

Auxiliary Reins

Someone, at some time, is bound to tell you to use an auxiliary aid, such as a martingale or a draw rein, to give more "power" to your hands when the pony gets out of your control. Well, that's only proper, isn't it? You have to be in control. In some countries, novices can even ride dressage classes in running reins. Surely that's OK?

Well, no.

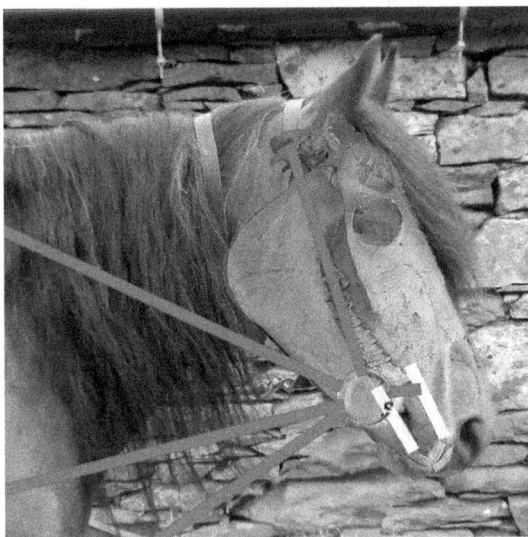

The various pulls effected by auxiliary reins along with the rider's rein

I've seen photographs, recent ones, that show that even people who love their horses dearly can get their equipment spectacularly wrong. Remember: The mouthpiece of the bit obeys the laws of engineering and moves to the opposite side of the cheek ring in reaction to a pull on the rein. Look where those pulls will make the jointed bit sit in opposition to them.

Jointed Snaffle With Running Rein

The "sliding side rein", "Viennese rein" or "running rein" acts from the centre of the girth up to the bit, then back to the girth under the saddle flap. It's even recommended in one of the "train your horse to drive" books. It offers a downward pull on the bit if the horse gets its head above a certain position. It should be fitted loosely. It often isn't. Exactly the same things happen if a running martingale is adjusted too short and alters the direction of the rein from the rider's hand.

The trouble is that when the pull on the horse's mouth is shared between the basic rein and an auxiliary rein, the angle of pull gets lower. The mouthpiece rises and gets closer to the teeth as well as squeezing the tongue and lips, and the central joint is lifted and pushed forward and it hits the palate.

The only way the horse can escape that palate strike is by pulling in his head and neck. What we should be asking him to do is to carry his head with the muscles under the neck relaxed. The problem is that a tight draw rein and a tight noseband will compel him to use those muscles to actively back off the bit. He may also use his tongue to hold the bit against his palate and prevent it constantly hitting him. The lower jaw can't relax because it is locked into position by the noseband. You have set up stiffness – a conflict that can only be resolved by the horse submitting, in the wrong way, to pain. This is NOT what training is about. A martingale or draw rein must NOT force the pony to endure the bit poking into his palate when his head is in the desired position.

Is There An Alternative?

There are LOTS of alternatives. Look in any bit catalogue, for a start, for French link, Myler or Sprenger KK snaffles. Look at mullen mouthed bits, or even straight bars.

I still prefer a solid mouthed bit because the behaviour of my animals suggests they like and accept it. The bit in this photograph has a mullen mouth. It curves gently over the tongue and has eggbutt sides that prevent any of the pinching you'd get from wear on the holes for the snaffle ring. All my driving bits, too, have mullen mouths or straight bars. (The only single jointed snaffle I possess was given to me in a "museum piece" 1930s hunter bridle. It's too big for any animal I have ever owned, and rusty, to boot.) Anybody can bridle my ponies with the mullen-mouthed bits I use. Carriage driving work doesn't upset them.

Their mouths are just normally moist. They don't drool excessively or create froth. They don't throw up their heads or fuss. They follow the bit easily, they have brakes and they can be steered by release of pressure. And they only bore down when they want to snatch a mouthful of grass!

Forget any auxiliary reins that attach to or run through the bit. If your horse throws his head about, use a standing martingale on your cavesson noseband – but if you change his jointed snaffle bit for almost ANY other bit AND ride with kind hands, he will probably stop throwing his head anyway.

Forget additional nosebands. Take the flash attachment off your bridle.

So please – if your horse evades the bit – if he tries to avoid being bridled, throws his head up or pulls down on your hands when you take contact; if he opens his mouth, "needs a flash noseband" or "has to be ridden in a martingale" – and especially if you are still using a single jointed snaffle – then please do as I suggested at the start of this piece. Go out and put your bridle on him. Stand at his head and move the bit. Lift the rein. Take contact. WATCH. Observe his reactions. He can't tell you in words what your hands and the bit are doing to his mouth, but his behaviour will.

Physical damage is done to horses' palates, tongues and lips every day. Emotional damage is done to their trust in a rider's hands. Is that fair? Is it kind? Is it necessary? Read this again. Study the pictures and think about it.

I Am Not A Lone Voice

Here are a few links to web sites that discuss bit action and specifically the single jointed snaffle:

USA: College of Veterinary Medicine: Dr Hilary Clayton for the US Dressage Federation

http://cvm.msu.edu/research/research-centers/mcphail-equine-performance-center/publications-1/usdf-connection/USDF_Dec05.pdf

and http://cvm.msu.edu/research/research-centers/mcphail-equine-performance-center/p\ublications-1/usdf-connection/USDF_May06_Clayton.pdf

Sweden: Sustainable Dressage

http://www.sustainabledressage.net/tack/bridle.php

Germany: Sprenger Bits

http://www.sprenger.de/open/language_id/2/action/standard%3Bdetail/menu/267/M/BFyCCw

Their diagram of the horse's jaw is inaccurate but they have at least designed a bit that attempts to avoid palate pressure and pinching.

USA: Myler bits

http://www.overafarmstud.co.uk/contents/en-us/d63.html

The photo of the Fell pony skull is used courtesy of

http://www.skullsite.co.uk/Horse/horse.htm – the skull is in Tullie House Museum, Carlisle.

Other photos of the horse's jaw bones can be found in Roberts, T (1971): Horse Control and the Bit, Roberts, Richmond, South Australia

Two Pelham type bits, 2013

I frequently tell my friends, that out of every twenty bits I make, nineteen are for men's heads and not more than one really for the horse's head. (Benjamin Latchford, 1871: The Loriner.)

Let me say before I start, I KNOW that there are large gaps in what might be said in this article – but please, bear with me.

I am not a riding teacher or a horse breaker. I have been a harnessmaker, so the areas I'm equipped to look at are the leatherwork and hardware we use on our horses. Training of the horse and the rider are important, but all training is going to be easier with suitable equipment than with equipment that hinders the message getting through to the horse.

I'm not going to advocate one bit over another. I'm just going to point out some facts. What I write will almost certainly conflict with other things you've read or with common assumptions, but if you go out to your horse and actually test you may find those common assumptions are inaccurate.

Always remember that bit makers are in the business of selling bits, so they describe all kinds of actions that may make you buy their variations on the basic designs. Don't put too much trust in their bit descriptions. Make your own judgements.

Make those judgements by observing your own animals and thinking. I hope the information here will slot into whatever else you happen to be doing with your equine/s.

I'm only going to look at a couple of bits that I find suitable for what I do, which is occasional driving in the show ring and regular driving exercise/schooling/leisure, with Fell ponies.

Tongue, lips and bars

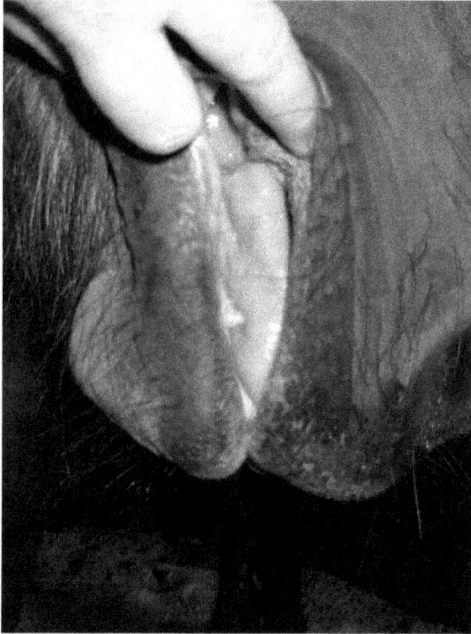

The tongue completely covers and protects the bars of my Fell pony mare. X-rays of horse heads (Sprenger, 2010) show that even in "well bred" horses, the tongue fills the mouth space.

A straight bar snaffle bit sits across the tongue and lips. It's the simplest and most logical bit to understand and use. It beats me why we don't see more people using it.

Bits that are straight but with a low central port, particularly a wide one such as Sprenger's Comfort Mouth, enable the bit to fit precisely over the shape of the jaw at the bars – but they still sit on top of the tongue and touch the lips either side.

The mullen mouthpiece

The mild curve of the mullen mouthpiece sits over the tongue and, in action, unlike a single-jointed snaffle it moves slightly away from the palate. The shape is easiest to see on this snaffle bit.

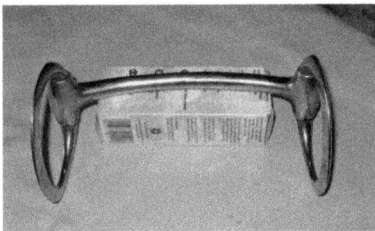

Showing the shallow curve right across the mouth space.

This mouthpiece rests on the tongue and the lips. I've used mullen mouths for years on my own ponies and never had one object to them, so I've not had reason to try any of the other options.

Glory and Arch mouthed bits, and flexible "happy mouth" bits, fit much the same, with varying degrees of precision. Some horses prefer a close fit, while others prefer the slacker fitting of the mullen mouth. They still have to fit over the tongue.

High port bits sit on the tongue, but when they are in use the mouthpiece rotates so the port rises to press against the palate. No horse deserves such treatment. High ports are also said to "accommodate the tongue" so the bit acts directly on the bars. No bit should ever act that way. The only time a bit can act on the bone and gums of the lower jaw is when you pull so hard on a single jointed snaffle that it does the nutcracker "squeeze". If you ever fit the bit so low that the horse puts his tongue over it and the bit sits directly on the gum and the jaw, the immediate wooden feel and loss of control should convince you that "direct action on the bars" is not a good method of communication.

No bit can ever act solely on the corners of the mouth, either, no matter what any bit catalogue asserts. The tongue is always there and is one of your main means of communicating with the horse.

Liverpool driving bit with Mullen mouth

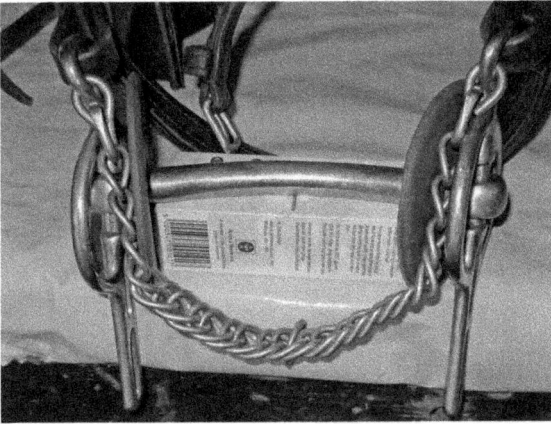

Top / rear view of a mullen-mouth Liverpool bit.

From top to bottom: The outcurved cheek eyes are important for native types with wide mouths, to give room for the widening of the native type face at the molar teeth above the bit. The curb hooks are easy to use, the points are rounded and they turn away from the pony's cheeks.

Cheek guards

There are several reasons why I prefer to use cheek guards with a Liverpool. The sliding mouthpiece of this bit often has "stops" at top and bottom which can be sharp-edged and can cause rubs or pinching. Guards prevent them causing sores. They take up the slack at the mouthpiece if you need to buy a wide bit to accommodate a pony face that broadens quickly at the cheek teeth. They keep slobber off the rein billets if you are using rough cheek or either of the "slot" rein settings. Also, guards discourage you from fitting the curb-chain too tight.

Putting the heavy rubber guards onto this long bit involved a basin of hot water, followed by two shoe laces tied through the centre hole of the guard – one to a weighty kitchen stove, and the other to a belt around my waist! I have found that cheap guards made of thin rubber will tear rather than stretch, so you might as well split those tidily and lace them on.

The Liverpool bit has a ring that runs right round the mouthpiece – behind and forward. This example has two deep slots down the cheeks, which would allow me to use my $7/8^{ths}$ inch wide driving reins through them IF I really needed to. The forward half of the ring enables "rough cheek" rein setting, but it can actually be a disadvantage in this bit (which I'll talk about later).

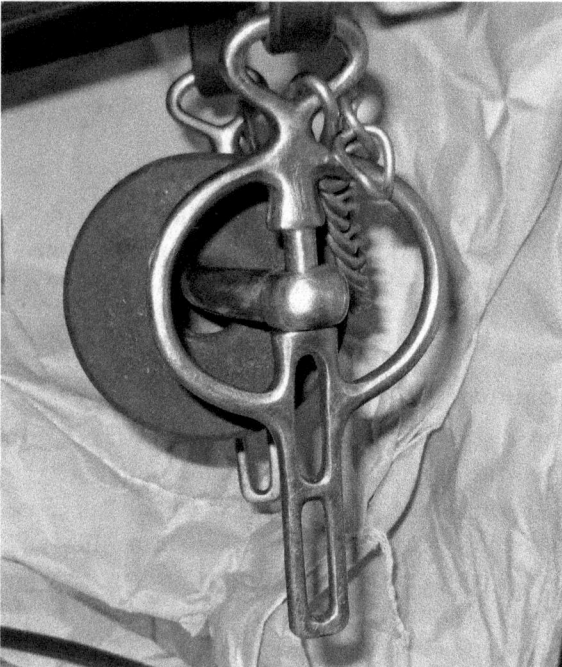

Four options of rein settings

A typical Liverpool bit has a loose mouthpiece, permitting up/down movement of the mouthpiece and a swing in/out of the cheeks. Because the mouthpiece is loose, you need to fit the bit slightly lower than you would fit a snaffle, permitting some play. This point is often overlooked.

Some horses like a loose mouthpiece, others don't. There are Liverpools with non-sliding cheeks that still swing, and there are fixed-mouth Liverpools, that are intended for use in pairs driving but may also suit horses who don't like the "play" that sliding or swinging cheeks permit.

There is leverage available in this cheek-style because of its length, both above and below the mouthpiece. With the rein set anywhere below the mouthpiece, the cheeks go back, the eye goes forward and that tightens the curb-chain. The bit rises in the mouth and slides up the cheekpieces, which adds somewhat to the leverage below the mouthpiece.

The rein settings starting from the ring (snaffle) setting and going down to the bottom slot become progressively more powerful. The maximum leverage available here, with the rein on the bottom slot, is 2:1 – 2 units acting below and 1 unit above the bit. This proportion is fairly standard for any curb bit.

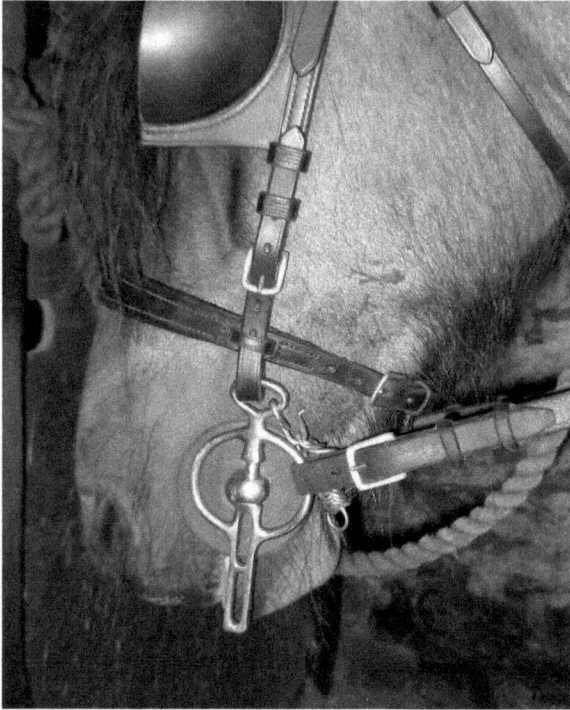

Plain cheek or smooth cheek rein setting

This is technically a "hybrid curb" bit, but since in driving we only use one rein at each side, buckling in the rein at this ring setting will act directly on the mouthpiece, making it a loose cheek hanging snaffle. A line drawn from the direction of the rein meets the mouthpiece precisely, so it can NOT apply leverage, therefore it can NOT apply curb or poll pressure. Hanging snaffles don't apply poll pressure either. They can't. It's a law of physics.

Rein pressure at this setting doesn't rotate the mouthpiece in the mouth, and the cheek pieces of the bridle are not put under tension. In fact, you can see in this photo that the "eye" of the bit has risen slightly and is not supported by the cheek pieces at all.

The curb-chain has no effect with this setting, except to stop the hooks flipping about (though it should still be turned, on fitting the bridle, till it's flat.) The "fly" link hangs from its lower edge. Strictly speaking, for driving the fly link should be taken off, as there is no provision for a lip strap on a driving bit and so the fly link has no purpose. This double-link chain is smoother than a single-link one, though single is traditional for driving.

Note that this driving bridle has the standard English design, with keepers at the sides of the noseband for the cheekpieces of the bridle. Such a noseband should be fitted below the cheek teeth – the keeper inside the noseband can cause pressure if you don't. The noseband is just touching the front of the nose when the bit is at rest, and should have two fingers' sideways space behind the jaw. This example, at this height, should be one hole looser.

Cheap and badly-measured nosebands that are too short behind and too long in front will make the bit cheeks poke forward in an ugly manner, like tusks. They also tempt you into fitting the curb-chain too tightly because they hold the eye of the bit backwards. More about curb-chains later.

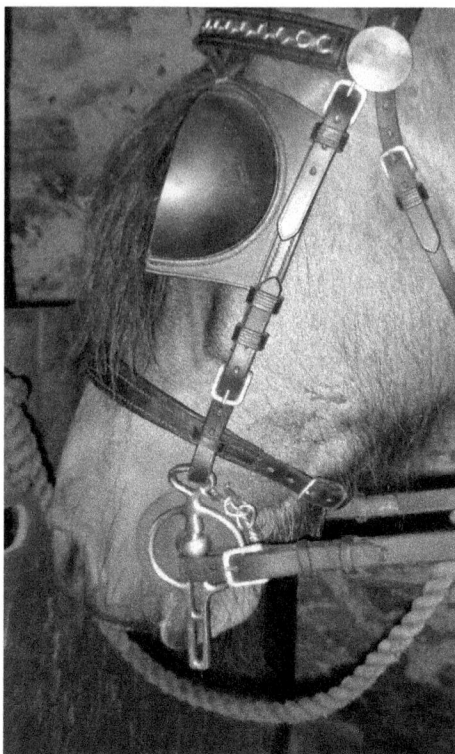

Rough Cheek rein setting.

There is very little leverage on the bit with the rough cheek setting but the rein itself often prevents up and down movement of a sliding mouthpiece, which – again – some horses may like and others dislike.

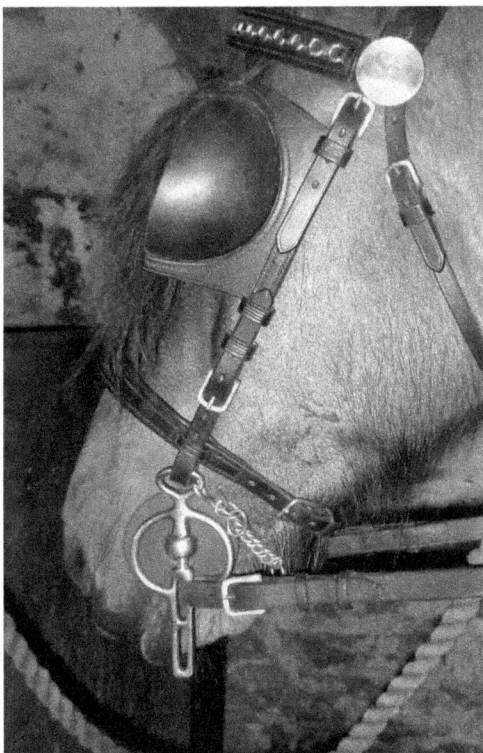

Top Slot rein setting

The rein on the top slot gives a little more leverage, but the slot-to-mouthpiece distance is still less than the mouthpiece-to-bit-eye distance, so the ratio of leverage is still less than 1:1. Tension on the rein makes the mouthpiece slide up the cheek of the bit and the eye of the bit go forward (notice how the cheekpiece of the bridle is now at the rear of the bit eye). This forward movement tightens the curb-chain. The bit mouthpiece lifts and rotates slightly. The curb-chain here could be one link longer and the noseband one hole slacker.

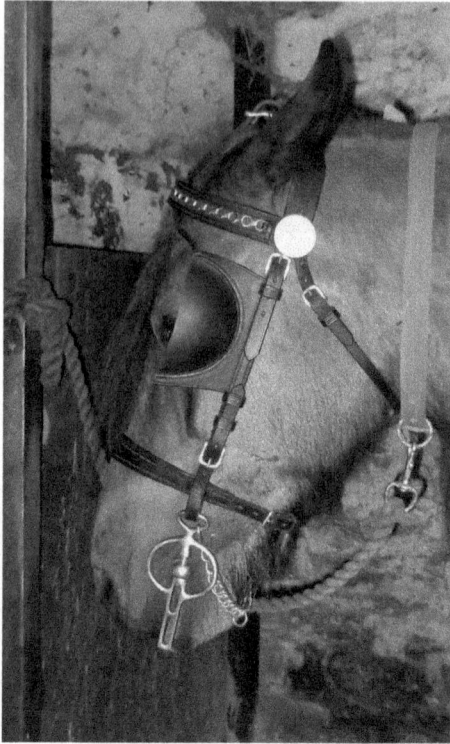

Curb-chain completely slack.

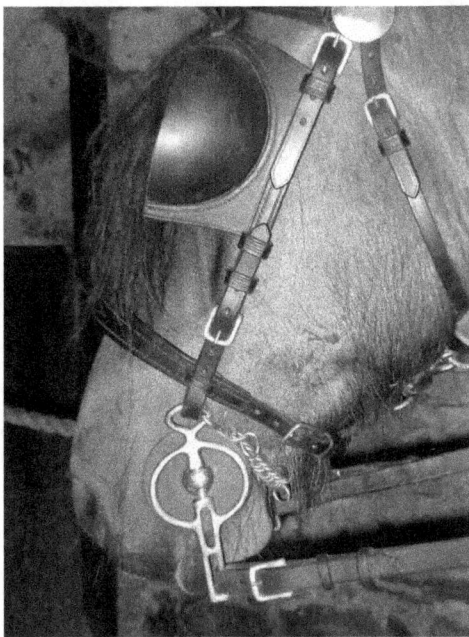

Reins on bottom slot, "the duffer's hole".

The mouthpiece has now slid to its highest position on the cheeks, and the movement has rotated it in the mouth. Although the curb-chain and noseband were not obviously tight, the mare really doesn't like tension created by the reins at this setting – she has backed off to the end of her rope. The bottom slot setting is very open to abuse if it's used with a tight curb-chain and tight noseband.

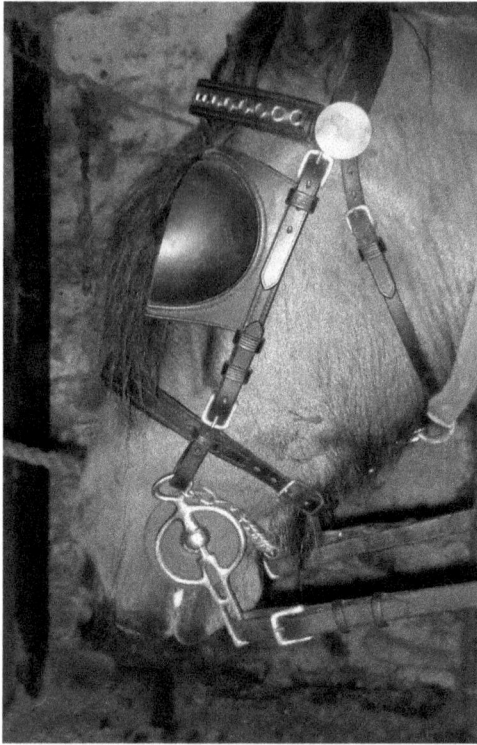

Slack curb-chain tightened by rein tension.

With the curb-chain slackened off completely, the noseband is now coming into play on the underside of the jaw instead of the actual curb. If the noseband were looser here, the bit would pull round to an even greater angle. Although the chain itself is barely able to touch the jaw at this slackness, it rises more than an inch in the centre when tension is put on the reins.

Mullen mouth Kimblewick or Uxeter

This version of the Kimblewick or Spanish jumping snaffle has a plain, curved unslotted mouthpiece. It has a swivel cheek that swings in or out, but the mouthpiece has no up and down movement. This curb-chain has a fly-link. With these cheeks, with slots for two rein positions as well as the plain ring setting, it is known as an Uxeter.

Uxeter side and front view

Top slot setting on this bit is exactly in line with the mouthpiece, so it offers NO curb or poll pressure. (More on "poll pressure" shortly.) With this setting the bit acts directly on tongue and lips, without turning the bit in the mouth, ie it lies still in use, like a Baucher or any other hanging snaffle.

Putting the rein on the lower slot of this bit gives a 1:1 ratio of lever action, the same amount of bit cheek above the mouthpiece as below. This is as "severe" as this short cheeked bit can get – and it is ridiculous to call it severe at all. The slight lever action merely turns the bit in the mouth, and puts some tension on the curb-chain.

Putting the rein on the ring is halfway between the two slots, giving a very slight amount of leverage (less lever below the mouthpiece than above) and a small rotation of the mouthpiece when rein pressure is applied. The curb-chain tightens a little and the cheek piece of the bridle is under slight tension. These are all small, almost "blurred" movements.

I've found the Kimblewick / Uxeter is not the severe bit it is often claimed to be. In fact it seems to be very forgiving. Its main action, like an unjointed snaffle, is from the pressure of the rein drawing the bit backwards in the mouth. A dressage expert might deride its imprecision, but it is kind. With driving reins, 12 feet or more between bit and hand, with all signals carried via 2 rein terrets, precision can't be achieved anyway. I have voice aids available to me in driving, so I go for a kind bit.

The example in the photo has a square cheek eye so the lift-and-tension effect is slightly more immediate than if the cheek eye were large and rounded (see the photos of the Liverpool bit, below) where the bit can turn and the eye slip across without disturbing the bridle. The Kimblewick / Uxeter is a convenient bit for leisure driving because the cheeks are so short they never catch in anything. They don't put off people you meet on the road who may want to pet the pony. There's nothing forward of the mouthpiece except the front of the cheek eye, so even if there is outward pull from the rein, there's nothing to press into the pony's face. She can also graze (when allowed) even if I don't take the bridle off.

I drive with the rein on the ring of the Uxeter. That's very similar to the setting I use if I drive in a show class, "rough cheek" on the Liverpool bit. My ponies like this bit.

Disadvantages of the Liverpool, and other hybrid Pelham-type bits

If the Liverpool cheek has 3 slots, it gives you 5 rein settings, but the cheeks will project too far beyond a pony's muzzle. That long cheek is really only suitable for horses, who have a mouth that is actually as well as proportionately longer than that of a pony, or of many cobs. 2-slot cheeks giving 4 rein settings are plenty long enough for a pony.

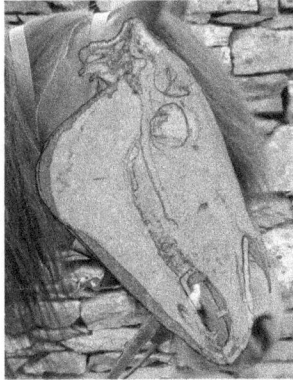

The orange/yellow skull is that of a horse, scaled to the same length as that of a pony skull.

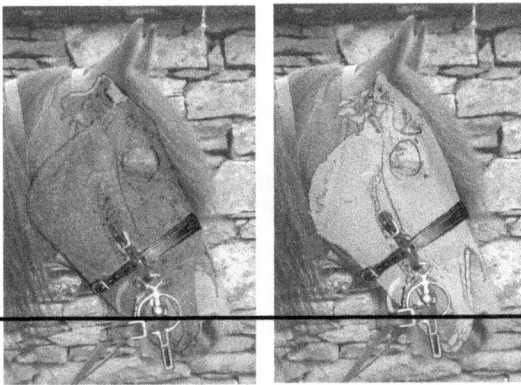

The horse (yellow) has a longer mouth-space, a higher palate and a finer lower jaw compared to the pony (in red). Liverpool bit correctly positioned, on left: Fell pony skull; right, Horse skull. (To same scale.) The black line shows the difference in bit height.

When a "hybrid" curb bit, such as the Liverpool or Pelham, is fitted correctly for height on a cob or native pony the curb-chain will sit neatly in the chin groove, but on the longer mouth of a horse if the mouthpiece is right then the chain can be too high up the back of the jaw. So, horses can be more difficult to fit with such bits. This is another reason why the true curb bit like a Weymouth has a fly link on the curb-chain and a position for a lip-strap. The lip-strap keeps the centre of the curb-chain in the right place, and stops it flapping as well as preventing the chain from being flipped off when the horse shakes its head at flies (which is the usual reason given!)

A difficulty with the swivelling Liverpool cheek is that any outward pull of the rein at the rear of the cheek ring will press the forward part of the ring towards the horse's face. For that reason it's not suitable for driving pairs, who should have a fixed-mouth version of this bit, or a bit without the forward part of the ring, which is really only decorative. It can be done without, as it is in the design of the Buxton, the Military/Elbow, and the Kimblewick.

Pelhams and Liverpools and other hybrid bits fit ponies and cobs well because these animals have a short mouth space. Horses are better suited by the classical two-bitted double bridle (Weymouth curb and single-jointed bridoon) and they have the jaw length to cope with both. Their mouths also have space for the single-joint to work on the tongue and lips, rather than pushing up into the palate.

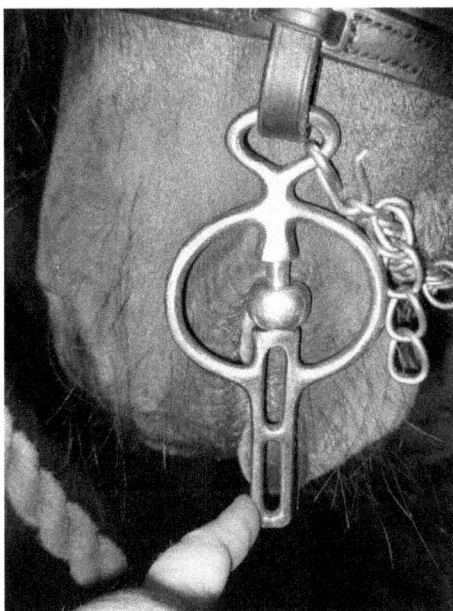

Above – the chain is fixed far too tight, permitting no movement of the bit whatsoever and forcing the horse to have the chain in contact all the time. This is severe.

Because the Liverpool has a curb-chain, which must be fixed on any curb bit each time you ride or drive, there is the possibility of fitting it wrongly. In the case of a tight chain the horse gets no "cue" from the driver using the rein. He can't respond quickly and so escape curb pressure by obeying. The pressure is there already, the bit cannot turn, and the cue happens at the same moment as the increased pressure.

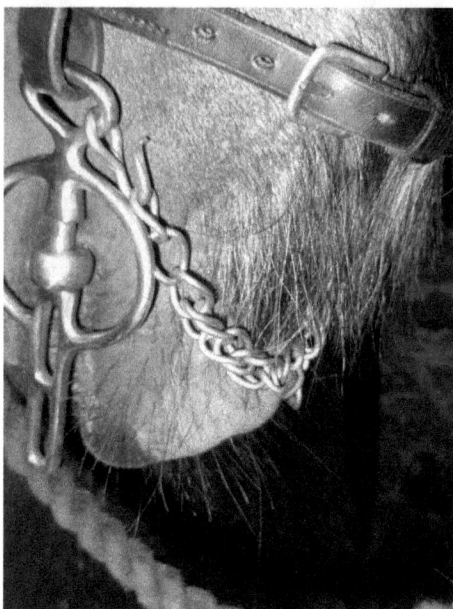

*Here, the curb-chain has not been turned to make the links lie flat;
it's been left "rough". This is severe.*

With the "roughed" chain there are aggressive points of pressure on the bones of the jaw. A combination of these two common errors would be torture for the horse. Small blame to him if he objects.

Poll pressure – a myth?

I conducted a straw poll (please excuse the pun) on the RED carriage driving forum about poll pressure. I asked them to put their fingers under the crown piece of the bridle and tighten the rein to the curb bit. Almost all my responses came from people who don't use curb bits and so before they tested they were only guessing.

On a scale of 0 to 3, where

     0 is "Zilch. No poll pressure."

1 is "I could barely feel the crownpiece move."
2 is "Mm, I can feel why they give to that."
3 is "Ow, that really hurt!"

All those who guessed chose 2 or 3 – they thought the poll pressure would be severe – until the testers began to send in their reports. Then the puzzlement began. My results, and the testers' results, were 0 and 1.

Let us "Go figure" why that was!

Liverpool bit at rest.

Liverpool bit activated by rein pressure.

Lower end of bit cheek swings backwards.

Mouthpiece rotates, presses back on the tongue and lips, and rises fractionally in the mouth.

Bit eye swings forward.

Crownpiece shifts fractionally towards the ears as the cheekpiece goes forward with the bit eye.

The curb-chain lifts a long way up the jaw as it tightens.

On the previous scale of assessments, when I put my finger in the following positions and applied "rein pressure":

Liverpool (bottom slot)

The cheekpiece swings forward with the bit eye; pressure at poll = 0, or at most, 1. I could barely feel the crownpiece move.

Mouthpiece rotates, presses back and rises fractionally in the mouth = 2. I can feel why they give to that.

The curb-chain lifts up the jaw and tightens = 3+ ! That really hurt!

Kimblewick (ring – the equivalent of rough cheek on the Liverpool)

The cheekpiece swings forward with the bit eye; pressure at poll = 0. Zilch.

Mouthpiece rotates a tiny bit, presses back and rises fractionally in the mouth = 1. The pressure applied is similar to the weight I put on the rein, like a snaffle.

The curb-chain lifts up the jaw and tightens = 2. I can feel why they give to that – but it doesn't tighten nearly as much as the Liverpool did, because the cheek piece above the bit is small and can't move so far to pull on the chain.

Discussion

The backwards pull of the rein on these bits does not apply pressure at the poll. There is just a barely perceptible change of angle in the crownpiece due to the eye of the bit going forward – a slight sensation of the leather moving a fraction of an inch towards the ears. I wondered initially whether it was significant that my bridles have shaped headpieces, which shift the leather away from the ears and allow the cheekpieces to fall further back down the face; but other people's tests with unshaped bridles also reported the same results.

Unless you have forced the bit so high in the horse's mouth that it jams on the molar teeth, there is no fulcrum effect at the mouthpiece of a curb bit and no perceptible increase of pressure at the poll.

It's the *rotation of the bit* over the tongue and lips that gives the horse his cue to yield. If he doesn't yield, the bit rises a little. It is the eye of the bit that is the fulcrum, not the mouthpiece. However, even the most severe lever action can only shorten the distance between the poll and the mouth by a fraction of an inch, and the pressure at the top is spread over not just the junction of the poll and the atlas, but right down the width of the face until it begins to narrow to the muzzle. There is far more ability to resist (hold still against) pressure in the bone and flesh of the poll than there is in the soft tissue of the mouth.

So it seems the main effect of a lever bit is the slight rise and rotation of the mouthpiece over the tongue and against the soft corners of the lips. The curb-chain should not come into play until both rise and rotation have been ignored. When the chain does make contact, it is very firm indeed on the underside of the jaw, and at that point there is no other increase of pressure available elsewhere – neither lifting the bit in the mouth, nor pulling down on top of the head.

There is a subtle difference of rein pressure between turning the bit in the mouth and applying the curb-chain. The longer the bit cheeks and the tighter the curb-chain, the stronger the power you can exert, but it's also true that the further the cheekpiece has to be turned to apply the chain, the more warning the horse gets before its power hits his jaw. The horse therefore has to be well enough trained to know that pressure means "yield" – and when he does so, the rider/driver has to be quick to release (and certainly not increase) the rein pressure that applies the curb-chain.

This, then, is why long-cheeked curb bits are not advised for novices, either human or horse: they have to be precisely adjusted and sensitively used, and they are very open to abuse. However, short-cheeked bits with kind mouthpieces, like the mullen mouthed Kimblewick may well offer "control" for strong ponies who resist single jointed snaffles. Perhaps this control is not because of their stronger action but because they are kinder and milder for short mouthed animals – and perhaps because the rider is being more careful, believing that the bit is severe!

Conclusion

Having done these tests, I shall continue to use my mullen mouthed Kimblewick for everyday work because I KNOW it is mild. It's certainly enough bit for my experienced ponies, and it's convenient for all the activities they take part in. I am, however, going to replace its curb-chain with the smooth leather curb I have tucked away in the spare room. I'm also taking the curb-chain off my Liverpool. I will never consider putting the rein in at either of the slots in the cheeks for my own ponies – they just don't need it. And exhibitors in any driving class that I am judging will have their bit fitting and use inspected with an even more critical eye.

References

Latchford, B. (1871) The Loriner

http://ia600305.us.archive.org/33/items/lorineropinionso00latc/lorineropinionso00latc_bw.pdf

Sprenger Comfort Mouth bit

http://www.horsebitbank.com/sprenger-comfort-mouth-pelham-new-644.phtml

Happy Mouths – X ray investigations of bits and horse mouths by Sprenger

http://www.horsedeals.co.uk/advice/equipment/happy-mouths/1661

Also well worth reading

Roberts, T (1971): Horse Control and the Bit, Roberts, Richmond, South Australia

Thoughts on Fixed vs Sliding Back Bands (SBB), 30 August 2008 and other dates

Sliding backbands are necessary for 2-wheeled carts and for 4-wheeled vehicles with fixed rather than independent shafts. I have driven over rough terrain and in local XC driving trials with 2 wheelers for 2 decades using SBB saddles and they emphatically have NOT caused tipovers. (Driver idiocy and occasional horse misbehaviour did.) Nobody is going to convince me that a fixed BB saddle would ever stop a 2-wheeler or a fixed-shaft 4-wheeler overturning. SBBs enable you to drive across a slope without shaft pressure hauling the saddle sideways. They make turning simpler for the same reason. They take out a lot of horse movement from the shaft behaviour, so it's more comfortable for both horse and human; and they absorb shaft movement over rough going so the saddle can sit quiet on the horse's back.

HOWEVER

SBB saddles are not appropriate for 4-wheeled vehicles with independent shaft arrangements because one shaft can slide low and the other high and cause all kinds of trouble for a horse in turns (behind the elbow, into the neck, etc). So if you are competing single across country in a 4-wheeler with independent shafts, as more and more Horse Trials drivers are doing, the dislike of the SBB saddle makes sense. It's quite easy to fix the BB so it doesn't slide though, if you already have a SBB saddle and want to move to a 4-wheeler with independent shafts. I had several customers who did that when I was making harness.

Otherwise, make life easy on your horse please. For a single horse in a 2-wheeler or a fixed-shaft 4-wheeler, SBB saddles are more horse friendly and more driver friendly.

What would you do? Le Trec! 28 September 2008

Our local BDS lady has just run one of these today so I'll describe how it was done. It was the first time she'd arranged anything of this nature, so some things worked and some didn't and next time (there WILL be a next time) it will be even more fun. Incidentally, there may well BE rules for scoring this sort of thing, but we couldn't find any so we ran it on our own ideas!

First of all drivers and horses were checked over for safety. We got marks knocked off for essentials missing (mobile phone, penknife, lead rope, headcollar under bridle, harness spares that fit; helmet, gloves; but also less-essentials like aprons). Harness and carriage suitability and fit were included, but the check also covered visibility on the road – horse/driver with Hi-Viz items, and in my case with cycle lights lit – and whether we were carrying any first aid equipment, like a ziplock bag containing a bandage, a sealed saline wash, water, and something to clean round a wound, like cotton swabs.

Next we went for an 8K drive, solo, at 5 minute intervals. This was done by reference to a printed guide; I believe other Trecs have done orienteering style drives, but in this particular venue only one route is really feasible so there wasn't much point in making it more complex. We had to drive at a comfortable speed for our animals and on this occasion no "window" of time was suggested for the distance – I think this will be clarified for next time as nobody really knew what they were trying to achieve without a target of any kind to aim for. Ruby, who knows the route by now having driven it four times over the years, knew exactly when she needed to step forward to make up time and when she would need breathers on steep hills. She was a bit puzzled by there being no hazards when we came back into the Park – she appeared to have been looking forward to the ducking and diving thing.

We finished the drive, our times were logged, and then we had a break for a couple of hours to cool the horses, to have lunch, and to inspect the "problems" or as the organiser called them "the twiddly bits". The overall time of this section was used to distinguish between results.

The problems were: the first half of a standard cones course; two "hazards" built of "road mending barriers", with lettered gates as per a HDT (or CDE if you prefer). These were not timed in themselves; walk past a flag hanging from on a horizontal stick, that swivelled on a short cane fastened firmly to a wooden base on the ground, in order to knock the flag with the offside wheel; walk up to a "box" outlined by cones, turn and reverse in, stand immobile for one minute, and walk out; walk (or trot) so that first your off side and then your nearside wheel passed between two pairs of parallel spars pinned down to the ground, w/o touching either; enter between 2 flags into a 15 metre circle spray-painted on the ground, turn within the circle without crossing the painted line and exit where you came in (easy peasy for Ruby who can spin the cart on one wheel); complete the cones course (which Ruby liked a lot, as it was very twisty).

Of these, I'd criticise the reversing manoeuvre, (1) because it was placed very close to the main road, where motorcycles were screaming past with some frequency. Just as I backed Ruby into the box successfully, two bikes went by, behind her, at high speed, which, since she was pretty collected in her reversing mode, made her stand on her hind legs. I have suggested that box is placed elsewhere for the next event we try. Also, (2) it was almost impossible for the pairs, with their 4 wheelers, to approach, turn, and get lined up to reverse successfully across the roughish grass, because any tussock could cause "bump steer" of the back axle and thus a complete failure to get the rest of the carriage into the box. Drive in and reverse out next time perhaps? I'm a bit sceptical about the hazards too.

I have several other suggestions that I'll put forward for next time, such as, driving into a rectangle or circle, halting while groom dismounts, circles the carriage at a walk, and remounts, horse meanwhile to remain immobile; driving into a box, groom to get out and move an obstacle (eg a plastic drainpipe laid on the ground or across two blocks or cones) so that the carriage can pass, and remount; collect and post a letter from/to a box, or a ball from/to a bucket.

We must have done all right today, in spite of the "motorcycle levade", as Ruby was second for the safety and presentation aspect, third in the drive and third in the "twiddly bits", and third overall. We had a superbly sunny and crisp day for the event and thoroughly enjoyed ourselves; I'd certainly compete or help at another Driving Le Trec.

November Drive with Ruby, 2008

Autumn has blown itself out with rumbles of thunder, hailstones, floods, and screaming winds, and the leaves have gone. The rivers are scoured and even the sheep are fewer; it's as though the gales have blown the lambs away so only the curly-horned tups and the old, heavy-fleeced ewes remain to shelter behind the walls and dykes.

Sometimes, though, even November relents, and the sky reverts to its forgotten blue.

I open the stable door and release Ruby, the Fell pony, who has been confined to quarters, not because her furry barrel body is unable to stand the weather, but because the ground is so wet that her hooves would mash good turf to a black pulp. She emerges politely enough, but heads up the yard at a steam-train trot, to reappear head-between-knees, doing handstands, emitting squeaks and snorts of pure excitement. She skates down the tarmac, bucks to a stop, turns in the air with a flurry of mane, and trots off again. I'm glad I didn't let her out onto the pasture.

After an hour or two of grazing, her claustrophobia has eased considerably and it's time to think of going for a drive to enjoy the warmth of the afternoon. Out with the harness and carriage. The brassware is dulled from lack of use, the wheels crusted with mud that I haven't had a spare day to clean off but I'm not going to waste the short winter afternoon on cleaning. It's collar on, straps buckled, and away. Ruby is as keen as I am to explore our lonely roads; the four walls of her stable must bore her as much as work tasks bore me.

Our neighbours too are making the most of the sunshine. The sailing instructor is unloading dinghies from his trailer and stowing them away for winter. A farmer has stoked his kitchen fire before he goes out on the quad bike, and the jet of white smoke from the chimney rises straight up in the still air. His trailer carries a barking dog and a plastic sack of feed for the sheep. Another is taking his tractor to the pumps to refuel; indicator blinking, disregarded, he's so busy "farming his neighbour's land" over the wall that he only sees us at the last moment, and has to pull into a gateway to let us by. Ruby, affecting to worry about the tractor's growling, arches her neck and lifts her feet high as she trots past: "See how active I am, you won't catch me, so don't even try."

Her unshod feet clop sharply on the tarmac, squelch over the grass verges, occasionally click when a stone is trapped in a cleft of her hoof then flicked loose again to rattle along the road. Once out of the village, the silence of open country, which is not silence but noise diminished by distance, sweeps round us and soothes us. I can hear the river churning, down at the bottom of the valley. A silver and red express gallops southward down the long rail embankment; a goods train, containers chained to its back, rumbles north with a steadier beat. The motorway hums faintly, constantly, in the background. Ruby's ears flick to and fro, absorbing every sound.

With the winter sun shining level across washed fields, things that were invisible in summer declare themselves once more. The rig-and-furrow of ancient ploughland stands out like ribs of corduroy. Lichens glow on the stones in circles of ghostly grey or acid green. Milky cascades of water from every field miraculously blend into a silky brown flow over the river's bedrock, clear and deceptively innocent, its only threat a creamy standing wave below each boulder. A burgundy-purple haze of little twigs crowns the silver birches on its banks, where charming pinky-grey fluffballs flutter nimbly, their prim black-and-white tail-feathers identifying them as long-tailed tits.

Ruby's sweating now through her thick winter fur, so we walk most of the way home, apart from the two hills where she prefers to trot. We power up out of the deepening shadows of the riverside, onto the open moor, back into the low, coppery afternoon light. A cock-pheasant races across a field, to join the sheep nibbling their trickled line of feed. If he's the one who has pecked my cabbages into lace and my broccoli into naked parasols, I'll look forward to having him on a platter at Christmas.

Back in the yard, the unharnessing follows a set routine. Ruby waits until only her collar remains, then tries, as always, to flip it off for herself. I give her a hand, and she works with me, lowering her neck, relaxing her throat so I can turn the collar easily and lift it over her head. She waits till I've stepped back, shakes herself thunderously then whickers to ask for her reward, her scoop of mixed grain and carrots.

Today's sunshine is unlikely to be repeated, so while she's munching, I wheel the carriage back under cover.

I take the risk of turning Ruby out into one of the empty fields, and it pays off; she's worked out her earlier need to bucket around and stomp holes in the grassland. I have a cup of coffee and a scone, and an hour later, when I go out into the dusk to call her, Ruby is still grazing peacefully within twenty yards of the gate.

As I clip the rope to her headcollar, and lead her back into the yard, the moon is rising, pale, over the edge of the hill. It looks full and contented, and so do we.

Ruby's good deed, 29 January 2009

We were supposed to be doing walking exercise but Her Ladyship had the wind in her ears and when we passed a field containing some ponies she hadn't seen before she just HAD to show off with her big flarchy trot and huge snorts. Silly madam. After that she tried to be silly at every car that passed. On the way back she did the same and at one point we were trotting so collectedly we were very nearly doing it on one spot, which felt quite explosive. However, she settled down again – she never does get out of control, though it often looks like she might. In fact, she settled back so well, when we were about half a mile from home I had time to notice that someone had un-padlocked, opened and left wide the little gate onto the main rail line. Knowing that now and again there are sheep loose on the road I thought that, even if somebody was working legitimately on the railway, the gate should be shut. So I swung Ruby round, placed her head-on to the open gate and said, "PUSH!" and she shut it with her nose.

I knew it would come in handy one day.

Newbie advice, 17 February 2009

> *Which horse? Which cart? so confused...*

This thread caught my eye because initially I thought – newbie and 2 year old? Uh-oh!

But I agree: of the three equines you mentioned, you are going to find the smaller pony easier to harness. So long as you remember that a 2 yr old is sometimes quiet because she doesn't know what's going on and may get sprightly once she begins to fitten up and muscle up and her brain kicks in ... Make haste slowly if you decide to stick with her.

Remember she's a baby and will be for another 4 years.

If you are a newbie to driving, make sure you know what you are doing when you work with her, because if you plan to keep her, you will be keeping whatever you teach her during her formative years – be it good or bad. Older horses that have seen more are able to forgive mistakes, but a young horse is learning what you ask and what you permit. So try hard to get it right.

Of the 2 vs 4 wheels argument, my personal choice is the 2 wheeler, using harness that gives balanced draft for that vehicle (You'll be sick of reading our advice to "go and get Barb's book on Understanding Harness"). Sliding backband, open tugs, adjustable balance. This is comfortable for pony and people.

I personally dislike the 4 wheeler over rough ground because you get two jolts for every bump (one for each axle). Riding in a two wheeler is akin to riding a horse, while riding in a 4 wheeler is more like riding in a car. You do need an "active seat" to assist the balance for 2 wheels, unless it is very heavy to begin with – and for the little 12.3 pony it won't be.

I have some safety reasons for my choice of a 2 wheeler:

A young horse can't jack-knife a 2 wheeler if it spooks or backs up.

It's easier to handle driving through gates if you drive alone (not recommended, but it is pretty well my only option and I have a good many gates to deal with on narrow roads where the 4 wheeler doesn't make life easy.)

It's often easier to buy a vehicle with 2 wheels that has a well placed step for easy entry – 4 wheelers tend to challenge me! though it does depend on the build.

An old friend of mine, Fred Todd, now dead, alas, once told me that in his experience a two wheeled cart was superior to a four wheeled one for heavy work PROVIDED it was properly balanced (ie, loaded by somebody who understood what he was doing). As an example he cited a black Shire horse that he'd worked with, who could shift – say – a ton, on a 2 wheeled cart but jibbed at the same load on a four wheeler. He did give me an explanation of why, and sadly I am only hazily remembering – probably something about the line of draft of the 4 wheeler effectively requiring the horse to lift the forecarriage as well as pulling the load. Plus, I suspect, the larger wheel diameter of the 2 wheelers – always easier on the horse than small diameter wheels. Andrew Pringle, a surveyor for the Royal Agricultural Society in 1794, said much the same; that 4 horses each with a single 2 wheeled cart could move a greater total weight than the same horses harnessed as a team to one 4-wheeler.

Fred was not a fan of 4 wheelers for competitive cross country work and when he was National Singles Champion way back in the early 80s he drove exclusively 2 wheelers (but I must point out that back then *everybody* drove singles across country in 2 wheelers).

Some American 4 wheelers have no "cut under" for the front axle to turn. These I believe to be dangerous for a young horse and newbie driver, because in case of a spook or need to turn sharply the front wheels come up against the body and things can break.

So I'd stick with 2 wheels.

Ruby and the trainspotters, 9 April 2009

Things have been pretty busy here for me. I've changed to working for myself after redundancy from the University Computing job. I now build web sites and manage them, and I write, and I'm planning on doing my BDS Level 2 exams / units in order to get my teaching ticket. So with Ruby and the self-catering cottage next door, life is pretty full.

Weather's been rubbish the last few days but despite strong winds today, it wasn't raining, and I thought I'd drive Ruby. She'd been in the stable all day yesterday because the weather was foul. Did a quick bit of shopping first because I think most shops will be shut tomorrow, and I noticed on the way home that there were lots of cars parked at the railway bridge, which usually means a special is due through and the "chuffographers" are all setting up their tripods and video cameras. They're pretty bad at parking, and spectacularly good at blocking the place up, our roads being only just wide enough for 2 cars to pass at the best of times.

Hung about a while in the yard at home, keeping an eye on things, and the crowds got bigger.

Anyway, "steam specials" usually pass through around mid-day so I got Ruby out of the stable at noon and sure enough, there's a little train,with steam engine and "banker" engine (unusual) and two carriages, poop poop, chuffing merrily north. Good, thinks I, that's that, the chuffographers'll all be gone by the time I am yoked up to drive.

Ruby's shedding hard so the grooming and harnessing take up another 25 mins. Off we go … and the car numbers if anything have increased! Hm, what do they know that I don't?

People parked in front of our house; man with camera talking to postie, who's blocking the road; the postvan mirrors are obstructed by talking man, so postie doesn't see us.

Patiently whistling to ourselves we stand behind the post van until he notices and moves on.

OK, we avoid the main hill out of the village (still double lined with cars and tripods) and go to Scout Green. Nice and quiet. Couple of standard trains go up and down the main line. Ruby's driving nice and straight and steady. (Did I mention that her inclination to drift right was cured by re-aligning the cart shafts? Duh.)

Down to Scout Green, hop off and do the gate there and travel on. Hmm. People all over the open fell, some running towards the railway.

CHUFF CHUFF CHUFF HOOT HOOT. Ah. Another steamer is coming up the gradient – this time working hard, black smoke, ten coaches, people waving, cameras going like mad. We pause in a handy space between cars so as NOT to be under the railway bridge when the dragon goes over … And Ruby stands like a rock, just watching. CHUFF CHUFF CHUFF HOOT HOOT. No problem. Good girl, on we go. Of course now everybody's mad to move on … idiots coming round corners without really looking. Watch out Ruby, park on the grass again till they clear the blind bend under the railway bridge … trot on … and walk again because there are chuffographers walking up the road, thrilled skinny at having witnessed A Proper Train going by (so what, they were ALL like that when I was a kid!) and not taking any notice of our unshod footfalls behind. So we walk along between the double row of cars and people, and a regular goods train comes north, heavy laden, grinding along, wheels squealing. Ruby doesn't like walking parallel to that; the track is only thirty yards from us. "DO I have to walk? I want to run away." We walk. She does a very collected, can-I-be-naughty trot until I tell her to calm down, nobody's going anywhere. The train is finally past and she's still in walk.

There's a queue of cars leaving this scene – for some reason there are men with a cherrypicker lift on the back of a truck, doing things to the motorway bridge 100 yards ahead. Everybody is backed up waiting for it to move. Ruby goes into Traffic Mode and is patient. We follow the truck up under the motorway underpass, and have to wait for it again at the next underpass (the motorway is in two separate parts here, north bound and south bound, so 2 underpasses). She's very relaxed but interested and taking it all in. Long wait. I stay just short of the tunnel so we don't have to wait in the shadows and echoes. When eventually the truck gets its lift packed away and departs, we have 3 cars ahead and at least 6 behind, so I park up by the next gate and they all overtake and rumble over the cattle grid. But one nice fellow stops and opens the gate for us. So at least SOME trainspotters have common sense.

After that it's just a case of listening (as well I can for the wind) for cars coming up behind and needing to overtake. Lots of hand signals. Ruby is getting good at telling me if she hears traffic and I don't – the ears turn back, and she moves over to the verge. Got to love that intelligent brain.

Coming home down the hill where the double line of cars were before we set off, there's nothing left but tyre marks in the mud. But she'd have made nothing of it if they'd still been there.

That's my girl. Have a nice feed. Go and tidy the grass in the yard for me.

SONNY "THE STROPPY TEENAGER"

(Blog posts), June 2009

I had the interesting experience today of driving both my mare Ruby and her son, Sonny (it wasn't me who named him). Sonny is an 8 year old dark bay Fell gelding who came to my friend David Trotter for some mild discipline since he had "got boss of" his breeder. He's been with David about ten days and has now had his head turned gently around.

I sat in the exercise cart today while David drove, and I took some photos and video.

David Trotter preparing to take Sonny out for a drive

Next week Sonny rejoins his Mum at our place, just to widen his experience and make sure he is obedient to a woman's instructions as well as to a man's.

It'll be fun to see how his Ma greets him when he arrives. She has missed having other ponies to play with. And it will be fun having another pony for me to play with too.

Sonny's Visit to Greenholme, 15 June 2009

I'm not posting much at present on the RED list as we are busy. Ruby's younger foal, Sonny, now aged 8, has come here for two weeks of mind-broadening.

Ruby – though delighted to see him again yesterday – has decided after 36 hours that he is just a stroppy teenager out to steal my affections, and is disciplining him accordingly.

I drove him for 20 minutes today, so from now on I'll be including him in my time-challenge record posting at the end of the month.

Hope everyone else is having as much fun as we are.

Sonny's visit to Greenholme (2), 9 June

David's done the groundwork and it's just a case of spending a week or two filling in a bit more experience. Sonny is coming here early Sunday morning and David is going to give me a hand to introduce him to my cart with its bigger and more visible wheels. Then I will give David a lift home. I might drive Sonny out later in the day when he's had time to cool off after coming over Pikey [big hill to the south], but before he's thought about getting fresh again. Stabling him with straight hay-and-water and no hard feed has done wonders for his figure and also his attitude. Like his Mum, he slonks a bit at walk unless you nag him. He still peeps at things, but that's just greenness, nothing nasty. Time and miles are the cure for that. Danny is booked to come and shoe Ruby and I've left a message that I also want him to handle Sonny if he comes while Sonny is here. I know he and Sonny have had their differences, but I have a strategy ready.

Sonny's visit to Greenholme (3)

I turned Ruby out early into the field so the two adjoining stables would both be empty for Sonny's arrival. David appeared on the yard just as I poured my breakfast coffee, but I went out to see how things were going. Roger had driven up in the car following David and Sonny with the exercise cart, so he was already standing at Sonny's head while David unyoked and unharnessed. "He came over Pikey just grand," said David. "Got into trot to keep up his momentum and just kept going. Never bothered about the motorbikes either, and we met quite a few."

Sonny was quite sweaty after doing four miles over hilly country, and ordinarily I'd have washed him off, but I thought perhaps that would be a question too far on his arrival in a completely strange place. He was a bit worried by Sammy the sheepdog who made a couple of dashes at his heels as we walked round to the stable, but he only went a stride or two and obeyed the halter.

The stable was another matter. Outside the sun was bright and the stable looked very dark! He jibbed, but David told him firmly to "walk on" and after a moment's consideration Sonny walked in.

I left Sonny to look round while I fetched a haynet, and David and Roger went off back to Tebay, since Roger had to go to work. Once the haynet was up, I walked out to collect Ruby. Typical of his family, as soon as Sonny realised the door was shut, he started trying the latch.

Out in the field, Ruby had her head down and was hoping nobody was going to take her away from the grass, but she came in obediently. At the gate she must have smelt Sonny, because she stood very still and he let out a series of loud whinnies. So in we went. Mother and son met nose to nose over the connecting door and stood like statues, breathing deeply, almost kissing, for several minutes, before Sonny's sniffing became too much for Ruby and she let out the classic indignant-mare squeal.

Graham wandered out to have a look and I went back for my breakfast. The coffee was still hot.

An hour later when both were settled, I took the grooming brushes and gave Sonny a firm going-over to loosen the sweat from his coat. He stood quietly, so that's no problem. He wasn't sure about me handling his right ear, which has a matted bit on the ear-tuft, but I persuaded him it was all right. I'll trim off the tuft, which is probably catching on things apart from my brush. Must find the round ended scissors (you don't use them much with Fells!). Then I picked up all his feet. After I'd handled the left side he said, "No, I know what you want but I'm not going to pick up my right fore." So I moved him about until that foot had left the ground, and asked again. He made me use two hands, but he picked it up, and the right hind, peacefully. That's going to be something to do at least once a day then.

Ruby meanwhile stood yearning over the partition, "Groom ME, groom ME!" and scratching her neck on a handy knot in the woodwork (which she hadn't had access to when in the other box.) I fetched a saw and got rid of the knot, and gave her a fuss and a bit of hay. Silly old dear.

Sonny's visit to Greenholme (4), Sunday, June 14, 2009

Jen (our daughter) arrived this lunchtime, with Rob (her partner) and Naomi (our grand-daughter). We shut the gates, hung the CAUTION – LESSON IN PROGRESS sign, and brought both ponies out and tied them in the sunshine while we fitted harness to Sonny. Lots of fiddling, all very good for him. He stood well and even when we decided to trim the matted bit off his ear he didn't make much of a fuss. Jen cupped one hand round his eye like a blinker while I nipped off the "felt". He tries to lean on you to stop things he finds annoying, but he doesn't thrash about or kick or rear, so gentle persistence is working. He actually rather enjoys having his ears scratched, once he's let you get your hand up there; the eyes go all sleepy and he leans on your fingers. We picked up all his feet again too. He wasn't actively naughty, just a bit stubbornly uncooperative. His feet do need a trim so if Danny isn't coming soon I might get the rasp out and have a go at them where the excess growth is cracking. Mind you, steady work on the roads should sort them out.

Interesting how the pony's movement is shown up by the places where wear and overgrowth occur in the hooves.

We fitted all the harness and brought out the carriage. Graham was doing some maintenance on David's exercise cart, so instead we showed Sonny the cross country cart with its big wheels. This involved letting him come up and sniff them, then Jen led him round to the other side (horses' brains need to accept input from the left eye AND the right eye separately). I walked round the yard like a daftie pulling the cart while Jen led Sonny after it, circling in both directions, so he could see how the wheels behaved. Much interest, but no panics. Good. Rob and Naomi sat on the barn steps and made cheeky remarks about Grannie having got the sequence wrong because the pony was following the cart. Ha ha.

We fitted the carriage to Sonny after that. He accepted pretty well everything, which is as it should be, after nearly 3 weeks of trotting round Tebay with David and the exercise cart. He was a bit puzzled about the shafts bumping more freely in the tugs (David's cart is a nip fit, rather like a pair of nutcrackers!) but accepted it. More adjustments to the harness followed. More scratching of his ears and picking up of feet. All good stuff. Lots of praise.

Then it was "take it all off time", and Jen saddled up and introduced Sonny to the mounting block (highly portable home made thing) which we'd plonked in the middle of the yard. We edged him up to the block and she leaned across him then mounted. He was okay with all this as he'd been ridden before, and I left her to walk him around the top of the yard while I harnessed Ruby and put her into the carriage ready to go. Opened the gates, walked Ruby up to top yard and let Sonny see the whole thing, before setting off for a quiet walk up to the top of Whiteham.

Both ponies walked out well and Jen gently convinced Sonny not to try being silly. He tried one shy, and didn't bother again.

While we were talking Jen said he had been unusually reactive when she introduced herself in the stable. He had known she was there, but when she touched his shoulder he "turned himself inside out". So the quiet stance and the gently sleepy eyes are not entirely to be relied on. Sudden explosions like that make you wonder if someone has at some time been very rough with a pony.

We walked all the way up to the top of the common with Ruby leading Sonny, or Sonny alongside the carriage to watch the wheels, which he didn't mind at all. He also obeyed when Jen stopped him well short of the cattle grid while I took Ruby on and turned her. She then asked him to lead the way home; classic early mounted work. Put the experienced pony in front on the way out, and the youngster in front on the way back. He walked well and Jen collected him and asked for trot as they went up Daw Bank. Which he did nicely on a pretty well loose rein.

By now we'd been working with or around him for over 2 hours, which would have been too much for a young horse, but as he's 8, equivalent to a fairly mature teenager, it didn't seem to overface him. We gave him a carrot, and Naomi helped give Ruby a handful of feed, then we turned both Mum and son out in the field for half an hour to finish their socialising and have a nibble of grass. Jen didn't let him drag her about on the way to the field – he had to walk away and back several times and behave properly before she would let him through the gate.

Ruby demonstrated her athletic trot for us with huge gusto and Sonny bounded along after her in canter. She's already put him in his place once or twice, the initial delight at seeing him having faded into parental responsibility!

Jen and Rob and Naomi went out to bring them back in, after we had all had a drink and done some jigsaws indoors. Ruby kept looking back – she appeared to be worried that Naomi was with Jen and Sonny, instead of herself. She is so maternal. Sonny followed her into the stable without argument – an improvement on 9 am this morning.

All in all, a good afternoon's work. Tomorrow, I'll drive him.

Sonny's visit to Greenholme (5), Monday, June 15, 2009

Ruby was scowling and squeaking and stamping at Sonny yesterday evening and he was sulking, not eating his haynet, but by breakfast time he'd eaten up.

More education today. Danny the farrier was due to put a set of shoes on Ruby. I left Sonny standing tied to the big pine tree across the yard. He also had a wagon-rope about 1 cm in diameter round the tree and once round his neck under the headcollar, tied with a bowline so it wouldn't tighten, and placed six inches back from his poll so it wouldn't do any damage. I knew he and Danny had had "issues" previously and he'd pulled tying points out of walls. I wasn't going to give him any excuses.

I picked out his feet ready for trimming, all round, and he co-operated. "This is all getting to be old hat," he said. Fine by me.

Danny arrived and we chatted while Danny shod Ruby, then he moved to work on Sonny. And Sonny, though a bit "numb" about giving his feet to be trimmed, didn't even offer throw himself about or object. So we gave him lots of praise.

When Danny had gone, I put Ruby in the stable with some more hay, and went back for Sonny. As we walked down the yard he shied as though the dog had rushed at him – which I knew it couldn't because I'd tied it up short. He stepped on the edge of my boot and effectively pinned it to the ground so I rolled over. But he didn't go anywhere – just stood there, being a big numb teenager. Graham took the lead rope while I dragged myself off the floor, and then I put the boy away while I had a cup of coffee and a think. I know he did this with David Trotter – stood on his wellie and felled him. So after my think, I tied up the dog elsewhere, picked up a length of alkathene pipe and took Sonny for a walk round the yard. I had no intention of hitting him – the pipe was just the right length to poke him in the shoulder but not splinter if he decided to jump or lean into me. And of course, actually being a wise pony, he didn't. So more praise and he got put away with his haynet (and Mum) once more.

Later on I got him out again (still with the pipe for reference!) and harnessed him up. Lots of fiddling and chat. I put him to David's ex cart and drove him round the yard, turning right and left. He was fine. I made him stand once or twice and wait for the command to move on. Then took him back to the tree and tied up. Chatted, fiddled and faffed (he probably thought, bloody women!) then untied him, and drove round the yard again and up among the trees, and turned in places I hadn't turned before. Made him stand some more. Lots of praise because he was getting everything right. This time when I tied up he was unharnessed and I led him back to the field – still carrying the pipe because we were going down the yard where he'd shied both today and yesterday. And he walked circumspectly and behaved.

I turned Ruby out with him and finally had time to inspect my Ariat boot – big tear at the welt where his foot had pinned me. Still, it could have been my toes. No complaints.

Sonny's visit to Greenholme (6), Tuesday, June 16, 2009

Not so good today, at least to begin with. I think it's probably the grass yesterday – as on Sunday they only had less than an hour out, whereas yesterday it was nearer 5.

I put Sammy the sheepdog on a short rope in a different place for Sonny to look at and not have the excuse of "oh he startled me". I brought Sonny out just after 10 am, after he'd had his morning haynet (which he isn't mad keen on). I tied him to the "patience tree" and groomed him, and harnessed him up. He was okay. Then I brought out the cross country cart, which he'd seen on Sunday, and let him look at it, then I brought it up and put the shafts round him. Scuttle, fidget, quiver, "Oh my, that's dangerous." So I let him settle, and took it away briefly and put it on again. More fidgeting. I fastened him in and let him stand.

He did a lot of wandering from one side to another, so I set him up with the wagon line again in case he got really stroppy. I'd put on coat, hat and gloves to go out driving, but I discarded the idea, and shut the yard gates. I sat with him for an hour while he fiddled and faffed about. Every now and again I went and walked round him and shoved the trap shafts about, bumping them up and down and side to side, and pulling and pushing the trap back and forth. He fidgeted a bit each time, but less, until eventually he didn't really bother. He spent some time rubbing his head on the halter ropes and trying to get his head under them to bust them. It didn't work, mainly because the tie level is higher than his withers and he can't get any purchase on the rope by snagging it over his poll. He's obviously done this a few times and been able to escape.

When he had stood quiet for a while I took off the cross country gig and put the exercise cart back on him, which he didn't fuss about nearly as much. He's now standing for another hour, with a haynet (and refusing to eat the hay). I think the photo for this one needs a caption of Harry Enfield's teenage monster saying "It's NOT FAIR."

It doesn't matter which cart he accepts, since he isn't going to be a driving pony. What matters is that he stops buggering about when he doesn't think he wants to do something.

LATER

Having let Sonny stand for another hour, (like a pot of tea stewing) I went out and put on my hat and gloves and prepared to drive him round the yard. Jen's driving pupil Mike turned up and seeing the CAUTION sign on the gate he parked the horsebox outside and walked in to see what was going on. He introduced himself to Sonny, who'd calmed down by then into boredom, and I asked him to unclip the rope while I drove Sonny round the yard. After his three hours of standing, Sonny went willingly and only tried to second guess the turns once.

Then Jen arrived, ready to teach, and as this little 5 minute trip round the yard was a big improvement on Sonny's earlier attitude, I took the cart off and unharnessed him. Jen saddled him and we put him into the stable to stand with another haynet while she taught her lesson to Mike and his pony Dennis; and I took Ruby out for a drive. His whinnies for his mother were pathetic but we hardened our hearts – even Ruby by then had got fed up with him and didn't bother to respond to his shouts.

An hour later again, after Mike and Dennis had done their thing, Jen brought Sonny out, checked the girth, showed him the mounting block once more, and rode him into Greenholme and up the hill onto Whiteham, and back. She made him walk and stand, walk and stand. He tried shying once to each side and then gave over. She chatted to Willy Kipling in the village ("That's not your Mother's horse." "No, it's out of Mother's horse." "Ah. It's nice though. And is it naughty?" Hmm ...) Sonny fidgeted about but Jen didn't let him eat grass (which was what he wanted) or move on till she told him. They had some discussions about standing still on the way home, but she came back happy with him. She led him back to the stable and he was really listening to her – when she stopped, he stopped, and when she walked on, he walked on, on a loose rope. This is the result we are looking for. So although it was a long day, by 3:15 pm there was a definite improvement to be seen.

I turned him out with Ruby while I tidied the stables for the night, and he had a good roll: "wash that cart right outta my hair!" I brought them both back in after half an hour. Ruby was busy scratching on a low tree branch and made me walk all the way down the field for her, but Sonny came cantering after his mum in case he was going to miss something. While I took Ruby indoors he had a good long drink, and then let me clip on his lead rope and lead him in. Walk with me, stop with me; walk with me, stop with me. He's improving.

Sonny's visit to Greenholme (7), Wednesday, June 17, 2009

Yuck – pouring rain and wind this morning. Jen arrived shortly after I'd fed the beasties and tidied up the stable. Sonny ate his carrot and spurned his haynet, wanting to eat Ruby's soaked hay instead (which he couldn't actually reach). Bet he regretted that when Jen marched in and saddled and bridled him.

I was just going out to visit one of my web clients, but seeing that Sonny was circling the mounting block without getting anywhere near it, I went over to give a hand. He tried creeping backwards while Jen was mounting, but a firm hand on the headcollar under his chin stopped that. She climbed up and he settled. We must practise the mount/dismount stuff tomorrow, but p**sing rain is not the time to do it, and so I got the car out of the way and left Jen to carry on his ride after I'd gone.

She took him to Scout Green, basically because it's a sheltered route where you can do a 2 mile ride out and 2 miles back without opening a gate. He was happy to go out, OK with going out solo, was forward and obedient. Jen was riding him with a very light rein, almost none at all most of the time, just using leg to move him onward. At the road junction where we've twice turned towards Ewelock Bank, he whinnied for Mum, but when Jen gently took up contact on the rein he went on OK. He spooked a bit at the bridge at High Scales (oooh, rushing water and a bridge) but went forward when Jen insisted. She rode through to Scout Green and he walked through big puddles just fine.

Coming back, she put him on the grass at Beckside lawn – mostly to see what he would do – and he offered to trot so she let him, and he put his ears back and bronked, two or three dirty big bucks with his ears back, so she knew it was naughtiness and not ONLY excitement. She sat him, and when she picked up the rein he put in a sudden stop (which she said was the most unsettling thing he had done!) and froze as though he expected to be beaten. She moved him on at a strong working trot all the way up the bank from Beckside and over the fell at Whiteham and he gave no more problems.

In the village once more, she asked him to stand and wait, and he did, looking about but not moving his feet. If he fidgets, speaking "Stand" and "Wait" gently, with loose rein, will keep him still – if he does move, simply lifting the rein a touch is all it needs to stop him. Yesterday he fidgeted, and crept backwards, but today despite the excuse of awful weather, he stood well. He walked home fine from there. Jen says, "he just needs to be ridden with seat and leg, from back to front, and not hung onto from front to back." He feels solid as a ride, not wobbly like a young green horse, but a lot of this is down to his physical maturity (8 years) and his square build – very short back and broad chest.

Jen said he flinched at her getting off in the yard, but walked about quietly after her on a loose rein and didn't make any fuss about going back into the stable even though Ruby was busy investigating both stables (making sure Sonny hadn't got anything nice that she hadn't got). Tomorrow we will drive him out, then do some mounting and dismounting practice.

Incidentally, his mother is bossing him too. Ruby was never Top Dog when she was at Sedbergh. She had borne him and Belle, but Boxer (Tebay Vespa) was Top Dog. After Ruby came to me, Sonny's youth and strength must have been more than a match for Boxer as he aged. So their positions are reversed while they are here: Ruby is gaining self-respect, and Sonny is having his dented. Both of which are very good things.

Sonny's visit to Greenholme (8), Thursday, June 18, 2009

Jen arrived shortly after 9 am and we brought both ponies out to be brushed over and tacked-up, Sonny at the tree, Ruby outside the end stable. The weather was windy with brief, heavy showers but both were relatively laid-back about it. There's a lot to be said for Fell ponies :)

After yesterday's through soaking Jen had cleaned saddle and bridle and saddle soaped them. I had opened up the curb hook on the bit, to make it easier to remove the curb chain when unbridling. Previously it had been tight and difficult to remove, which agitated Sonny unnecessarily. David had spent half an hour teaching him to open his mouth for the bit (because he was being obstinate about it) and now he'll open his mouth, and more importantly his teeth, to let you slip the bridle on without fuss. All you need to do is put the bridle in position with the bit under his nose, and he'll do it when you say, "Open."

Jen had put the reins onto the (Uxeter) bit at the plain ring setting – instead of the lower, curb setting as we'd received it from David. Sonny doesn't seem to need the curb setting. Taking hold and "grabbing him" by the bit just doesn't work. He needs to be ridden forward from the leg, and then will round up nicely into a good outline, and ask, "Where's the bit? I need to know you're there." A light rein contact is all that he then needs, and he'll work in a nice outline on no contact at all if you just trust him to do so.

I harnessed Ruby to the carriage and peeked round the end of the stable to see whether Jen wanted any help with Sonny today. She led him round the mounting block but then ignored it. She tied him with the usual quick release knot to the tree at the high ring that she could easily reach from his back, parked her long dressage whip through the stirrup keeper on the saddle, and mounted him from the ground. He was foiled. She then pulled the quick release, and carried the lead rope as well as the reins for the rest of the ride. (She used to do this when breaking youngsters at Trotter's yard.)

We walked down to Bretherdale road-end, for a change, and then up Pikestoll which is steep. Part way up we met a county council 3-ton pickup coming down, so it, and we, each had to edge over to enable us to pass. At the first farm gateway – where Tom always leaves silage bales in winter, so it's full of black plastic – we made the ponies walk over the plastic, then walked back down to the road-end. Here we parted company: I went to the bridge, and Jen rode Sonny up Bretherdale, then we both turned, and came back to pass each other. This was complicated by the pickup truck returning from Bretherdale behind Sonny, and a tractor with (?fencing?) equipment on it following me and Ruby. I parked in Tom's farm lane, Jen rode Sonny to join us, and the motorised traffic moved on before we crossed, and turned, and joined up again to walk back up Pikey for a second time. Jen put Sonny in front and he walked away and trotted nicely up to the second gateway. Here we turned again, and came back down. It all sounds a bit boring to describe, but enlivened by the brisk breeze and occasional showers, it was actually quite pleasant! At the "black plastic" gateway we met the tractor again and the ponies were both very good about walking over the plastic to get off the road; scary stuff but very much "old hat" now not only to Ruby but also to Sonny. On a loose rein, Sonny in fact stood the tractor better than Ruby, who wanted to make an excuse to jump in front of Sonny. Down the hill again, along the level to the bridge; I suggested Jen use her leg on Sonny to move him sideways across the road a few times, while she had level straight going and no traffic. He responded easily and without flapping.

Up the hill to the house, over the brow and down into Greenholme. No traffic, no fuss, all very boring, just as it should be.

Jen rode Sonny down to the beck, where there is a slope into the water. I didn't expect her to pick a day when the beck was running a bit high to ask him to walk into water, or else I would have stopped her, since everything had gone very well up to that point. They had – not an argument – but a minor discussion, on the bank, with Jen asking Sonny to step in, and Sonny saying, quite mildly, that he didn't think so, thanks.

I have to say I think he was right, as the water was still coloured from yesterday's rain and he could not be sure of his footing. We know it's a sound bottom, but he didn't. However, he didn't do anything naughty other than stand still, and he could easily have ducked Jen with a well timed buck. So she got off and got back on him while his feet were planted. No arguments.

We'll save crossing water for a nice hot day. He'll be happy to splash, when we've trotted over Pikey to the ford at Roundthwaite, where I can get Ruby and the carriage across and there is room for Sonny to follow Mum.

We went home, and I trotted Ruby away from Sonny, who preferred to investigate the track to Brown Bank barn – possibly thinking it was like the track up to David's buildings! Anyway, Jen let him look, and then brought him home.

We've mucked out the stables (always easier with 2 people!) and turned the ponies out for an hour's grass while the wind is there to keep off the flies.

Of course, the hour had stretched to 2 by the time I got round to bringing them in. I put up a haynet for Sonny, and Ruby's usual flake of soaked hay in her half-barrel. I shut the yard gate, opened the field gate, and walked down the field to catch Ruby, who walked quietly in, picking bits of grass as we went. Sonny came wandering along a respectful 20 yards behind. I put Ruby indoors with her mugful of feed, leaving a tablespoonful on the windowsill for Sonny. He was still 20 yards from the open gate, but looking for me, so I called him, and he trotted up and let me lead him in ... walk with me, stand with me ... he is better at this than Ruby is, now.

Sonny's visit to Greenholme (9), Friday, June 19, 2009

More blustery, showery weather this morning. In contrast to yesterday, both ponies were sharp and eager to go: Ruby clattering about and not wanting to wait for Sonny, Sonny swinging about and not wanting to wait for Jen to mount. Maybe two hours of spring grass is more than they need. Jen walked off and left Sonny tied to his tree (they must be well acquainted by now), and when she came back he stood OK for her to get up.

We walked from Daw Bank to the electricity substation past Selsmire farm, a distance of about two miles, and back. The idea was to get Sonny quietly across the two motorway bridges, and past a field of young horses whose curiosity can be upsetting as they trot, splash and canter along their side of the field fence.

We met a good deal of traffic, a couple of 4-wheeler wagons, couple of tractors, lots of cars. Everything very circumspect, unusually so, which was fine of course. Sonny was less fidgety once we got going. He was very nosey this morning, wanting to watch the men rebuilding part of Brown Bank barn, and Jen reported that he was fascinated by the idea of the traffic disappearing under his feet on the motorway bridge, and had to stop and watch it reappear – "ooh LOOK" – on the other side. He thought it was the strangest thing he'd seen in ages. Passing the young horses he just quivered, and didn't do anything silly, as the newest of them, a bay filly, trotted alongside Ruby in the carriage.

We trotted a little distance of the homeward journey and Sonny behaved well. He even stood to watch a big heavy goods train chugging up the railway line, and one of the aforementioned wagons creeping past us at Bridge End with its air brakes hissing. He was more bothered by the fact that Ruby was keen to go and was doing some backing, hence squeezing the amount of space poor Sonny had behind us. He led happily as we trotted up the brow to home and Mum hammered after him in racing mode.

As the field is getting a bit wet after all this rain, both ponies are back indoors. It will be interesting to see how they behave tomorrow with no fresh grass inside them.

PS Ruby trod on the back heel of my OTHER Ariat boot with her damn great steel clog, so now I have a slightly ruined PAIR. Do you suppose – like live items – Ariat boots have a Time To Die?

In the late afternoon the weather changed from blustery and wet to blustery and sunny, so I put the two beasties out in the little paddock while I mucked out and did-up for the night. I tied Sammy up short so he couldn't nip any heels as we passed by.

When I came back for them Sonny had a dicky fit because he didn't hear me coming for the wind and I "just appeared" round the end of the field shelter. However, he didn't go anywhere, just leapt a foot in the air. I caught Ruby and Graham looked after the gate while I walked her in, not realising I'd closed the yard gate onto the road so it didn't really matter if Sonny went walkabout. Sonny came out and went back in through the gate, so I walked in and called him and turned sideways so I wasn't threatening him, and he came up to be caught quietly.

Ruby is looking like a racing snake in her summer coat, and Sonny is beginning to shine too, and continuing to lose fat off his neck and belly, so he is starting to look like the pony he ought to be.

Sonny's visit to Greenholme (10), Saturday, June 20, 2009

Jen was here and grooming Sonny before I rolled out of bed this morning, so the poor fellow had to go to work without any breakfast – like he's getting anything other than a tablespoonful of mix on his windowsill. He hadn't polished off all his hay (Ruby leaves NOTHING) so he probably wasn't empty, but he did look a lot more trim than when he arrived a week ago. He needed the lung space however as Jen, having thoroughly brushed out his mane and tail as well as his body, rode him over Pikestoll to Roundthwaite. The idea was to see if the watersplash there was easier to use than the river in Greenholme. It turned out the bank was a bit steep there too (I haven't used it for a month or two) so Jen just walked him around some big puddles until he had to get his feet wet. Then walked him on the other rein, ditto. On the way back they met a sweeper wagon preparing the road for resurfacing, and Sonny stood quietly while it whisked and whined past. They walked back over Pikey and met me and Ruby as we trotted up to Dyke farm. He was more bothered by Felicity's dog Molly, who was running about in the field, than any of the things he had met. He walked quietly on down to Greenholme while I turned Ruby and followed him back. I saw them trotting nicely up the brow to home.

Jen reported he was "running on empty" as far as energy went, which is probably true, but it did wonders for his figure. We brushed both ponies off and turned them out in the paddock, which has a good deal of grass on it, as Graham shut it up for a week to let the docks die back after spraying. They had a couple of hours on there and came in thirsty; when I checked the water tank I found a dead bird in there, so no wonder they didn't drink. I must go and bucket out the decaying remains. Yuck.

Tomorrow's North West Driving Club drive is on, as we all seem to have asked every roadman we met whether they're resurfacing round the village tomorrow – they are not :)

I suggested Jen check Sonny's feet. If he is being a bit reluctant now on account of them getting short, we might need to Easy-boot him tomorrow over these fresh chippings. Ruby's size 2's fit his back feet, but not the front ones, even though I rasped the outer rim; he didn't bother much about Jen trying the boots on and she turned him out in them so he could accept the feel of them. She's going to ask Ali Morton if she can borrow a pair of her 3's for tomorrow and the remaining week of Sonny's stay with us.

Sonny's visit to Greenholme (11), Sunday, June 21, 2009

The ponies had breakfast and some hay today before we got them out to go down into the village and meet our Treasure Hunters. Sonny wore Ruby's size 2 Easyboots on his back feet, and was happy with them although he was puzzled by the crunching noise they made on the fresh chippings on the road!

We only had two people driving after all. Pauline's horse hadn't been shod because the blacksmith had brought shoes that were too small, and Alicia who had been going to drive just gave apologies. So we had Ann with her grandson David as groom for her black Shetland, and Ann Marie and Roger Harrison with their grey one, and Sonny and Ruby who weren't taking part because I'd set the clues. We walked the ponies to the village and gave out the clues (there were 30 questions) and let the drivers go off at their own speed and their own time, while we just nattered with Pauline, then we set off as well. Sonny was very well behaved. I had meant to take a photo, but the camera was lurking somewhere dark and I didn't have time to go hunting for it, so tough.

We walked and trotted up the hill and over the motorway, and encountered lots of Sunday traffic, some of it much less considerate than weekday traffic. Bikes and motorbikes, people walking, chuffographers sitting with their scary tripods waiting for trains on the main line, parked cars, a wagon, several big vans, impatient car-drivers, and people walking dogs. We diverted from the route to go down the Martinagap track, and Jen used the far end of the track to try walking Sonny in circles in open grassland. He did this very well, responding solely to her body and legs, without needing the rein. He didn't try to rush into trot, or to buck. She left it at that for the time being (too big a field to want to try anything argumentative, and not ours!). We went on down into Orton village, which was busy, with what looked like an entire Mazda car rally parked outside the chocolate factory. We used the Treasure Hunt route round the village, and through the narrows I occupied the middle of the road to discourage a car driver behind us who badly wanted to overtake where it was unsafe. Jen and I both indicated we were turning right, and got out of the way ASAP – Sonny showing good acceleration when asked. Then we took some detours through the far side of the village, and Jen asked Sonny to walk down the beck side, which he did, but he wouldn't put his feet in the water even though it was clear and with a sound bottom. She didn't make a big issue of it as it would have made a mess of somebody's nicely mown grass.

We trotted out of the T junction by the school, out onto the main road again, and walked back through the village, turning towards home. After trotting up Stephenson's Brow we caught up the two Shetlands whose drivers were picking up clues at Mazon Gill Cottage. Ann suggested we overtake her, but I said we'd wait until we got out of the dip, so oncoming traffic could see us; in any case, we were going to trot home by the wider route and let the two Shets go on collecting clues. This worked well, and Ruby and Sonny went on "leap-frogging", overtaking each other at walk or trot, all the way home. Jen trotted Sonny home up Daw Bank (and had a few strides of canter) while I checked the date on Yew Tree farm which I had used as a clue but kept forgetting to write down (1675).

Back home, I unharnessed Ruby and brushed her off; she was hardly sweaty at all, but Sonny was – we had, after all, done a good six miles.

Ruby the Racing Snake

Slimline Sonny

Jen got a bucket of water and a dandy brush and gave him a wash. He was very good about this and didn't make any fuss. Then we smothered both ponies in fly spray and put them in the little paddock while we buzzed back to the village green with the answer sheet and the rosettes. Lots of chatting and "what a pity there weren't more people to enjoy that lovely drive" etc.

We came away when the midgies started to bite, and we brought the ponies back indoors for the same reason and gave them a slab of hay each.

So Sonny has been to his first social drive out. He was a little star for the whole 2 and a half hours. He deserved his yellow rosette.

Two for tea...

And tea for two...

The only blot on his copybook for today was that he didn't want to go back indoors after he'd been out for these photos! But he only pulled back once and then gave in and followed me. I daresay he was thinking he only had to obey Jen. Tough luck Sonny.

Sonny's visit to Greenholme (12), Monday, June 22, 2009

Jen came while I was at work and took Sonny out. She put the Easyboots on his hind feet, and reasoning that if her bum was sore from the saddle his back would probably be a bit uncomfortable too, she decided not to ride. Instead she brought out the black harness and set him up for driving. He accepted all this until she put the crupper under his tail, which made him tuck his bottom in. Graham came and put a hand on his rein and talked to him, and he settled down again all right even with Jen clanking the chains about and fiddling with the harness. She brought out David's ex cart and put it on him – he fretted and fidgeted a bit, but when she stayed relaxed and told him not to be such a fairy, he settled down. He pretended to fuss about going down the yard, when the breeching came into play, but again soon settled into his work. He was a bit lazy going out – hardly surprising after his quite long ride yesterday – but stood well for her to pretend to adjust harness and re-fasten one of his boots at the Selsmire substation layby. Jen reported that he needed "a lot more rein" in the carriage, as he definitely missed the leg contact and "wobbled about" a lot more.

On the way home he trotted steadily past the young ponies and walked down the hill into the village despite there being a large sheep-wagon coming down the hill after him. Jen let him have 30 minutes in the paddock with lots of fly spray but put him back indoors after that because despite the spray, the flies were biting.

Sonny's visit to Greenholme (13), Tuesday, June 23, 2009

Jen's coming later today to teach a lesson so Sonny, officially, was having a day off. However, I thought that because he'd been awkward about being harnessed and yoked up yesterday, it would be good for him if I did it again today.

He stood nicely and accepted all the harness being put on. His mouth was open, splonk, for the bit well before I got it anywhere near his nose. He didn't make any fuss about the crupper, and he didn't fidget when I put the ex cart on. I untied him from the tree and he started to lean on me, so I tied him up again and got in and out of the cart, and sang, and bounced about, and rattled my feet on the boards, and he just… stood… there. I got out and in and out again, and untied him, and he just… stood… there. So I got in and asked him to come around and move on, and away we went. I drove him to Tom's "black plastic" gateway, then up to Bretherdale cattle grid and back, and up the brow towards home. Sonny trotted nicely each time I asked him, and although he wasn't very enthusiastic at starting, each time he got better.

I drove him past our gateway and he planted his feet and effectively said, "BUT you've passed it! Are you stupid? We go IN here, not PAST."

"Tough luck, Sonny, we are going to Greenholme whether you want to or not."

But he just… stood… there. He was willing to stand forever despite being smacked, but by turning him one way and then the other I got his planted feet to pick up and move. Quite suddenly he gave in and started walking again. Of course I relaxed the rein, stopped tapping him and gave him lots of praise the moment he shifted his weight forward. We walked down to Greenholme and walked a right-handed circle on the green, but he began to resist again when I suggested a left handed one, because it TURNED AWAY FROM HOME. Little banana-brain stood there planted once more. So I turned him right, until a left turn would be "homeward", and we did a left handed circle that way, and trotted home. I took him round the yard and up among the trees, and turned left, and behold, he could do it. He made no fuss about standing at the tree to be unyoked and unharnessed, so I smothered him in fly spray and turned him out with his mum in the little paddock. (She's horseing, and because there's a male pony in her company she is showing it, despite the fact that he's her son, and a gelding!)

Sonny's visit to Greenholme (14), Wednesday, June 24, 2009

Sonny and Ruby had their breakfast hay and were comfortably nattering over the intervening panel in the stable when Jen came to take Sonny out. This time, as she's finding the 17 inch saddle that came with him rather too deep for her comfort, she used my Thorowgood 17 1/2 inch synthetic, which is very nice to ride on. With its endurance pad underneath, it gives a really wide bearing surface so is likely to be comfy for Sonny too. She mounted off a tack box outside the stable, and Graham let them into the field. Jen reports that Sonny expected to go wild – after all, this is the field where we let him and Ruby go to graze and play – and he walked "with a quiver" for some time, but when she sat still and let him quiver without picking up the rein or kicking him on, he decided he would rather wait to be told what to do. She does think though, that if she had grabbed him by the bit, he'd have tried having a gallop and a buck.

After they'd been walking big circles for a while, and up and down the rocky bits of the field, I went out to take pics. That was the only time Sonny planted himself! Jen moved him from side to side with her legs, and backed him a few strides, and after that he went forward again nicely. She trotted him in big circles and figures of eight, and up and down the slopes, and he offered her a canter so she let him stride on.

They walked in after that, doing more big circles away from the gate, and Sonny behaved well in spite of the 7 or 8 clegs on his neck and flanks. Jen unsaddled him and walked him down to the hosepipe – which he thinks is a snake. He wasn't very happy about being washed, but when he realised that the water cooled him off and got rid of the flies, he tried very hard to be brave (better than Ruby who swings about when washed).

I had cleaned out the stable and given both him and Ruby fresh hay and water, so they are now indoors away from the heat and the clegs.

~~~~~~~~~~~~~~

LATER

The afternoon cooled pleasantly around 4 pm so I harnessed Ruby and set off to Greenholme. She was happy on a loose rein, walking nicely, so we just kept going, up the hill towards Orton, left at the guidepost for Scout Green, along to Sproat Ghyll farm where the cows were being turned out after milking. We walked along behind them and behind the boys on the 4 wheeler motorbike who drove them into their field and shut the gate. We passed the couple of cars that had been held up by meeting the cows, and walked steadily on. I saw clouds of pollen being blown from a field of flowering grass, and the gate of the Roman road bridleway was open so we trotted up it, just to the brow; turned there and came back. I was glad we had gone up, because the view across to the Howgill Fells was fantastic, all the way from the Lune Gorge round to Wild Boar Fell beyond Kirkby Stephen. Amazing how the view opens out with just another fifty feet of elevation. Ruby strode on happily back to the guidepost and steadily trotted home. I was very proud of my cheerful, shiny mare.

I put both ponies out for half an hour while the breeze was there to keep the clegs off, and mucked out and put hay and water in for them. They didn't really want to come back in, but they didn't object and Sonny managed to be brave about the dog, without trying to crush up to me for safety.

I took Ruby out in the afternoon – which was one of those annoying drives that start out badly, not because of anything Ruby did, but because we had only just left the yard when we encountered a large Manitou loader towing a large flat farm trailer. There was really nowhere to go but home, and although our road is very narrow, poor Ruby did her best to screw the carriage round in its own length, and very ugly it all was too, with the wheels scraping the wall behind me and Ruby trying not to get the shafts hooked up in the sheep netting on the wall in front of her. We got turned round and went back into the yard to let the loader go by, and then I had to take Ruby out of the carriage and spend the next fifteen minutes with a mallet and cold chisel whacking twelve inches of solid rubber tyre back into its channel on the inside wheel. *F***ing road chippings, f***ing farm equipment, grrr grrr grrr.*

I finally got the carriage hooked up again and took Ruby along the road for a couple of miles, hoping the tyre would continue to settle into the channel as we went. Eventually I found a nice, shady, grassy roadside with no biting flies, where she could graze for ten minutes and I could recover my lost temper. She trotted home from there in good style, and I was pleased that when we met the Manitou loader again the young driver pulled in where there was plenty of room, and let US go by in return for our gesture an hour earlier.

Ruby didn't appreciate me giving her a wash when we got home, but a scoop of mix, a clean shavings bed (thanks to Jen in the morning who had tidied up my hasty picking-over) and a slab of soaked hay, soon made her forget her grumpiness. Sonny said he'd rather like some of Ruby's mix, too, but as he still had half a haynet left, I told him he'd have to make do with a clean bed. And so did Ruby.

The tyre isn't right but I think it will hold okay.

Sonny's visit to Greenholme (15), Thursday, June 25, 2009

The ponies had their usual breakfast, some mix (half a scoop for Ruby and a handful for Sonny), a bucket of fresh water and some hay, while I tidied the stables. I was puzzled by a sploshy-sploshy noise coming from Sonny's side of the partition so I looked over to see what he was doing. He was picking up a mouthful of hay then shaking his nose in the water bucket, dabble-dabble, to wet the hay before he ate it. Obviously the idea of Mother's soaked hay appeals to him.

This morning was cooler with a fresh breeze and the ponies were much more comfortable than they were yesterday in the heat with the flies bothering them. We worked in the hayfield (though it's just being grazed by sheep, that's still what we call it), with both Ruby and Sonny. Jen said Sonny was very ready to go, but she just sat him quietly, with a very light contact on the reins, and walked him round the perimeter of the new territory for a good twenty minutes to let him calm down. Ruby, in the carriage, also walked quietly. Eventually we were walking round each other, passing and repassing, closing in and moving away, standing and moving off again quietly. Jen got on and off a couple of times. Sonny was very well behaved.

We moved into trot work on big circles after half an hour or so and both ponies were obedient and sensible. The only time there was any argument from Sonny was when Jen took him back into the other field and worked him up and down the banks, cantering him up towards the paddock and turning away in trot. Ruby and I were just coming up through the gateway and couldn't see Sonny for the hedge, when there was a loud CRACK! and Ruby shot through the gateway in three strides of a gallop. I picked up the rein and asked her what was the matter, and she calmed down again, "Oh, wasn't that for me?" Jen said Sonny had planted himself once again, so she gave him a proper smack on the bottom with her long whip to convince him she meant it when she said, "Walk on." The crack had echoed all the way down the field! After that she cantered him in a circle, and he was obedient, so then we all walked quietly back to the yard to take some photos. Jen uses a handy technique for remounting, eg after opening a difficult gate – which would be useful for his owner, in case Sonny takes it into his head to be silly about being mounted in a different situation from our yard.

Sonny's visit to Greenholme (16), Friday, June 26, 2009

I woke very early and was up and about by 6.30 so the ponies had not only had breakfast but digested their hay too when we got them out at 9.30 and brushed off.

Jen took Sonny into the field and mounted him by the gatepost there, just to let him be mounted in a different place. I followed when I'd harnessed and yoked Ruby. Jen and Sonny were already walking the sheep off the hayfield so we joined her.

A stag and two hinds cantered out of the Nursery wood and across the river, over Tom's fences, across the road, and away over two walls, running from Mr Allen's motorbike as he "looked" the sheep. Jen was astonished at how large red deer are – she was only a child when she met any close up, at Lowther Wildlife Park. The horses didn't bother, for once; Ruby has got quite sparked up at times when we've put-up roe deer close at hand.

It was all very laid-back today; the weather was fresh and cool, Ruby was chilled and Sonny relaxed, despite several hours of grazing in the paddock yesterday afternoon and despite the clegs fastening on blood at every opportunity. I didn't get bitten – I must be doing something right! Jen rode Sonny up and down the slopes, circled at trot, and cantered him frequently, which he evidently enjoyed. She also went on working on ground tying – throw down the lead rope and he will halt. He was confused though when I asked if he was reacting to the throw or the rope ... she moved her arm without the rope and he thought about stopping, then didn't. Bright boy! The memory of his crack over the backside evidently held good; he didn't "plant" himself at all today.

Keep the lead rope attached to his headcollar – it's easy to carry the rope. Loop it round something (like the gatepost) while you get up. Hold the rope, not the reins.

Throw the rope loose (Sonny by now allows you to flip it round his head like a skipping rope and doesn't worry).

Lean forward and catch the rope ready to carry it again. Sonny often lifts his head to make it easier for you.

Jen's working on ground tying, but although he is very good about it, he is still likely to wander, so he hasn't got the rules perfectly right yet :)

I moved the sheep away from the yard gate a couple of times with Ruby, who quite enjoyed being a sheep-herd. Sonny saw Jackie Taylor and her son James walking up the road, and pricked his little ears and asked to investigate, so Jen told him to canter after them, which he was delighted to do. He saw that they had a dog, and was curious but not too bothered. I took Ruby for a nice trot along the wood side and back, and we both really enjoyed that. She wanted to tank through the gateway (also remembering Sonny's crack over the backside yesterday!) but I made her walk back in quietly.

It all made a nice change from sorting out web forums and damn-awkward trolls :)

Photos of tomorrow's schooling session, I hope. Today was too laid back to bother :)

Sonny's visit to Greenholme (17), Saturday, June 27, 2009

Yawn. A slow start this morning! I fed the two nags but didn't tidy the stable (BAAAD mother!) Jen, Rob and Naomi came today, Naomi having determined that she, too, had to "Boss Sonny!"

We were going to work in the fields again, so Jen opened the field gate and shut the front gate – our cottage visitors having gone out for the day – which meant the "Caution – Lesson in progress" sign was visible to the roadside. Of course, then James Beevor, Big Time Boy himself, ignored the sign and came bowling in, leaving his bike at the gate thank God, but getting thoroughly in the way. That meant there was me, Ruby and Naomi, Jen, Sonny, Graham talking to Big Time Boy, Rob taking photos, the Allen family and their farm bike driving a flock of sheep down the road and back to their field after clipping, and Sammy lurking behind my car ready to tell Sonny off if he put a foot out of line.

Poor Sonny, he just couldn't handle all that information at one time. He managed to behave until Jen wanted to mount, then had a small "backing" explosion. Jen got up, and made him settle, then got off and went through it all again. Ruby, Naomi and I didn't see all this, but I heard Graham offering advice so I poked my head round the corner to see if it was OK to set off with Ruby; got the nod and went quietly away down into the field.

Sonny was gobsmacked that Mother had gone without him! Usually because we've had more stuff to attach (like harness and carriage) we've followed him, and not the other way around. Ruby was pretty chilled. Naomi was asking questions of me about "why did the sheep need to have their fur taken off," so I didn't watch Sonny working in, but Jen says he was pretty keen and for the first time she needed to have a contact on the bit as she circled him at walk around various of the smaller fields, before she joined us in the hayfield. Once she'd brought him along he was sensible and walked, trotted and cantered on either rein without being naughty despite all the clegs that were about. I did wipe a few off Ruby with the tip of the whip, but she wasn't as covered in them as Sonny was, poor lad!

When we got back to the yard Naomi wanted to sit on Sonny, so Rob popped her onto the saddle in front of Jen and Jen walked him around the yard. They took some pics of Naomi sitting on him at the tying tree, and as by this time he'd decided perhaps small children were not actually Martians, he was very calm about it all. It helped that Beevor had gone, too!

Sonny had another hosepipe wash – having got quite sweaty in his tizzing and his workout in the field – and Naomi helped me to take Ruby's harness off (Oooh, Grannie just couldn't manage all those big buckles on her own). We turned the two ponies out in the paddock and mucked out (Naomi, Rob and Graham sitting on the field wall like the three wise monkeys) and went off to the pub in Tebay for lunch. We brought them back into the stable after that, as Jen said, "I think four hours grazing yesterday must have been too much for Sonny!"

Sonny's visit to Greenholme (18), Sunday, June 28, 2009

Sonny spent breakfast time at the tying tree, with his tiny mouthful of hard feed and a small haynet. It's so sweet how he lovingly licks the bowl, over and over, to get the last trace of flavour. Jen and I shut the roadside gates, and mucked out the stables. Ruby makes an awful mess now Sonny's here, because her soaked hay is at one side (she pushes the half-barrel to where she wants it) and Sonny is then behind her, so she tramples the muck and wet shavings into a right old soup as she turns from food to grooming and bossing, and back again. On her own, she is fantastically tidy. She wandered between stables while we brushed and shovelled, pushing the door to and fro with her nose as required.

Jen found Sonny was fine today – a touch wary of the watching visitors' children, but she took him round the corner to the field gate to mount, and he settled. They went up Bretherdale in order to do "getting on and off and opening and shutting gates". All well. He wants to be off as soon as remounted, but this should improve with practice, and the "rope round the gate stoop" method (see earlier blog entries) works to prevent difficulties. The ground tying is working well – Jen dropped the lead rope yesterday by accident while crossing the yard, and he stopped at once!

Today Jen put him across the fellside grass on Nichol Hill, and he listened and didn't pull or buck. Asking for changes of pace mainly on the voice and not the rein, "up, up up" will lengthen his trot or get him into canter, while "steady" will bring him down. She worked him up and down hill, in circles, rounded up a few sheep, jumped him up a bank onto the road, paddled through the beck, and had a thoroughly good time. Limited grazing time has clearly helped once again – that and a calm yard, of course.

He had another bath when he came back and now we've swapped stables – Ruby is in "Sonny's side" and vice versa – to see if it helps with the Feng Shui…

I took Ruby for a drive over Pikey just after lunch, to check how far the road resurfacing extends, since Sonny will have to go that way to return home. Luckily the chippings end just after Dyke Farm's gateway so he won't have them tearing up his feet after that. Ruby didn't attract too many clegs on our journey, and didn't sweat too badly either, but still quite appreciated a wash off when we got home, which makes a change as she usually fusses a bit. The clegs were bad, so I left both ponies indoors with haynets.

I had to beat part of the tyre back into place on the carriage wheel again though, as we'd needed to turn in a narrow lane at Roundthwaite on account of Jackie Parsley's tractor and hay trailer.

Ruby's side of the stable is blissfully tidy once again. Sonny's is a bit messy. The odd thing is that he's almost permanently in the dark as he WILL keep shutting the top stable door. Ruby doesn't bother with it but he does.

Sonny's visit to Greenholme (19 and 20), 19th and 20th June 2009

Jen and I took both ponies for a quiet ride out to Scout Green, with Naomi as my passenger on the carriage. The weather was heavy and the clegs were biting, so we just wandered peacefully up to the top of Whiteham and across the bit of open fell onto the Scout Green road, and back. Sonny was quiet and steady apart from a startle when he brushed Jen's leg against one of the flimsy "loose chippings – max 20mph" signs on the roadside, so she spent a few minutes walking him up to other signs and kicking them with her boot! Of course he just stood there and said, "whatever …" We also practised leapfrogging each other along the road; Jen would walk or trot Sonny past Ruby, then I'd do the same with Ruby passing Sonny. Both ponies were calm, to the extent that I could brush clegs off Ruby from all sorts of places with the tip of the driving whip. The only time she startled was when Jen clapped her hand over a cleg on Sonny's neck with a tremendous crack! like that of the whip a few days ago. Other than that, it was all quiet.

We washed off the ponies and then put fly rugs on them. I didn't have my camera out but the picture they both made was hysterical – Ruby in white mesh with ear caps and navy edges, Sonny all in lilac with red leg straps. They didn't fuss about their strange attire until they were loose in the paddock, when Sonny took one look at Ruby and exclaimed, "Oh my God it's a ghost!" and Ruby dashed off saying, "Where, where!" The two of them then high-tailed it round the paddock, stepping and snorting at each other and generally being silly for a good five minutes before the lure of the grass settled them down. We gave them an hour and then put them back indoors with their haynets.

My bedtime "haynet check" revealed another side of Sonny – when I hung the haynet for him, Ruby came to help him taste it over the partition, and he snapped first at her and then at me. Unfortunately for him, I'd seen him coming so I put up a fist as he swung his head, and he smacked his cheek teeth on it and rebounded with a "What the hell was that for" expression. Unlike the brightest horse we've had he didn't then repeat the misdemeanour to see if he'd connected his action with the self-inflicted punishment.

Bye-Bye Sonny, Tuesday 30th June

Alison arrived prompt at 9.30 and we tacked-up Sonny with his nice clean saddle and bridle.

Naomi helped by kissing him on the nose at every opportunity.

Alison mounted to practise handling the lead rope as well as the reins, and ground tying. We let her take a stick with her, one that some boy visitors had collected a few weeks ago – on the principle that if she carried a stick she wouldn't need it and if she didn't – she would!

She walked him up and down the yard, and then set off for home, with her husband John following in the car.

Bye-bye, Sonny, be good!

RUBY (2)

Ruby, Solo once more, Wednesday, July 1, 2009

Sonny has now gone back to his owner. Just heard from Alison that she and Sonny had a good time on their ~10 mile ride home; both getting very wet in the heavy showers, but it was nice warm rain! and he's going to get daily rides out from now on. Great. Hope he will continue to be a reformed character.

I have been vastly amused by Ruby's reaction to Sonny going home. I kept her indoors all day (mainly to save her from the heat and humidity and flies, in the nice cool stone stable) and her response to the empty box next door is to USE IT AS HER LOO – she has left a huge pile of muck in the middle of the swept floor. Her "own" box is clean. So much for missing her darling offspring!!

This morning I was waiting for the post lady to come, as I had three letters to go, but by 12 noon I thought she'd probably not got anything to deliver to us and would not turn up, so I went out to muck out the stable and of course, while I was shovelling, she arrived and left without my letters.

So I harnessed Ruby and trotted down to Orton Post Office (a little over two and a half miles away), which is also a very nice local shop and usually blocked up with parked cars, but I've found if I time my visits for lunch hour, I can park right outside. Then I can get off the carriage, not let go of the reins, and post my letters in the wall box safely.

Ruby was very sober as she trotted in the midday heat. I let her walk through some of the shadier patches along the road to cool off – luckily there were few flies or clegs about.

At Mazon Gill where last week the road had begun to collapse into the culvert over the gill, there were temporary traffic lights to control the traffic passing the large JCB digger and the road-mending wagon and the big hole with men shoulder-deep in the culvert. Ruby stood like a champ while one of the workmen jumped up and down in front of the sensor to try to get it to change the lights for us! She trotted by the wagon and digger, glanced briefly at the submerged men, and went on down to the village cool as you please. On the return journey the digger was working and when he saw us waiting again at the lights, the supervisor of the gang made throat-cutting TURNITOFF gestures to the driver. He kindly stopped the engine and we went by peacefully – however, as I thanked the supervisor I did tell him that really, Ruby has an ambition to drive a JCB. She has an engineering turn of mind and if allowed, she would probably try all the levers with her nose.

She's now out in the field in her "ghost suit" and I've spent ten minutes refilling all the spray bottles with my home-made fly repellent after I realised that during Sonny's visit we used up most of the last batch.

Round trip, Pikey, Tebay, Orton, 6 July 2009

The hot weather has cooled a little here in Northern England. My honeysuckle hedge has nearly gone over, and the midges which lurk in its trumpet shaped blossoms are also fewer, so Ruby is happier, although still going out to graze wearing her "fly-armour" – and still scratching a bit overnight in the stable.

David "I just enjoy the challenge" Trotter, who introduces horses to harness at Tebay, came over yesterday morning with a driving pad, an old Cottage Craft type made of webbing with a steel tree. He'd been long reining a mare and she'd spun round on him and snapped off one terret. Could Graham and I replace the terret? We said yes, as although I don't do harness repairs commercially any more (are you listening Mr Tax Man?) David still asks me to keep his gear usable.

So off he went homeward, and Graham took the pad out the workshop. When he began to drill the brass foot out of the socket it threaded itself right through into the padding, so I ended up fishing with long nosed pliers for this loose lump of brass. Luckily the pair of terrets I still had in the leftover stock had the same thread, and I asked Graham to cut the screw-feet short so they wouldn't make pressure points under the pad. (I'd noticed a few months ago that when David put the pad onto one of his visiting horses, it had flinched a little and resisted in its neck when he girthed up. Those terret points were the reason.)

It was by then early afternoon and Ruby was still in the stables, having eaten up her soaked hay and begun to get bored with swinging the connecting door to and fro. The return of the pad would be a good excuse for a decent drive out.

On Saturday she had been lively, not really naughty but keen and inclined to express her *joie de vivre* by bursting into canter. I thought, a trip over the 4 miles of hill to David's would be ideal for sobering her up a little. So I fastened the mended pad up tightly with its own straps, tied it to the carriage seat, and with

Ruby in a surprisingly calm frame of mind we set off over Pikestoll, the big hill to the south, en route to Tebay.

Did I say the weather had cooled? It rained and we got pretty wet going over the top! I decided that if the sun came out by the time we got to Tebay, we'd do the "round trip" and come home via Orton, reasoning that the Sunday car drivers would have no excuse for not seeing us in our fluorescent gear and with our twinkling bike lights. If the rain carried on, I'd turn round and come home over Pikey because it has far less traffic (little to none).

Ruby was interested in the pony mares and foals in fields along the way but the gradients soon made her concentrate. She's got her "haytime runny nose" right now despite being dosed with Piriton and despite her own hay being soaked. Having seen the clouds of grass-pollen blowing off a neighbour's field last week I couldn't really blame her for doing a bit of nose blowing as we climbed.

We've been doing a lot more work this year since I ended full time employment, so as soon as I saw that the road markings had been ground off ready for a resurfacing I got Danny to come and shoe Ruby – there's a limit to the number of times I can wrestle with Easyboots in a week. And it did free up the boots to use on Sonny while he was here. Her shoes were gripping well. Down the tree-lined hedgerows on the far side she was happy to trot, although I walked her on the steepest bits because the fresh chippings of the surface would be vicious to stumble onto. By the time we got to Roundthwaite the rain had stopped and all the wet leaves were twinkling in sunshine.

I posted a couple of letters in the box at Roundthwaite; we do this on occasion, so Ruby is used to standing close to the wall while I push the letters through the slot. Then we went on towards the A685, the Appleby to Kendal road. Traffic here is less forgiving than on the back roads; the A685 is wider and has sweeping curves that invite fast driving. Ruby trotted over the motorway bridge and the railway bridge, and faced oncoming motorbikes, and put up with swishing tyres passing her, and I just let her swing along and talked to her, and she didn't flinch an inch. Here and there through narrower stretches we had cars queueing behind us, but then I held the middle of my carriageway and didn't give anyone chance to risk overtaking us on blind summits. And, I have to say, most drivers know when they should be patient – after all it WAS Sunday!

We arrived safely in Tebay and delivered the mended pad to David, chatting while Ruby stood on the pavement and got her breath back from the long trot on the main road.

"Which way are you going back?"

"Well, the sun's coming out again, so I think I'll go through Orton."

So that's what we did. Five easy miles, compared to four of hard work over Pikey. I walked Ruby on the quiet and wide stretches through Tebay, where cars could easily overtake, trotted her where the road was narrow, and round the motorway roundabout, and past the old fish farm and the grazing Shetland ponies, the bridge at Bybeck with the young Fell ponies who whinnied and trotted uncertainly towards us, the rushy field where I bought my Fell x Arab Kestrel as a foal. Here the road becomes a series of switchbacks, and it's a game of cat and mouse to make sure you aren't in a blind dip when traffic comes over the brow behind you. Ruby handled all this well. I pulled in on one of the lay-bys to give her another breather.

Through Orton the traffic was peaceful but large – many of our neighbours are completing their first cut of silage, and the roads are full of tractors with booming silage trailers going out empty to the fields, returning groaning and fully laden. Ruby merely tilted her head to look up at the height of them, and kept trotting. If there was room to pull into a gateway and let traffic by, she responded instantly to the lightest rein, and stood (eating the chest-high grass of course! could I begrudge it to her?) until I asked her move on again. By then we were getting back into our usual territory and her interest in the scenery was starting to fade; but the views back to the Howgills were sharp and clear against the stormy sky, and I was happy just rolling along at a good trot with the carriage balanced and barely swinging.

Down the hill into Greenholme, where we met a car and another tractor and trailer who waited for us to clear the hump-backed bridge over Birk Beck. I turned Ruby up the hill for home and she sprang it – and I burst out laughing and let her bowl on.

I think our nine mile drive probably scored at Sue 9, Ruby 1.

"Bucking strap" vs "Kicking strap", 12 August 2009

A friend of mine currently has her (British standard) Shetland mare in our stables while she works through a buck-and-kick issue in our quiet location. The kicking-strap is mandatory for her. However, despite the strap being tight when standing, Shets being Shets, and little, there was an occasion when the mare kicked and got a leg over the trace. Driving her for half a mile like that, uncomfortably, till there was a safe place to stop seems to have been more of a deterrent than the kicking-strap itself, as she hasn't done it again – so far. The strap stopped her getting that leg over the shaft though, or launching her heels over/through the dashboard.

The old friend is the most determined and bloodyminded woman I know: she's a retired doctor and a carriage driver since she was knee-high to a grasshopper. Equine dentist and vet will be called when needed even if she can't afford food for herself. So if there IS anything physically wrong with a pony it will get put right.

We haven't had a kick from the Shetland in over a week; not since the pony realised that kicking hurt her. She's an alpha mare, that's her main problem. If you're not a convincing leader, she won't trust you, she will take over. My friend has only had geldings before, despite her long experience.

You bet I am being careful – many thanks for your thoughtful remarks. I have had, and got rid of, kickers and rearers, on my own account. I haven't persuaded this owner to give up on the pony (who has actually been reasonably good this week and only misbehaved a little – backing – through fright at a very close and large truck on a narrow road.) I have however talked the owner into buying and wearing a helmet, though she said at first that she didn't care if she got killed, until I pointed out that it was me who'd have to drag her home and bury her!

The runaway Shetland, 16 August 2009

Looks like my friend has finally made up her mind that this pony doesn't respect her. Though the pony has behaved itself for the last 2 weeks, she doesn't feel she is sufficiently in command to take it home and drive without my support, and she's finally admitted the mental strain is more than she can take.

I have sent her on to a neighbour who has a nice little 5 year old pony for sale, unbroken but firmly and kindly handled, just ready to go into work. A clean slate. I've told her to forget about doing the groundwork herself and get one of our friends, who trains ponies on a regular basis, to do it for her. At pushing 80 years old, walking her dogs is enough of an effort, let alone long reining a pony to traffic proof it.

16 August 2009

>*What will happen to the Shetland?*

Well, there are a few options. She's a pedigreed mare with show ring successes so she could go back into being shown in-hand, or for breeding – she is a proven brood mare. She could go back to her original owner for those purposes.

I could not recommend her as a driving pony for a novice, nor as a child's pony because she is clever and pushy and can nip if she thinks you've got food.

Once you've got her respect she has a terrific work ethic so if someone came along who was capable of getting that respect AND had enough driving skill to take her down the road and use her kindly but firmly every day, she'd be a really useful, smart, tough little work horse. But people like that don't come over the horizon too often and if they do, they probably aren't in the market for a spoiled pony.

Trying out a new horse?

I'd be looking for safety first. You'll see at once whether the horse is the size (and possibly colour) and type you have in mind. This is what I personally would do:

* Ask about the horse's age (you can check teeth to verify this) and supposed previous driving experience.

* Ask the horse's name (everyday stable name) before approaching to introduce yourself to him.

* Handle the horse all over – head, shoulders, body, quarters, tail, feet. Both sides. Be wary of any areas of reluctance to accept you; odd shaped feet, lameness, unusual lumps, bumps, scars, or white patches from saddlery or harness – how were they acquired and do they have any impact on behaviour?

* If you're comfortable with the reactions, ask if you can harness the horse yourself while someone assists you by heading the horse. Is there any resistance to the collar being put on, crupper, breeching, saddle being girthed, bridle/bit? Note any oddities in the bit or the harness – why are they there?

* If you're comfortable with the reactions, ask to long-rein (ground drive) the horse rather than immediately putting to. Check what commands the horse should know and whether he responds as you expect when you use them.

* If you're comfortable with the reactions, ask to be allowed to put him to the carriage or cart, yourself, again while someone assists you by heading the horse. Be wary if there is any reluctance to stand still, or nervousness. The handler's reactions might also tell you quite a lot, body language rather than verbal is hard to fake!

* If you're comfortable with the reactions, go for a quiet drive – arena or trail will depend on your location but if you can do arena first then trail that would be ideal – with the handler/seller

as your helper. Does the horse stand quietly while you mount the cart, wait till told to move off, and does he move off willingly when you give the command? Does he walk actively and cheerfully, without wanting to rush into trot? Does he steer sensitively at a walk? Does he trot straight, without grabbing the bit or having to be pushed into trot? Does he go by traffic and scary objects without fussing? When you turn for home does he stay light in your hands, and not want to tear back to his stable? When you get back is he OK to pass the gate into the yard and obedient until you tell him he can go in?

Basically you're looking to go through a mini version of the steps you'd take to train to harness. A genuine seller should let you take as long as you want – you need to be happy with your potential purchase.

If you like what you've experienced so far, then it's down to whether you like the style of the horse and you "click" with each other. Some of that is gut feeling. You'll put up with odd quirks if you like the horse, and be endlessly irritated if you don't. A bit like partners really :) except partners can be expected to earn their keep whereas a horse just goes on eating!!

Mr T comes home, 21 October 2009

It's a day pinched from nowhere, today! My Wednesday web client doesn't need me till Friday, and the severe weather warning of heavy rain and high winds has just not happened – it's grey but calm and moderately warm. So I went driving.

I may have mentioned that my old driving pony – Mr T – has been away on loan for 3 years with a friend, whose husband, despite borrowing him to drive, never actually did so. Husband is now too unwell to drive, so Mr T has come home again. Now aged 22 years, he is very fit and well, very kind and willing, but still an utter wuss about things he perceives as dangerous.

He lived at our place for 13 years from 1993 to 2006 but of course in the last 3 years there have been changes around the area, like pony-eating black and yellow striped "visibility" ends added to roadside crash barriers, and heaps of an unusual grit mixture, black with white flecks, that the Council have provided this year for use on icy roads in winter. It doesn't heap at the shallow angle of sand, but much more steeply, and god only knows what T thought the heap was beside the railway bridge; judging by his horrified immobility, he must have thought Hallowe-en had come early. But the express train … thundering underneath the bridge while he evaluated the horrible Heap Monster … he was totally okay with. He went over both motorway bridges okay, or he would have done if the speed-camera van hadn't shut one of its doors as he approached, and while he was worrying about that, he didn't hear a car quietly overtaking him, so when it appeared in his field of vision he turned himself inside out.

As for the rebuilding work going on at a recently unsold farmhouse – well you know how ferocious a one-man concrete mixer can be. Mr T shrank from 13.1 to about 12 hands. The builder turned the motor off, and T went by on pins. I think he'd have passed it OK anyway, but the kindly action certainly did help. I just sat and talked him through it, and laughed inside.

Yes, "that's not stupid, that's smart and alert". Poor old T had forgotten that his cruel "real mother" makes him go out solo instead of with my friend's big brown mare who protected him and gave him courage. I'm afraid he'll just have to learn to be brave by himself again. If he does his "shrinking violet" act when he's in the lead of the tandem, Ruby (who gets BIGGER when she thinks there is a hazard) will prance right over the top of him!

I wish Ruby would walk the way T does, though – as though he's a Man on a Mission. He really is a terrific walker.

Now we're home, I've just been widening the steel arch inside the driving saddle I'm using for him. (Don't try this at home – I know what is inside *my* saddles because I built them, and I know how much pressure I can put on them and where. You can't do it with a traditional tree made of wood because it would break.)

I can't remember which pony I built it for, probably Fred the Welsh Section C, but it is tending to slide sideways on T because it's a touch too narrow and isn't sitting correctly. Having added a good 15 degrees of width to it I expect it to sit much closer now and have a better, broader, contact on his back, so I can girth it a bit tighter without causing pressure points. The sliding backband still moves freely. It'll be something fresh to watch for on tomorrow's drive.

Mr T and Ruby are out in the paddock, he's had a two seriously good rolls and she's demonstrated she's still in season (she came in the moment T arrived), and now they're both grazing happily.

Tonight I'm going to a horsey quiz where a friend of mine is getting an award for horsemanship – this year she has won the British National Pony Pairs driving championship. Life is good.

Flooding in Cockermouth, 21 November 2009

Rob and Jen have been flooded out. Their house is at the junction of the rivers Derwent and Cocker (hence Cockermouth). Where we live at Greenholme, some 50 miles from Cockermouth, we are on a nice little hill above the Birk Beck which meets the Lune about a mile downstream. Graham and I are OK. We get lots of wind and rain, hence very soggy land, but are very unlikely to be flooded out of the house like they've been. At 600 ft above sea level it would need quite a flood to cause us to take to the boats.

Mr T decided that being stabled was not fun this morning and when I was mucking out he made a run for it (well, a steady amble). It has not been a bad day here – very mild and with some sunshine! – so I shut him and Ruby out of the stables and the hay, and let them wander round the tarmac yard; and by afternoon they were hungry and very happy to go back in.

Rob and Jen, Naomi and the cat are all moving into the holiday cottage.

Blinders / Blinkers, 2009

Lots of reasons for – and some against. Someone must have thought they were necessary – after all, it's extra work for the harness maker and extra $$ for the buyer, right?

Many horses driven single can cope with seeing "everything" and some are calmer if they can do so. I've had several Fell ponies who were trained in open bridles and are equally happy with or without blinkers (winkers / blinders). I had one mare who was trained open, and got jittery if she was harnessed with blinkers; though after 5 years of steady work she didn't mind them if we were showing or doing a wedding with a smart harness that had blinkers.

Some military teams (4 or 6 up) drive without blinkers, such as the Royal Horse Artillery in Britain. But these use postillion riders and are not driven from a box on the carriage with long reins or with a long driving whip – both of which demand eye protection for the wheelers where the leader reins pass the head.

Then there are animals who get distracted or worried, and for them a half cup or full cup blinker is helpful. You can turn their heads away from scary objects and the object effectively "is not there" because it is hidden by the blinker. I've had a couple (one hot, one not) who were much more relaxed when wearing blinkers. Sounds stupid but it's true.

So – it's partly local fashion or tradition, and partly to do with the temperament of individual horses, and partly the nature of the job they are doing, that dictates whether a horse goes in blinkers or an open bridle. If you are not showing or going to any fashionable meets, it may not matter which you choose, except to you and your horse. But exercise caution...

The safest way is to have your animal trained without blinkers first, then repeat the training with blinkers if necessary. The frequent remark that blinkers "hide the wheels" from a horse is a bit of a red herring IMO – any horse in harness who doesn't know he is pulling a carriage/cart is either really stupid, or has been constantly tied up in side checks – because in normal harness he only has to turn his head round to see the object. And I'd rather not drive a horse who would be frightened of seeing the carriage, but that may be just me.

If you think your horse sounds like a good candidate for trying without blinkers – do some work on the ground in the open bridle without the cart, and go through all the training steps again, like dragging a tyre or log, and having a friend bring the cart up behind and letting him see it follow him as he walks. NEVER just replace a blinker bridle with an open one and expect a horse to behave the same when hitched – many have not been trained without the blinkers and there's always the chance that those will run.

Keep us posted if you decide to try it!

Spring, maybe! 20 March 2010

I've stopped counting our Driving Challenge hours as with all the disruptions we've had in the last 6 months the driving has kind of taken a back seat.

We have my old Fell pony Mr T back at home after his long-loan ended, and Jen has got quite enthusiastic about driving him in the 4 wheeler carriage she got off Ebay for £300. Its body was rotten but the undercarriage was sound, so my husband has carefully rebuilt it using the rotten timber as a template, and remade the shafts to fit a 13.2 instead of the very ugly sawn-down shape that must have been fitted to a Shetland! Mr T seems happy in it, and his elderly hocks are very pleased that the brakes relieve him of the weight of the carriage downhill. The carriage has been painted bright red and is known as the Fire Engine. Since my 2 wheeler also has red wheels and shafts, we are fairly easy to spot on the road, quite apart from our bike lights and reflective/fluorescent vests/leg wraps.

Grand-daughter Naomi, aged 4, has her own seat in the back of the Fire Engine, with an extra back-rail, but usually prefers to come with me and Ruby in the 2 wheeler, which she scrambles up into like a monkey. We had a pleasant drive this afternoon despite the chilly wind. I drove Ruby, and Jen drove Mr T, who is capable of outwalking Ruby (a different story when they trot, however!)

Naomi is getting quite adept at recognising the trees along the roadside; she knows a beech from an ash by the shape and colour of the buds, and is getting excited at seeing the first flowers coming out in the gardens (snowdrops and early crocuses) and the early lambs in the fields.

When we got home she scrambled down and headed "Ruby the wild horse" while I got down, and then when Jen arrived a minute or two later Naomi did the same for Mr T. Since both ponies had done a brisk 6 miles round Orton village and back, and were very ready for their suppers, they weren't exactly going to run away from the feed-room door, but it's good to see that even a 4 year old can get the safe procedures right with practice! She helped to make up the feeds (Mr T, now 23 years young, is starting to have loose teeth and needs his fibre in the form of soaked grass nuts and fibre nuts, so Naomi loves sloshing the water into the mix). And of course she is even keener on giving the ponies the buckets of feed.

So a good day was had by all.

Both ponies preparing for Easter drive, 2 April 2010

We've been working Mr T and Ruby, our Fell ponies, towards the Easter Monday Drive. Jen has been driving Mr T in her "fire engine" 4 wheeler while I use my normal 2 wheeled marathon cart.

Recently she bought a set of webbing harness, from Slovenia (in very unsubtle hi-vis scarlet and black to go with the fire engine's red paint). I have plenty of other harness to use on T but Jen wanted her own set. She has found that he goes better in its breast collar than in my wool-faced full neck collar – the line of draft being quite high, the neck collar was tipping a bit and he wasn't really settled with it.

The other thing she found yesterday was that the webbing holding the crupper dee at the back of the pad was a bit frail – it unravelled and pulled out when Mr T sat back into into the breeching. Thank heaven he's a steady old pony who's been there, seen it, done it and got the T shirt. With a green youngster the breeching suddenly dropping round the hocks could have been disastrous. T was very patient and stood talking to Ruby while Jen hauled the breeching back into place and put the crupper backstrap around the pad. Everything went fine from then on.

Jen checked all the other loops of webbing that evening – tug loops up from breast collar and breeching were all heat-sealed and soundly stitched. We'd just assumed that the loop holding the crupper dee would have gone right round the saddle tree as I would have done with my own webbing/leather saddles. Though the reins were too short and the traces too long, with those points sorted out by the local saddlery she's happy with a cheap purchase. We'll have to watch how it stands up to regular work; the eyelets for adjustment, especially, may not be sitting in sealed holes.

Today we drove down into Orton village, a round trip of about 6 miles, with both ponies swinging along for long stretches at a good, rolling trot, that lovely rhythm that you get when they've really settled into their work and can go for mile after mile without need to be steadied or chivvied on.

We walked most of the last mile home and they came home relaxed and only slightly sweaty. The winter coats coming out in handfuls and the summer coats look really well underneath.

Have a happy Easter, everyone.

A cold Spring drive (long), Tue, April 13, 2010

We've had nice weather for the last few days and the ground is beginning to dry up, but we're still limited to driving on the road for the moment because it's lambing time and fields are full of sheep and twin lambs.

Jen, my daughter, and Naomi (aged four and a half) are driving out with us since they're living next door till their flooded house is refurbished. Jen's teaching driving, using Mr T and her four wheeler, but that's undergoing bearing renewal right now because one of the wheels started binding yesterday and my husband has stripped all four wheels out and repacked two of them – new bearings purchased for one axle and bearings on order for the other (I don't know why the two axles are different; maybe it was just a home made carriage!). So with the 4 wheeler only having 2 wheels on, today Mr T got to go out in the green gig while I drove Ruby in the cross country gig.

The wind was from the northeast and it was COLD. We bundled Naomi up in gloves, salopettes and a hooded jacket under her riding helmet. Despite the snowman outfit she managed to climb up into the gig beside me and take up her "practice reins" – which are a pair of webbing riding reins that I've taped to the rein rail so she can pretend to drive. She really wanted to use Jen's scarlet driving reins but we thought it was probably safer not to have 15 feet of webbing liable to trail overboard when she forgot about them.

Ruby likes having Naomi in the gig with us and gets very grumpy if Naomi spends any time with Mr T when she's around. She stood like a rock while Naomi scrambled into the vehicle; I didn't tell her to move off, I just tucked Naomi up inside a big rug, making Ruby practise waiting, and Ruby was calm enough to watch Mr T disappearing out of the yard without us and not shift a foot. In any case, he has a let's-get-to-market-type walk and it's often good for Ruby to have to stretch her stride to catch him.

We walked into Greenholme, and after we'd crossed the hump-backed bridge Jen set Mr T into trot to tackle the hill. It also got him past the pony-eating orange concrete mixer that lives at Bridge End Farm where the house is being renovated. Ruby sailed after him and they breasted the hill in fine style and just kept going.

The ponies have been in work now for a couple of months and they're getting quite fit enough to do the work we want so we were just looking for a leg stretch today; a long steady trot out, a breather and a long steady trot back. I didn't have the GPS with me but I could tell we were only doing about 7 mph. Once they get into their rhythm they swing along without having to be pushed. Today, they would have done the same if Mr T hadn't been completely flummoxed by the fact that the service area's road was closed for maintenance; there were cars and vans parked on the grass verge and the roadway was closed off with a strip of red and white plastic hazard tape that fluttered and rattled in the wind. From behind I saw T's head and ears start to rise, and knew the anchors were going on! *Tape is deadly you know, look at all those vans and cars it's killed!*

So I pulled Ruby out round him (to her great pleasure) and gave him a lead. She'd had a cough and a snort to clear the muck out of her nose and there was no pause in her stride as we bowled up past Selsmire farm and along under the beech trees to the guidepost for Orton and Shap. This is about 2 miles from Greenholme. It's at the bottom of a slight slope so I walked Ruby down and we parked ourselves in the angle between the Greenholme and Scout Green road ends while the ponies had a breather, and with the wind so cold and their winter coats almost stripped out they were hardly sweating. They didn't take long to stop blowing. Jen got down to lift a shaft tug one hole to improve the ride of the green gig. We watched odd bits of traffic go by and then set off for home again.

Ruby once more set a steady rolling trot, hitting the hills with determination and turning back an ear to listen to Naomi, who was making plans for how when she was bigger she would be able to ride Mr T and Ruby and give them exercise so I could stay at home and work, though she admitted she "couldn't ride them both at once." (Hmm!! Am I being organised by a 4-year-old?)

On the way back Ruby gave the road closed tape a wide berth and pricked her ears at it; Jen drove Mr T up to it and he wasn't too happy but he trusted her. We trotted all the way to the railway bridge above Greenholme, and then walked down the hill. Ruby was very pleased to be in the lead as we turned the corner up the hill to home; she gets irritated if Mr T is in front at that point, and yesterday we had quite an argument about what pace she would use. In front, she is all smiles and biddable; behind, she will put her chin on her chest and snort and pull and bounce and fall in on corners – and falling in at a fast trot when the inside is a solid stone wall is not a good idea. Luckily, she knows our track width and even when she's arguing she gives the wall good clearance. Today, it was Jen's turn to hold Mr T back, and both ponies trotted up the sharp bank very calmly.

After we'd unharnessed and were brushing the ponies down Jen mentioned that the hame tugs on Mr T's collar were marking the inside of the shaft leathers.

Ruby and Mr T got their scoops of mix as a signal their work was finished, and while Jen and Naomi "the hosepipe queen" tidied the stable I decided to try a spare pair of 22" hames I'd bought off eBay, to see if the higher draught point would put the tugs in a place where they didn't rub on the shafts. As I unfastened the old top hame strap I found it had split where it passed through the buckle tongue and it was only holding by half its width – about a quarter of an inch!! I suppose I'd forgotten how old that strap was – it had come secondhand with a collar, and until Mr T came home from loan it was just there to hold the hames on his (unused) collar; never really thought of using it.

And then I forgot how old it was and we both forgot to check it… Yesterday's trip with the 4 wheeler and the binding wheel must have finally done for it. Our guardian angel was looking after Jen yesterday I think. The [webbing] bottom hame strap with the stainless steel buckle was fine.

So once the ponies were turned out in the paddock, it was off to the spares boxes to find two newer (and shorter) straps for the longer hames. Luckily the hame tugs are removable ones so that changeover was very simple. I may treat myself by making a couple of new pairs of hame straps – shall have to see if I have the right width of buckles.

No doubt Naomi will want to know how to do that too.

Sue

Dalemain "Packs and Tracks", 17 May 2010

I spent a day at the Fell Pony stallion show on Saturday (I was scheduled to go to a FPS meeting *after* it, but had to deliver some books before the *start* of it!). Friends kept asking why I wasn't competing in the driving class, and made fun of me until I reminded them I drive a mare and have done for the last 6 years, while the driving class is for stallions or geldings. And also, Ruby's been in season all week. It could have been, er, entertaining.

Anyway, Mr T was being kept back for another job on Sunday. My daughter Jen and I took him to a "Packs and Tracks" demonstration day run by Cumbria Bridleways, at Dalemain House, or Mansion as it prefers to call itself. In the morning we were first on, with an audience of approximately four, which gave Jen a chance to school Mr T by warming him up and doing a dressage test. During the rest of the morning we talked to visitors about driving, and after lunch we did a cone driving demo with Mr T and Mike, one of Jen's pupils brought his Welsh mare to join in. ... Mr T was a complete star and loved showing off through the cones, we had people all around the ring who were wowed by his agility at 23 years of age, and Mike realised he really was brave enough to drive in public. We even got a photo of him smiling. Another long day, with more catching up with friends.

Mr T had today off, while I dragged me weary bones out to give Ruby some work – necessary because she had had 2 days off! She's been powerfully in season for a week, and has harassed Mr T to death while she's out in the field, although she's been very chilled-out when working. She apparently screamed for Mr T most of yesterday while he was at Dalemain, when normally she doesn't care two hoots about him, whether at home or absent! She's been interested in anything that looked stallionly as we passed with the carriage, but amazingly, completely obedient :-)

Today I decided to go towards Howe Nook, which is a farm about 4 miles from us that stands next to the Roman military road. I had a letter to post, so we went down into Greenholme first, where we found a very large tractor pumping slurry from one huge tanker into a smaller one. Brum brum slurp. Ruby – who is mechanically minded – walked quietly past it and parked by the post box so I could slip the letter in. Then walked round the tractor as if it wasn't there, and set off hotfooted for home! Er, no, Ruby, we need to do just a bit more than 300 yards down the hill... so she came round onto the Orton road and trotted up the hill, and past the services, and over the motorway, and trotted, and trotted, and trotted. I gave her a 5 minute breather walking down to the Orton guidepost, then along the Shap / Howe Nook road, and trotted on after that. She was most interested in a Fell mare and foal on the other side of a wall, but the mare very carefully took her new baby away from the scary horse with wheels!

I gave Ruby another breather just below Howe Nook, then turned for home. She was feeling well but obedient, and I decided to give her a treat by trotting down Martinagap Lane, which is a green lane / bridleway where we have permission to drive when the weather is dry. Ruby strode on happily, bumping over tractor ruts that had dried solid, until a double bounce dislodged the 56lb weight on the back step and flipped it over, so its carpet wrapping no longer deadened the rattle. It wasn't going to fall off, as it's strapped on, but I didn't want to do the rest of the drive with 56lbs clanking on the aluminium; so I asked Ruby to walk, and then got my headcollar rope and tied her to a bush while I righted the weight. She thought that was good – nice long fresh grass to eat, yum! And as it turned out, that little glitch kept us nicely out of the way of a batch of trail motorbike riders snarling along the road, and all 12 of them went by without any inconvenience on either side. So I wrapped up the headcollar rope and hopped back in, and we went home. Ruby was still feeling very well so I just glanced at my watch to see what time she'd make – she did two miles at 16 kph. I think she's fitter than she has been for quite a while.

Nice Drive, 21 May 2010

Suddenly, the cold northerly wind that we've had for nearly 6 weeks has gone away, and it's warm, almost hot, here in Cumbria!

I fed both ponies this morning, which I haven't done myself in recent weeks because Jen, my daughter, has been teaching using Mr T and she often gets out before I do. However, today she's taken Naomi in for day surgery to remove those chemotherapy lines – last step back to normality for our 4½ year old grand-daughter, after nine months of cancer treatment. So Mr T and Ruby had their soaked sugar-beet, soaked cubes and half scoop of mix, and a wee bite of hay to keep them happy till I came out around 10:30 am to tack up Ruby for a drive.

Mr T stayed in, and apparently spent most of the hour and 20 minutes that we were away, bellowing for Ruby.

She never bothers to answer him while she's working. Work, for her, comes first; she just loves doing it. We walked for a mile, up the hill past the motorway services, then I put her into trot, just an easy jog, about 11 kph, nothing strenuous. The birds are busy here – most are already nesting, the blackbirds singing their hearts out and the crows dive-bombing the local buzzard in case he takes a fancy to their nest site. It's been a late, cold spring here, and a very dry six weeks or so. Some of the fields that are usually wet, and heavily overgrown in seaves (soft rushes) have burst into shades of palest lilac pink as the cuckoo-flowers (lady's smock) have come into bloom. I've never seen them so exuberant, it's quite remarkable. Further on, there was a soft, sweet green smell that I couldn't place at all – perhaps the smell of beech trees, because there is a long line of them beside the road, all big mature trees, smooth barked and newly in leaf and already casting a dense shade.

The oddest item on our daily drives has now gone – an abandoned fireside armchair that's lived for some weeks beside the electricity substation and has been nicknamed "the electric chair" and "the throne of power". I'd seen it previously in the rear of the pickup belonging to the man who took away our broken washing machine; maybe he left it there to make room for his next collection! Perhaps he came back for it. I hope so – it was quite a nice chair, much too good to waste!

Ruby kept up the trot for a couple of miles, then we turned towards Sproat Ghyll Farm (smiling at the travelling butcher who was reading the newspaper while sitting in the cab of his van, in the shade of the big sycamore on the corner). I kept Ruby trotting till we reached the farm, then gave her a few minutes on the grass verge, in the shade, while she caught her breath. That took very little time! She was nibbling the hedge inside the first minute, and moving off within another two or three. I walked her back towards the junction, and she dealt quite composedly with a very large, wide Manitou loader that came bumpety bumping along the road to turn in at the farm. She didn't mind its size, but the unpredictable bumping did cause her to shy a tiny bit when it was level with us. However, she never makes much fuss so I just told her quietly to go on walking. Once we'd passed the butcher's van again, I set her off in trot and she picked up eagerly for home. I really wanted to make sure she is fit to do a fast, hilly marathon drive of about 6 miles, with 3 or 4 obstacles, on Sunday, so I took up the reins two-handed, which always alerts her that I want more energy. Quite how she knows that I've changed my grip, I'm not sure – perhaps I take a stronger hold two-handed. I have noticed, too, that I compensate better for her naturally convex right side this way, and she strides more evenly; which must say something about my perception of rein pressure when driving coachman style, I suppose. Anyway, she flew home at a rolling 16 kph. Heading into the breeze, she actually cooled off as she did so. She is getting very fit, and her massive quarters are really hard-muscled.

She was still warm enough when we got home, though, to appreciate a wash off, without grumbling and swinging about!

Dalemain Event, 23 May 2010

I drove Ruby today at our North West Driving Club's "Fun Event" at Dalemain House, near Ullswater (they have a website, dalemain.com – go and enjoy the lovely photos). I've been able to get a lot more work into Ruby this year and she's pretty hard and fit. We both love doing this little event, because it gives us a beautiful drive out through the newly leafed woodland of Dalemain's estate, the first and last thirds being on private tracks or through the fields and the middle section passing through the village where I lived when my husband and I were courting.

Ruby just loves being able to do lots of work on grass.

Someone asked me today how long the Dalemain event has been going – well, I remember stewarding in May 1984 when they managed to fit in a dressage test as well as a marathon and cones (and it SNOWED, whereas today was red-hot), and that wasn't the first year it had run. I don't think we have missed a year there except in 2001 due to Foot and Mouth restrictions. That's some record. And I've lost count of how many times I've driven the marathon route, yet every time it is more beautiful, with the trees all bursting into leaf, the wild and garden cherry trees all in flower, the fat young lambs scurrying off the track as we trot by – and this year, fresh gravel on some of the more heavily worn sections, oh bliss! I remarked to Mike, who grooms for me, that once upon a time ALL our roads must have been rocky and rutted and only occasionally gravelled. Really, we are very spoiled these days with our tarmac and our pneumatic tyred cars!

I pushed Ruby for speed along the early level stretches, and when I let her stride out on the grass she really powered along, hitting a strong canter to get us up the hill to Dacre Castle, then catching her breath while we stopped and opened/shut the gate which let us out of the fields and onto the road into the village.

Ruby skated a bit going down the slope to the bridge, but I just let her pick her own speed, and once we'd crossed Dacre Beck we saw the long climb of Vicarage Hill ahead of us. Now, Ruby's climbed this hill every year (occasionally twice a year) since 2005 and she knows it's a long tough one, so it's to her credit that she stuck out her neck and said, "Bring it on!" and never broke stride all the way up – though the trot did get quite short as we neared the top. I let her pick her own speed and catch her breath as we eased back down the other side (managing not to mow down a gang of walkers), and after dodging into the fast traffic on the Ullswater road we were let into the fields again 100 yards further on through a stewarded gate. Ruby hit the grass with gusto and powered up the slopes. This is the other bit of the drive that I love – the huge views across to the Northern Lake District Fells, Saddleback to the north of us, and Cross Fell to the east, still with a crust of snow at the steep edges of its flat summit, all under the wide, clear blue of the sky. And then, once we reached the top, through several field gates (where each time Ruby got another breather), we had a glorious long sweeping slope of clean green grass, down towards the pink sandstone facade of the House and its terraced garden. Ruby just loved this stretch, and we sailed down to the little stone bridge that took us back into the East Park.

Since the event is a driving trial, we had hazards to negotiate (4 this year) but as this is a recreational driving list I won't go into detail, other than to say that we did all of them, and Ruby behaved very well and enjoyed them. Last year I drove her past ALL the hazards bar the first one, because she had got it into her head that she was going to be the brains and not the brawn of the outfit, and was going to belt through any gap she could see! This year she was very biddable apart from one gate where she just focused on the wrong space and had to be reversed out of it. Which she did obediently and quickly (I love my 2 wheeler). She also behaved impeccably in the cone driving, though I always have to remember how quickly she reacts to rein changes, and make sure I don't oversteer. The more I can leave her alone and just suggest changes of direction, the better and more accurate she is.

What pleased me most was that there was plenty of steam in the tank when we needed it. Since Ruby has had issues with mild COPD over the last 2 years I was very happy that she could do this testing hilly drive, and make the necessary times, and come home – yes, sweaty – but not stressed or unduly out of breath.

So, Ruby, Mike and I had a really lovely day out. Not so (these are the odd bits) my friend Margaret, whose latest small pony ran away with her twice during the day; nor some new friends who had brought their lovely big black-and-white driving cob so he could just watch the action as part of his education, and whose trailer turned over on the motorway on the way home. I think they're all physically OK, but I'll have to wait to hear more during the coming week.

Mr T was very happy to see Ruby when we got home! They both had a nice long graze in the field, pleasantly fly-free in a strong breeze.

6 June 2010 – Appleby Fair traffic

Normally I write about my drives out with Ruby the Magnificent in order to share the pleasure that carriage driving gives us. My driving is my recreation and I come home soothed in mind and spirit. Not so today. I'm BOILING.

I took Ruby out by herself because Mr T has had a few days off to ease a windgall on one his hind legs, and Jen didn't want to work him hard today. So I packed up two plastic bags full of other plastic bags for "recycling" and strapped them to the cart seat before setting off towards Tebay over our big hill, Pikestoll. Since Pikey is a long hard haul, and I intended to go right round the circuit which is a distance of 8 miles, I let Ruby stroll along to warm up at a walk. I stopped at "Tom's gateway" about a third of the way up to move the midge-repeller from the top of the collar, where it was touching Ruby's wither, and clip it round the stem of the saddle terret. I don't know if these sonic repellents actually work but when you've got a midgey farm and midge-sensitive horses all routes are worth trying. At any rate, the repeller (which is solar powered) didn't give any other problems in its new position. However, midges were the least of Ruby's troubles on the drive!

It was all very peaceful over Pikey and down to Roundthwaite road end, where we paused for quite a while, waiting for a clear run out onto the A685. Ruby tends to think that once a car has passed it is time to move out, whereas I could see traffic coming from much further down the road. The traffic wasn't actually heavy, but the cars kept coming. She was very good though and trotted straight out once the road really was clear. We kept a nice steady trot going over the motorway and railway bridges, up into Tebay and to David Trotter's house, where I left the plastic bags for him to reuse in his greengrocery deliveries. Then we went on our merry way through the village, through the narrows, down the hill and round the motorway roundabout. Keeping ourselves to ourselves, warning people of our presence with our flashing lights back and front.

Most people whom we meet on the road are courteous and smiling, and I smile and wave at them because I'm happy and why not share it? So it continued, until we were leaving the roundabout, when Ruby scooted because she saw a motorcyclist. But it was nothing serious, and I still managed to signal which exit I was going down. As we continued along the Orton section of the A685, however, I began to realise that there was a good deal more traffic than I'd expected; possibly leaving the motorway and heading for Appleby, where the Fair Hill gipsy gathering is coming to a close. Were they all horse people? I seriously doubt it. Horse sense was certainly not in evidence. When we approached blind summits where nobody should overtake because they can't see if anything is coming, they overtook. When I signalled them not to overtake because, sitting higher than the cars, I could see oncoming traffic, they overtook. When a convoy of foreign registered cars came up behind me and the first one pulled out to overtake, they all overtook, as though an umbilical cord might snap if they were separated – never mind the fact that the oncoming traffic had to stop for them.

I kept Ruby pounding along at a good straight trot, but her 11mph was just not fast enough for the idiots. I don't mean that everyone who followed me was a fool, because I was aware of one car that sat politely twenty yards back from us for at least a mile; but my verbal commands along that stretch included several cries of greeting to members of the Head family [work it out], and my coachman style driving gave ample opportunity to exercise my whip hand in certain unconventional signals.

Do cyclists have these troubles? They are equally vulnerable on the road. How do they deal with them, I wonder?

Once past Orton, where we left the Appleby road, courtesy and good humour returned, and perfect strangers waved and grinned, just the way it all usually happens. And Ruby walked and cooled off from her frenetic two miles. When we passed the youngster being schooled on the lunge at Selsmire farm, and he used our passing as an excuse to squeal and buck in circles, she only flicked an ear and told him saddles weren't that big a deal. She ignored the inquisitive Shetlands and the farm bikes, and only wanted to get back onto the yard and scream to Mr T that she hadn't abandoned him, she still loved him, and she was home.

And when I turned her out with him she squealed and told him to get lost!

Nothing went wrong on the drive. We drove to the rules of the road. So if you were in your car on the A685 this summer Sunday lunchtime, heading for Appleby, and if Ruby and I held you up for a few minutes until the road was clear, then I apologise, and thank you for your tolerance. But I'm also furious at the idiot behaviour we encountered.

"If you risked your life and ours by overtaking on a blind brow, on a blind bend, or in the face of oncoming traffic, or if you forced me to rein in my horse as you pulled in front of me, then please tell me – what was so important, on a Sunday lunch time, that you couldn't be patient for those few minutes?"

So come on Google, index this lot and let the idiots read the things I didn't have the chance to say today. If they can read.

Treasure Hunt, 20 June 2010

Busy busy busy.... I hosted a drive today for our driving club and although we didn't have a huge turnout we all had a lot of fun. I gave everybody maps and directions interspersed with clues that were mostly things to find along the route, though here and there when the drive passed through open countryside I added in a couple of general knowledge questions. I put up CAUTION – HORSES signs along a narrow stretch of road, and got everybody's mobile numbers in case I needed to get in touch with them en route (my number was on all the pages of the route / clues). Everything went okay but you never know!

It was all very relaxed. We all met on the village green. Everyone drove at their own speed, separately if they wanted, or in groups if they wanted. Even the competition-fit pair just chilled out while the driver and passengers enjoyed the views. With a cooling breeze, and the sun shining on the fells, it was perfect recreational driving weather. An old friend, who's been looking for a replacement driving pony since her old Fell died, came over just to spectate. She has taken a pony on trial that sounds ideal – she had had a test drive with him in his owner's set of harness held together with baling string, with a dirty bit that was half an inch too small, and with the traces wound round the shafts to shorten them... but the pony never put a foot wrong, and if he'll put up with all that crap he'll certainly bloom in Margaret's four star care!

After the drive I marked everyone's answer sheets while they saw to the horses. The pair went paddling in the river, and had a nice long drink and then grazed beside the horsebox. Some drivers took their ponies back to our yard where they'd parked, one stopped off at her home to wash off and turn out the pony and then came to the finish in her car; then when all the ponies had been seen to we all had a good gossipy picnic on the village green. And when everyone, horses and human, had gone home, I took Ruby out for a drive along part of the route to collect my CAUTION signs, and we had a really nice relaxed time chatting to neighbours and visitors that we passed along the road. I even met a Morgan (the sports car not the horse) and directed the driver to his destination, with mutual expressions of admiration for each other's form of transport.

Now grand-daughter Naomi, who has supervised Ruby being rubbed down and fed and turned out in the top garth with Mr T, is flouncing round my garden dressed up as a fairy – complete (as all gardeners should be) with pink wellies. What a hoot.

Skelton Show (Mr T), 4 July 2010

We've been so spoiled with all the dry weather here that it comes as a shock when wind and rain return as they have today. However, if it refills the streams I can stand it.

Ruby and Mr T are out in the small paddock. It's all they've been permitted to use, since the keep for the neighbour's sheep was getting short on the main fields, and the sheep pay rent.

Ruby has her blue weatherproof sheet on, and Mr T, who doesn't have much fat on his ribs these days, has an old stable rug under his waterproof and a smug smile on his little grey-flecked face. He is due his day of rest because he's worked all week with me, getting everything right to go to Skelton show yesterday.

I've pretty well decided that I am not going to "do" showing any more – getting it all cleaned, assembled and loaded exhausted me by Friday. But, having done all the work, and having stated that we were only going in order to get the judge's signature on the BDS form and not to win, I was able to enjoy just being at the show and nattering to people as I got ready for the class at lunchtime.

Mr T loved it – party time in a nice grass field, what's not to like? He heard a whinny once or twice that sounded like Ruby's best "girly" voice, and so he shouted back, but after that he took no notice until another Fell pony appeared in harness. (They are utter racists – they don't recognise any other breeds.) Mike, a local driver who has lessons with Jen, was grooming for me. He came early and collected our number from the Secretary's tent, which couldn't really have been much further away from our allocated parking area ... He returned looking as though he'd been on an expedition so I quoted at him, "I may be some time."

It's the first time I've been to this show in about 10 years and the show ground this year is half as big again as it was then; a very good thing, as I'd sworn I wouldn't enter again after the last visit, when we'd had nowhere to work-in and I'd sprained an ankle in a sun-hardened "cow pothole" as I stepped down off the horsebox ramp. But there was lots of room this year! The driving "ring" was being used by people to warm up for other ridden classes and so we could use that, as well as the rest of the huge field. Also the drive out wasn't on hard roads but marked out round the top of the fields, so Mr T had great fun telling me that he was really a racehorse and could out-trot them all, especially down that hill where they were all tippytoeing along, why wouldn't I let him race them? But he's such a sweetie, when I told him to settle down he did.

In the main ring, when we went in for the presentation of rosettes, things were a bit confused! They had the driving horses, the Cumberland Wrestling, and some dairy cattle all in together. Mr T wasn't bothered by the wrestlers, but the very large cow that brayed (rather than mooing) puzzled him immensely and as he peered round his blinkers at her he kept sidling up to Mike for reassurance.

Mike really enjoyed the day and at one point said as he sat beside me in the carriage, "Who'd have thought I'd ever be in a show class at Skelton Show?" I had to point out it was really not all that big a deal. But, it was nice that we were all having fun, unlike the chap who had parked right next to the ring entrance. He had a spindle back governess cart, a grey Welsh pony, three children (possibly grand-children) and his spouse... he swore at wife, kids and pony indiscriminately while preparing for the class. I wasn't the only person who'd noticed some dangerous points about his setup which made his pony's life difficult; it expressed its discomfort mainly by jibbing but I wouldn't have been surprised if it had decided to run away, and he obviously thought so too, judging by the way he sat forward over the edge of the bodywork and drove with his hands nearly on its rump. There was a lot of unsafe practice in putting to and taking out as well. I had been thinking of going over to have a chat with him once I'd packed all our gear back into the horsebox (well, I'd talked to everybody else), but he was clearly a very angry person and his temper hadn't improved when he was justifiably placed last in his class... he was still swearing at the kids as he left. So I just I waved as he passed, and he grimaced and sketched a wave back. I wondered what kind of a life the family and pony have when they are not on a show field.

Meanwhile Mr T, wrapped in a fleecy rug against the chill breeze, slurped happily through his feed of soaked sugarbeet and fibre nuts, and when it was time to load he walked into the horsebox and hardly made a sound all the way home.

As Mike said of Mr T when we were unharnessing after the class, "Don't you wish they were all like this!" It was the understatement of the day.

Crupperless? Observations and thoughts, 22 July 2010

The midge season is easing up and so are the clegs (horse flies). They haven't been so bad this year as last year and the year before but poor Ruby still has a series of patches of bare skin where she has scratched horsefly bites over the past couple of weeks. She has two bare areas at the end of her dock as well – though they are mostly hidden by the rest of her luxuriant tail. I guess this is an area that isn't quite covered by her "fly knickers" ear-to-tail sheet. Anyway, since the flies *have* been getting at her despite all my attempts to prevent them, which means her tail is itchy when we first put-to, the crupper became a small issue and one I didn't intend to make any bigger. Taking into account some of the discussions on RED, and the fact that I needed to do some mending anyway on breeching hip straps and crupper, I got brave and took a sharp knife to several straps.

First I trimmed off the worn ends of the hip straps. The centre, the broad strap from which the two straps divide, is fine, so I kept that and trimmed the ends to a shallow V. I had a pair of tough single-strap hip straps that no longer fit any other harnesses, and have seen very little use, and don't fit either pony, so I cut them to size, skived the upper ends and made new ends for my hip strap out of them. Then I punched one hole in the centre by which I could rivet or lace the hip strap in a central position onto the crupper back strap, through a similar hole made where the hip strap normally lies, in its slot. That secured the breeching so it couldn't slide sideways in use – the crupper backstrap now having only the single attachment to the saddle, I didn't want it being dragged out of place accidentally. Though I wondered about the wisdom of fixing something that normally has a degree of slide, just as the sliding backband does. I trimmed the end of the crupper backstrap to make it look tidy, and put the crupper dock away among the spare straps.

The first fitting was interesting. I could see at once that the hip strap which has always sat directly over the top of Ruby's croup was not going to stay there now the crupper no longer held the backstrap in position. It looked, in fact, as though it would slide forward. That would put unacceptable stress on the rear hipstrap of the breeching so I lengthened the backstrap three holes to make the hip strap sit further behind her hip bones. Moving the hip strap behind the top of her croup lowered the breeching seat half an inch so I had to take up the hip straps by one hole all round.

I was very careful to adjust the tightness of the breeching straps on the shafts so there was just the right amount of slack in the breeching seat when the traces were taut. I didn't want the seat flapping about uncontrollably with any strong rhythmic motion like a good trot.

Then we went out for a drive.

It was a bit unnerving to watch the backstrap moving, but after a while I got used to the extra movement and was sure that the single rivet was enough to keep the whole thing centred. What I think I was seeing was the natural movement of the hip strap, that previously slid in the slot, shifting the backstrap. Ruby appeared unbothered by this extra bit of "flap" (more movement at trot of course), though I wondered how a green horse might have reacted!

We mostly walked that first time out, but today I've been observing again at both walk and trot. The hip strap wanted to lie forward at its normal place, since this was the right vertical position for its suspension of the breeching seat; and this shift forward inevitably slackened the backstrap. I think the only solution to that would be a shorter breeching seat, which would require longer breeching straps. I'm not ready to do all that.

I needed to shorten the hip straps by another hole all round, today. That made the breeching seat look a bit tight round Ruby's quarters, but on the move, walk or trot, it had a good amount of clearance.

Overall, the crupperless test has shown up how important it is to get the fit of the breeching correct. My harness which worked fine when both ends of the crupper backstrap were connected to saddle and under the tail, became far more obviously reactive to Ruby's big movement when the crupper was removed and the hipstrap fixed to the backstrap. The hip strap has a place where it's neutral, taking very little strain and holding the breeching seat at the correct height, but this doesn't coincide, on this harness and this pony, with the right place for working crupperless. It's also interesting that the usual "purpose" given for the use of a crupper, to steady the saddle when going downhill, appears not to hold true; the absence of the crupper had no bearing whatsoever on the behaviour of the saddle, which didn't move... because I had my breeching fitted correctly. And I now know two reasons why farm backstraps that are crupperless, have a padded lining underneath – one is to absorb the "flap" and the other is to hold the crupper more rigid along the back so that "flap" is minimised.

I'm already planning to sew a dee or a ring onto the end of my own crupper backstrap, round which I can put a pair of straps to hold the crupper, once I've replaced its single rather small buckle with two wider ones. This will give me the option of working crupperless when Ruby's got an itchy tail or dock – and it happens annually, so she needs this option – but of replacing the crupper for the rest of the year. I might do some testing with a shorter breeching seat that's hanging on one of the harness racks, too. I could swap that in for the crupperless periods and go back to the main harness once the fly season is over.

More Crupperless observations, 23 July 2010

Did another test today – and took photos. I'm not sure I'm quite happy with the new position of the breeching hip straps; setting them well back keeps the crupper backstrap in position, but although I've shortened the hipstraps to lift the breeching seat back to its normal level, something's still not quite right. I feel the seat may ride up if Ruby does her big trot. When we passed a neighbour who turned on his weed sprayer quite close to us, Ruby startled and the seat rose a bit high, which it doesn't do in its normal position – this may be due to the trace carriers lying that bit further back, ie the breeching seat ring where they attach is now further away from the traces as they run down to the swingletree. This might be tipping the breeching seat down at front and up at back when the traces are taut. Another run needed, perhaps, with longer trace carriers, to see if that makes a difference.

I'm definitely going to put the crupper dock back on this weekend, on a detachable basis.

Photos in my Sue Millard folder, and two videos on YouTube – I know you all need pictures of a horse's ass to study over the weekend!

25 July 2010

Decided in the end to go back to the crupper. If I were to go down the crupperless route, I'd probably make a new set of breeching hip straps and backstrap on the spider pattern, that divides from a ring right at the backstrap and can sit fore-and-aft of the hip bone. I think mine divide too far down and flap too much without the extra anchorage of the crupper. But my rebuild has given me a few more holes to play with for adjustment during fitting, so it's not all bad :)

25 Sept 2009

Be wary of simply removing the crupper-dock from a standard setup. If you have a hip strap that slides through the crupper backstrap you'll also need to fix that centrally to the backstrap in some way to stop the breeching seat slipping sideways, one side high and the other low. Spider breeching is fixed to a central ring

(I believe – have not seen anything other than side view photos) so it should always hang level.

Someone said cruppers were a hangover from work harness – that depends, as always, what kind of work harness. Plough and logging harness in England doesn't have a breeching to support, or shafts to carry, or any way of braking, so it doesn't need a backstrap or a crupper; it only has a strap over the back at the girthline, to check the the trace-chains. Some heavy cart harnesses only had a padded short strap carrying the breeching and hip straps; it didn't extend to the tail.

When I'm judging light carriage classes over here, I expect the girth to be snug, but not tight, and the backband and tugs should allow the shafts to float easily. I lift the shaft tip to see that this is possible, and to gauge how much weight is on the horse's back. Single horses/ponies here in the UK, with 2 wheeled vehicles, use the sliding backband and oval open tugs – we don't wrap our shafts or tie them down. I saw one small Shetland having to put up with tight backband and slack girth at a show this summer and the whole harness moved sideways when he turned or trotted, poor fellow. I did offer advice to his driver afterwards! The crupper-length fit for our English turnouts is just to be able to turn your hand's width under the strap, from saddle to tail, over the croup. A bit less for smaller ponies, obviously. You don't want the strap tight, but equally the crupper should not "hang" under the tail.

The breeching seat and straps should be fitted to act as brake before the crupper and the backband and tugs come into play. That usually means relatively high, round the fattest bit of the quarters. It also means the traces are best a tiny bit longer than you think is right, so that when the pony is in draught, the tugs lie a bit forward of the tug-stops on the shafts. Webbing traces are friendly in this respect because they can look spot-on for fit when standing, but will stretch a little under tension so that gives you the play you need in the breeching seat to allow movement, but still permit the breeching to act as brake before the other bits of the harness are affected.

But again, this kind of adjustment is only possible with the loose backband and SBB saddle. The American wrap strap setup is much more difficult to adjust to be horse friendly, IMO.

Rambling, now, sorry.

Funny Drive! 31 July 2010

I took Ruby out this afternoon, by which time she was very grumpy, having been indoors all yesterday, and having eaten all today's midday hay allowance.

We drove up Pikestoll, the big hill to the south, and at the top I turned in at The Dyke, where my friend Felicity lives. Ruby likes this option because we usually stand nattering then come straight home. Hard luck Ruby – this time, there was nobody in! So we retraced our steps to the end of the farm lane, and set off down the hill on the other side, to Roundthwaite. Unusually, we met three cars and were overtaken by a neighbour on a motorbike – nearly a traffic jam for our little road! – but we had room to find a bit of grass verge each time and Ruby didn't object to them passing her, though the grass was a great temptation.

Down the far side, there's an even narrower stretch of road with a stream on one side and a bank on the other, and here we met a large Land Rover Discovery (4WD) towing a boat, of all things, on a trailer. I tried putting Ruby up a bit of grass verge, but here it was a good 3 feet high at 45 degrees, so I shook my head and took her off it. The driver of the 4WD poked his head out and said, "Have you got any suggestions?" I told him that if he could go back straight, 5 yards, there was a tiny gateway hidden under the nettles and goosegrass, in which I could get Ruby and the carriage off the road. So that's what we did... he had about 6 inches to spare on my side and I didn't bother looking how much he had to spare on his! But he did shout his thanks as he went by :)

Down into Roundthwaite, no more traffic, Ruby doing her big walk and letting me know in no uncertain terms that she was grumpy and needed to work. We had some lovely big trots on the level stretches, and I took her through Roundthwaite and up to the viewpoint into the Lune valley, over the motorway and railway and river. Somebody had mown one of the banks, and apparently, under the bracken and grass etc, a bench-seat for walkers has been hiding all these years! Ruby didn't want to wait and catch her breath, so I turned her back homeward, and sampled the little tracks on the "moor end", which are used by the local farms to collect animals off the fellside. Ruby enjoyed that, trotting through little watersplashes and up and down over the undulating grassland. We trotted up the gravelly road to the top of Roundthwaite, turned at the ford, and came back. Ruby, having got her pipes cleared climbing the hill, and facing now towards home, was motoring. Now, as you've probably realised from the early part of this description, our road is NARROW. So I was gobsmacked when a cyclist suddenly appeared under my right elbow! He shot through past me, with no warning or greeting, and Ruby turned herself inside out as the "silent death" popped into her view. I said a few choice words as I collected her up, and then sat firmly in the middle of the road to prevent a second cyclist overtaking until I could move over and let him past safely. No word of thanks there either... well screw YOU, mate! I thought. Ruby picked up on my irritation, added it to her own grumpiness, and shot off after both cyclists at full pelt. Needless to say, when they hit the up gradient 200 yards further on and heard our hoofs approaching, they had to pull over to let Mrs Steam Engine pass by. I grinned and said, " Thank you!" Oooh coals of fire... She was so fired up by chasing the bikes that she trotted all the way up to the top of the hill. I stopped her there in the Dyke lane end, and let her catch her breath, knowing full well that when the cyclists reached the top they'd want to fly down the hill at 40mph – and no way did I want to be walking Ruby down the hill ahead of them if they were going to pass us again at that speed, without warning and minimal braking power. They did eventually pass while we waited, and they reached our house, nearly a mile away, before we were a quarter of the way down the hill.

Ruby did her best let's-get-the-job-done walk all the way down the hill, and gave me a great trot on the river level and up the bank to the yard. And then pulled faces at me all the time I was unharnessing and brushing her off. Didn't I KNOW, she was HUNGRY???

I fed her and Mr T, and they're now out in the little paddock, pulling faces at each other instead of at me. By, she's a cracking drive when she's cross!

Ride, Drive and Barbecue, 15 August 2010

No it's not a recipe. (I worry sometimes.)

Today the Fell Pony Society held a Ride, Drive and Barbecue at Murton, which is a tiny village on the East Fellside, under the slopes of the northern Pennines. Ruby and I set off early, leaving Mr T chomping the sweet grass in the field (and quite happy for his best girlfriend to let him deal with it all by himself.) We trundled steadily in the horsebox through Orton and Appleby (yes, the gipsy Fair Appleby) and along narrow lanes to our destination, where the grass, as Ruby saw to her amazement, was eight inches high and begging to be eaten.

I let her have a few minutes of grazing before I harnessed her up. My passenger for the day was the FPS secretary, Elizabeth. Once she had found us, we yoked up Ruby, put on our helmets and hi viz gear and turned on the bike lights on the carriage; and then we got up and went for a wander round the field, adjusting the seat for balance so we'd have a comfortable drive.

All the riders were mounting, and one or two ponies spooked at the 3 carriages so I kept Ruby out on her own until I saw the drive leader, Mr Howe, setting off down the track to the gate with his stallion Jake. Knowing that we wouldn't get any more warning, I sent Ruby off after him... and it's just as well, because Howie wasn't checking that he had all of us with him before he sent Jake off at a trot. We never saw the other carriage again until we got back to the field 2 hours later!

To start with, Ruby was excited, mostly by the sound of the riders behind us, rattling down the track as they set off on their 6 mile ride. She reckoned that there must be a lioness somewhere about, and if that was the case she wanted to out trot Jake so the lioness would eat him and not her. She kept creeping out into the middle of the road to overtake, and I kept putting her back, as although I know the area, I didn't know where the drive was supposed to be going! I learned later that on last year's route the

20-odd riders and 4 drivers had been all mixed up together and "it got a bit exciting" especially as "Howie had set off at a trot from the word go and never once looked back." Hence the riders going a different way from the drivers this year!

The drivers' route led from Murton to its sister village, Hilton, and round by Appleby Golf Course (the public road goes across it). Here Ruby was a bit worried by the golfers and their strange rattling equipment. I don't think she knew anything about the speed of golf balls, but luckily nothing struck us and we trotted on down to the gate at the other end, and onto the "back road" which crosses the main Appleby to Brough road, the A66. Ruby is well acquainted with road bridges with wire sides, so she wasn't at all bothered by the traffic hurtling along beneath us. At the next junction we had to wait, to get out onto the road, for a gap in a parade of very shiny veteran and vintage tractors, all having a day out in the sunshine. I mentioned to Elizabeth that it was nice to have Fell ponies who are unbothered by traffic. She replied that her two would have been in the next field by now! They are Ruby's half sisters, so that's just got to be down to lack of exposure to the big bad world, as neither of them are Nervous Nellies, and Vicky, in particular, shares Ruby's inquisitive and clever nature as well as her tilted eyes and wicked, turned-in ears.

The road into Appleby carried quite a lot of fast traffic, but both ponies were rock steady as cars whizzed by (and most of them were very sensible about passing the horses). Encouraged by this, when Howie asked (yes he did ask!) over his shoulder, whether we wanted to take the first road back to Murton, or go on through Appleby, I said at once, "Oh let's go through the town, and make a bit of a statement!" So we trotted down Bongate, and along the Sands next to the river, where in June the gipsy horses are washed and swum, and then up the long straight hill of Battlebarrow. Jake was flagging by then and halfway up he dropped to a walk, which quite miffed Madam Ruby who was sure she could have trotted all the way to the top. But with traffic

315

behind and oncoming, there was no way to overtake him so she could prove it!

Out of the town, Howie led us onto roads that I knew, past Fair Hill (peacefully grazed by sheep) and onto the road back to Murton. Jake by now was giving clear signs that he'd had enough, so as I knew the way back to the field, I offered to put Ruby into the lead. With Ruby trotting cheerfully out in front of him, Jake decided perhaps this new woman in his life *might* just be worth the effort of pursuit!

There were more vintage vehicles at Appleby Manor Hotel, where there was a car rally (Morgans, perhaps? I didn't manage to catch sight of a radiator badge to check) but after that we had the roads to ourselves again, with the high green slopes of the Pennines basking in sunshine on one side of us, and the Eden Valley on the other, blue with misty haze.

Ruby brought us home to the horsebox field in good style, and I washed her off with a towel soaked in cold water. She was sweaty but not blowing hard, didn't want a drink when it was offered, and was soon tucking into the luscious grass once more, while I wiped down the harness and put it back into the horsebox. The riders were all home already, but they had only done 6 miles, while my GPS told me we had done 9 and a half!

Gwendy, the third of our drivers, arrived back last of all. She had been shepherded by Elizabeth's husband in his car with its hazard lights on, so she had gone round a route that was a kind of consultation exercise, stopping to discuss directions at each road junction. Since Elizabeth had told me he has NO sense of direction, this must have been entertaining, but they'd got back all right!

Gwendy had come "on the hoof" to the venue, so she asked if she could tie the pony, Heather, to the opposite side of our horsebox from Ruby. We are former work colleagues so of course I said yes! We loaded my carriage into the horsebox, saw to the ponies, made sure they were securely tied but could reach grass and water, then left them to graze while we joined in the barbecue in the next field.

Lovely food and superb chutney and salads to go with it... enough said!

When I got back, Ruby had stuffed her face with grass, leaving the usual "Fell pony trademark" of a nearly bare half circle beside the horsebox. She really wasn't bothered about having any of the feed she usually expects on getting back IN to the horsebox, but being a good natured mare she clomped in and settled while I helped Gwendy re-harness and re-hitch Heather, to go 2 miles down the road to stay overnight with friends before going home on Monday.

I adjusted Heather's breast collar so it was above her shoulder and not below, and put the reins through the terrets on neckstrap and saddle – "Oh," said Alice, Gwendy's groom (who owns Heather) – "Do the reins go through both sets of those?" I assured her they did... When Gwendy had put-to, I slackened the backband so it could slide freely, checked the breeching (which was right), and then lowered the breast collar again by one hole so it made a better line to the trace hooks. Gwendy then proposed to long rein Heather IN her carriage down the slope to the gate, so I said, very kindly but clearly, "PLEASE get in the carriage and drive from the seat..." explaining that it only took a mis-step for a shaft to knock you over and then the horse, and the carriage, were loose. Admittedly, Heather is a stolid mare, steady in harness in an open bridle, and she was quite worn out by her long day ... but safe practice is still better observed, even at the end of a long day. And Gwendy, bless her, saw the point.

Ruby travelled well in the box on the way home. She started whinnying when we got within sniffing distance of the farm. Mr T shouted at her as we drove into the yard, and soon they were touching noses and discussing the deeds of the day... while I mucked out and unloaded the horsebox.

317

Must go and give them their evening hay now... and hope that at SOME point we get a load of hay to see them through the winter.

2010 – Managing two ponies

I can get one horse in shape, but not two – not if I want to do some writing and web work to keep the ponies in the manner to which I've accustomed them. It was easier last spring because Jen and family were living here (while their house was being de-flooded), and working 2 ponies together gets far more work into them than working one alone followed by another.

Hay has been really expensive this autumn and I've been lucky to get some reasonably from a friend; I've eked it out by giving Mr T mainly soaked sugarbeet and soaked very cheap horse nuts with 28% fibre in them. His teeth are getting wobbly and he doesn't cope so well with hay any more. Even so, feeding and bedding 2 ponies will have cost me £2400 by the end of this accounting year – that's 2/3rds of my earned income. No need to ask where my priorities are :) (Begging and a small pension!)

Give them their due, the ponies have earned a little with teaching fees to offset against their costs.

Mr T doesn't mind me working Ruby. At 24, he is still boss man and behaves in a very chauvinistic manner to her. When there is food, he claims it. When there is danger, he graciously lets Ruby face it first.

When Ruby goes out to work, T beetles about, calling for her, but that's worry, not envy. He still has all the instincts of a wild horse on the fell, and he doesn't like being alone – whereas Ruby, although she plays at being a wild horse with violent emotions, is actually very content to be an only horse and will make do with people as companions. She won't shout after T if HE goes out to work! OTOH if he goes out carrying Naomi and she doesn't get to do it too, she will punish him when he comes back.

318

It was quite interesting to watch Naomi ride each of them last Monday. Ruby calmly looked after "her" child; whereas Mr T, the little worrier, had to be reassured by Naomi that everything was all right.

Feather, August 2021

What a ragbag of inheritance our language has.

I've been pondering why the hair round the feet of horses and ponies is called "feather", in the singular, no matter how legs or how many horses we are talking about.

What other nouns behave like this? Wool, at clipping-time, is a mass noun; the fleeces (plural) as a whole are wool, not wools, though a grader at the mill would define different "wools" by their staple length and fineness. Fluff. We wouldn't call the fibre gathered by the vacuum cleaner "fluffs" even if it had come off several cats. A high quality duvet is filled with down, not downs, despite the filling having come from more than one bird. It's something to do with volume, mass or quantity. Some uncountable quality makes these things mass nouns.

Rice, gold, butter. Milk, honey, marmalade. Sugar, grass, sand. Hay, straw, bedding. Cutlery, furniture. Concrete. All these are mass nouns. Not pebbles, rocks, or apples.

So feather is a mass noun when it relates to horses, but not when it relates to birds! Feathers with an "s" are something entirely different, and structurally different from hair (which, incidentally, on humans, in English, is also a mass noun – we never say, "I love your hairs," although the French do!)

Why? I dunno. It just is.

ERIC "THE COMEDIAN"

One horse retires, another appears, 19 July 2022

I'm at the stage of retiring Ruby the Magnificent. Her arthritic joints are playing her up despite Bute. Until quite recently she would go out for a drive then gently put the brakes on at a downhill (or uphill if she thinks we'll be turning round and coming back downhill) but the last drive we did, she asked at every gateway and layby if we could turn round and go home. This is no longer the cheerful mare of 18 years ago who got better the further we went. I was very sad for her. So we went home.

Now I've had me little weep, and on Sunday I posted an enquiry among friends on social media, and within a couple of days I have made contact with the owners of a couple of potential understudies for the old star.

One is a Fell pony mare, brown (a 15% chance) and a driver (even rarer), but she has been unsound in the past (over 2 years ago) so I am waiting for a call from the vet who knows her, to see if he thinks she would do my job. Let's hope all goes well. The other is (shhh) a grey Dales...

So now Ruby can just mooch about and enjoy the summer. If she's miserable when winter is coming – then maybe it will be time to say goodbye. But if she's still happy mooching, it won't.

2 August 2022

I have been offered a "gift horse" on loan so I will be able to let Ruby retire gracefully.

I've been quiet-ish for a week, though, because Covid finally caught up with us. I think Graham had it last week, but he was just a bit sleepy and went to bed early one night – after that nothing. I did the commentary at 2 Fell Pony Display Team performances at a country fair on Sunday last, and thought I had an unusually sore throat – but I tested the following morning and there were 2 pink lines on the test so I've been sitting at home all week. Ruby doesn't mind. She is still "going short" and I'm giving her some extra herbal help with approval from vet, but it will only stave off the inevitable, which is that at 27 she has reached honourable retirement.

4 August

I should have gone to see the Ruby-understudy yesterday but I was still testing positive.

The pony is over the other side of the Pennines and he is an 11 year old grey Dales gelding, 14 hands ride and drive, and a former stallion. The first Fell I ever worked with seriously had been a stallion till he was 7 – Sleddale Angus – and he was an arbitrary prince who didn't believe his reproductive capacity had been taken away; but Mr T, whom you'll all remember, was gelded at 5 after a brief stud career, and he was an absolute sweetie, so I am prepared for either character and it is likely not a problem. This boy, well bred and with stock to his name, is known to his chums as Eric. He would be a long term loan, not a sale. He also has an excellent reputation. People who know him are emailing and messaging me saying that I won't be disappointed and that they are big fans of his.

So, I'm trusting I'll be testing negative by Tuesday and will be able to go and see him and maybe long-rein him, and agree terms with his owner if we are both happy.

I wonder how Ruby will feel about a new boyfriend.

She's very chirpy, and sound in the field (but she's only walking – not prancing and doing handstands!) and she walks down the yard fairly freely until the slope steepens, then she takes it carefully. It will be interesting to see how she reacts to the new boy. My stables are in a former cow-byre, two looseboxes separated by a solid gate and solid partition that the ponies can put their heads over. If all goes well next week then on "arrival day" I will have Ruby out in the paddock, unload Eric to the inner loosebox, then bring her in to the outer one and they can chat over the top all night before I even think of turning them out together. (If I did it the other way around with Ruby in the inner box, she knows how to open the door from that side and get into the outer one!)

If Eric is Steady verging on Boring he will do me just fine. But being a Dales I imagine he will have a smart trot!

5 August 2022

The imminent arrival of Ruby's understudy has prompted me to do something I've been thinking about ever since I was first able to use the old cow byre for ponies – make it easier to muck out! Cobbles are all very well, but they are beggars when you're trying to pick out wet patches from wood pellets or sawdust. I've cleaned down, put a layer of old clean bedding over the cobbles to level out the dips and fill up to the humps, then put down a pond liner sheet and gone on bedding with wetted-down pellets from there as if it's a concrete floored stable. It doesn't rustle (that was a worry!) but it's going to be a smoother surface to muck out. And for £35 for enough sheet to do two boxes, I thought it was a cheap experiment compared to poured rubber or concrete!

As it turned out, the sheets were not entirely satisfactory because they rumpled easily and being designed for ponds they didn't stand up to the wear of pony feet, but they allowed me time to settle both ponies in the adjacent boxes and learn their likely dunging patterns.

LATER

After seven weeks I replaced the pond liners with large offcuts of cow-stall rubber matting.

I went to Quattro in Penrith and came home with the farm trailer loaded with offcuts of matting. The biggest, heaviest mat was on the top of the load and I couldn't lift it. Husband had taken a neighbour's sheep to auction and had just come home from fetching same neighbour's medicines from the doctor's surgery. Messages beeped on the answerphone from other people wanting help / advice.

After a couple of hours of heavy physical work, solo, I got two stables half cleared of bedding to put them down on the floor, the cow stall seconds and off cuts jigsawed into the stables and the beds remade.

Can't help thinking though that the two not-very-tech-minded *men* who were concurrently trying to remove the wrong sized SIM card from a wireless modem (in a shed remarkable for its rust, wood dust, sheep-horn shavings and oil) might have offered that job to the *woman* with the Computing Master's degree, and unloaded the cow mats for me. (Life returns to normal, eh.)

The pond liners can be used to protect our winter log pile and keep rain from blowing in on the hay in the open storage shed. We waste nowt here, ye know.

Old and new – Eric, the 11 year old grey Dales, meets Ruby the 27 year old bay Fell.

7 August 2022

Had a cracking day at the Fell Pony Breed Show, building the cone-driving course, judging the Private / exercise show class and timing the cone-driving at the end of the day. A very interesting show class with three single turnouts and a not-very-united team of four Fells – the first time there has been a 4 in hand in the ring there, though we did once have a unicorn turnout of 3, some years ago. No photos though as I was fully occupied 😊 Also Eric's fan club were asking how he's doing!

8 August 2022

There is one thing about adopting a grey pony from a good home – when you're too knackered to hunt for a headcollar and a bucket, you can just walk up to him with a wet sponge to wash off his "green dapples". I don't know if his coat will always be this stain-resistant!

This afternoon I combined Eric and the harness for the first time with the carriage. He was totally unbothered about me fitting stuff and shortening straps on him and adjusting bolts on the carriage. [Note – he is a trained driving horse already – this is not his first-ever trip in the carriage, just his first with my gear and with me driving!] I got in and walked him round the yard a few times, then Graham opened the gate and we proceeded onto the minefield (in Eric's mind) that is an unfamiliar road. There were several stops to stare, but a gentle touch with the whip broke his trance each time and we proceeded peacefully down into Greenholme and up the hill to Whiteham. His trot was quick, cheerful and calm, and he wasn't bothered by a van and farm 'gator behind us on the way back. His main worries were Clumps of Heather That Looked At Him Out Of The Grass, and Pony-Trapping Road Markings – white triangles and give ways, patches of tarmac, even faint blue sprayed instructions, all had to be snorted over and danced around. He'll get used to those, so I just laughed at him and talked him onward.

Then he blotted his copybook mightily. We met two quiet, peaceful cyclists. OMG they were obviously horse eaters! He discovered reverse and put us squarely backwards into the ditch, managing to tuck a rein under *both* shaft tips at the same time – which takes some doing – perhaps he was a knitter in a previous life. Luckily the ditch was just deep enough to prevent him going any further so with a few smacks on the bottom he eventually re-engaged forward gear and pulled us out, and we retreated to the Whiteham road end to let the rather shocked cyclists go by. He is going to have to meet cyclists a lot, because this is a cycle route. Silly chap. We'd had a very successful very short drive up to the bike incident, and if I could have avoided that, I'd have been perfectly content with what we had achieved. I know he has quite a bit of experience under his belt so it's only a case of Dr Time and Dr Miles so we can build our communication system!

Anyone who wants to come here and cycle round the yard will be welcome…

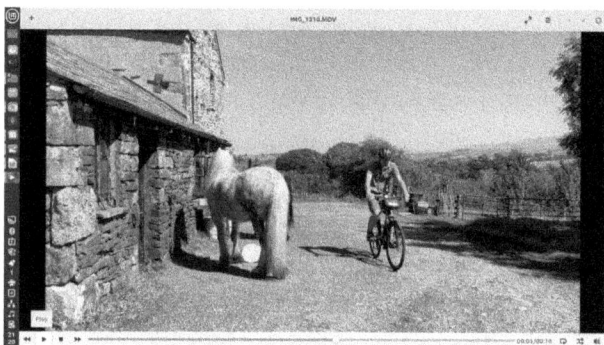

As you can see, Eric is utterly terrified of our neighbour's bike. Not.

10 August 2022

Our neighbour came up this afternoon and cycled round the yard, and Eric could hardly have been less worried. Standing tied, with Ruby, outside the stable; or approaching the stationary bike; walking round it to either hand; eating a carrot off it; having it cycle past him; following it; having it come past him from behind; with or without blinkers – he was completely unbothered. I led him about in his blinker bridle too, in case it was either the blinkers or the bit that had troubled him, but he was fine in that

328

scenario as well as walking round the bike and following and passing it and having it behind him. So what was troubling him the other day may not have been the bikes, though it was the sight of them that started him being silly.

I am going to drive him out again tomorrow with a friend of mine as groom, so if we meet anything she can hop off and walk between him and any scary stuff (there's a big machine parked up by the railway bridge that has potential). Little drives not too far from home will do for now!

11 August 2022

We have done another drive with Eric early this morning before it got hot. We were overtaken in the first hundred yards by three cyclists, of whom he took hardly any notice. (I said, "Go on – chase after them!" Which he did.) He did a couple of "reconnaissance" pauses to take in the topography. I don't mind him building his "mental map" for a minute or two on a drive. He dithered over a few patches of mended tarmac and damp areas of sheep pee, and he only had one tiny meltdown and that was at driving through an allotment field with NO FENCES and NO WALLS to define the road. He wasn't too bothered about the free-range sheep, but free-range grass was another thing entirely. We ask a lot of them, don't we – expecting them to ignore their surroundings, when knowing exactly what is in the vicinity would be literally vital in the wild.

We didn't go as far as any fields where ponies might come down to the roadside fences. Keep it all as positive as possible for these first few outings. He had a bath when he came home because he was very sweaty – his summer coat, like Ruby's, is beginning to shed, so the winter one must be setting.

His "power trot" registered at 19kph on the ride tracker.

11 August 2022

I thought I'd bring the horsies indoors during the hottest part of the afternoon so I wandered out to the field and shouted for them. They lifted their heads, swished their tails and looked at me as though I'd gone mad. It was too hot to argue, so I went back in the house.

By their normal tea-time, Ruby had brought Eric to the gate and they were both whinnying at me while I shared a scoop of feed between their two buckets in the feed room and sprinkled Ruby's joint supplement over her share. I put her bucket in the stable she chose a couple of nights ago, and Eric's in the other; shut the main gates and let them come in. And of course Ruby decided to eat Eric's tea and he decided to eat hers.

I had to lead Ruby into the "correct" stable and get her to tell him to shove off to his own side. Which, after a small hesitation, he did. #maresareboss

The following morning they were each in the other's space. Ruby had even pushed the door shut on him! And he's such a wuss, he hadn't pushed it open again.

I think they've decided now where they are happy (or should I say, Ruby has decided). Both beds are intact and relatively tidy and although she's flipped the bolt-stop she hasn't opened the door to go into the inner stable and push Eric around. It's taken a week.

13 August 2022

Today we made further progress in taking Eric out on our local roads. Jess (whom I've known for more than 10 years, but who's only recently started "grooming") arrived at 9am as passenger with a neighbour, Libby, driving her Fell mare Marnie. I had Eric harnessed and put to, ready to go when they arrived. Graham drove past him with the tractor and he wasn't bothered.

Eric heard Marnie before I could see her, so it was his lifted head that alerted me. I got in the Bennington and drove him round the yard a few times until they joined us. Jess then got up beside me with Eric and we followed Marnie into Greenholme, up the hill and over the railway bridge. It has high stone walls and metal railings that bounce the sound oddly, so that was his first challenge, which with Marnie leading he didn't worry about. Libby led us into the car park of the motorway services, where she handed Marnie to Jess and went in to the butcher's shop to get beef bones for her dogs.

Eric and Marnie stood and waited very beautifully and were admired by various mums and kids, and they didn't bother about the cars passing by on the roadway outside.

When Libby came back Jess rejoined me in the Bennington and we agreed to go a little further so Eric could experience driving over the two road bridges that span the motorway north and southbound carriageways. That also took us past two Fell colts in the field between the carriageways, who were very excited by two ponies-with-wheels passing by. I think Eric would have stopped at that point but he was persuaded into keeping going by Marnie carrying on ahead of him :D He wasn't sure about the crash barriers at either end of the bridges, but he didn't make any difficulty about passing them.

We turned at a biggish gateway a little further on, and trotted under control back over the motorway bridges and past the colts, past the services entrance and some more cyclists and over the railway bridge. We turned into the farm yard, where I suggested that Jess should get back in with Libby and I would follow them down to Dolly bridge, over Bretherdale Beck, and then turn away from them so they could go home southward and I could take Eric north and back to the yard. Which we did, without any problems. Eric fairly stormed back up the hill. I turned him on the layby outside the gate so that he got an easier turn up the slope into the yard – and also, so that he didn't cut the corner or get hooked up on the gate while also on the slope.

Eric was keen but biddable throughout, not pulling my arms out to keep up with the trap ahead. I could steady him back from a full trot to a gentle one and vice versa even if that meant Marnie got twenty yards ahead. He didn't fuss over following Marnie, or try to "sit in the boot" of the trap, or object to standing for ten minutes on the car park. He was just the gentleman I had been told he was, and listening both to bit and voice. I have him in a mullen-mouth Kimblewick, without the curb chain, the hooks secured close to the bit rings with plaiting bands. It was enough bit for control without the curb.

It's very hot today, even so early, so he needed a wash when I unharnessed. He doesn't mind being washed although for some reason he was surprised by having his muzzle sponged.

I am going to measure his neck again this afternoon and possibly buy a secondhand full collar for him tomorrow.

15 August

Eric did a good 4 miles today. I had him in harness waiting for Marnie, Libby and Jess to arrive. They were delayed, because I had asked Libby if she knew of anyone who had a 21 or 22 inch collar I could try on Eric, and as she had two to sell she had spent some time devising a way to carry one of each on the little exercise cart!

While I waited, I put to and drove him down to the next door farm – twice – and down the road towards the village, and round our yard, and over the ash heap that looks like the salt heaps he puffs about on our roadside, and practising neat turns to left and right with my usual voice commands, and standing quietly and waiting, and occasionally doing a controlled reverse. He knows how to do all these things but, as I explained to our bemused holiday-cottage visitors, he's on L-plates – he needs to practise listening to *my* voice instead of the ones in his head. So that was a good half hour of "little things" to be going on with until Marnie arrived.

Libby unloaded the collars into my feed room. She had tied them in pillowcases inside shopping bags, to the back of the seat rail. Jess came to sit beside me on the Bennington. We went down into the village, past a working concrete mixer, and up over Whiteham where he'd had the bike meltdown on Sunday. Then down to Beckside where we trotted alongside Birk Beck and followed the river to Scout Green. It's a narrow one-track road. Eric was very cheerful, enjoying a big steady trot behind Marnie but listening to my voice and hands, happily holding back down the steep drop to the beck, keeping back from Marnie's trap when I asked him to, powering on after her when I let him extend.

Coming back, I made him wait at Beckside to allow Marnie to tackle that steep bank uphill on her own. I knew she'd been working hard the day before so I suspected she'd fall back from trot to walk halfway up, and if Eric was in full flight pulling two of us he would catch her up but have no room to pass her and that wouldn't be fair on him. He waited without fussing, and when she'd completed the uphill (yes, the second half in walk) I set him off and he did it all in trot.

When we reached Greenholme I asked Libby to let Eric lead for the last 200 yards back to the yard, and after a wobble or two he complied.

After Marnie had gone, I washed Eric off and tried the two collars on him. He sometimes resists the collar being turned (not surprising when the collars I have are a bit small!), so the Polo mint trick came into play – once the collar is ready to turn I offer a mint at his shoulder level, his head comes down for it and his throat relaxes, and I swing the collar over. I'll add a word to cue the relaxation.

The 21 inch wouldn't go down to his shoulders, but the 22 did. It's possibly a touch snug at the top, but he's in high condition and he's going to lose a bit as he gets fitter. I think if I work him in it – perhaps after soaking the top half and stretching it – it will settle to his neck. My hames fit it at the draft point but leave a little room at the top so that may allow the collar to widen. I'll work him in it tomorrow and see how things go.

Ruby greeted Eric's return with pleasure – she's decided today to come into season, so she's feeling gentler than usual and later out in the field he got away with nipping her neck and mutual grooming, oo-er!

16 August

Today it's cooler and Jess arrived in good time while I was harnessing up. The collar went on easily and we drove 2 and a half miles along yesterday's route with Eric solo. He was really listening well and managed to skirt the salt heaps with only a slight huff and swerve! He did ask if we were going to turn round at points where I had done so yesterday but accepted my Keep Walking with equanimity. Most of the drive was a discussion with Jess about harness parts and purposes (she will never look at coaching scene Christmas cards in quite the same way!) Eric was very happy with his collar. I know he has worn one before, and the mint trick worked well to get it turned on and off. He powered up Beckside bank without a hesitation and did most of his work in trot (always confidence-giving). When we got back, there was a perfect oval of sweat on both sides of his neck with just a hands-breadth dry at his throat so I think the collar will work well for him. I washed him off when we got home and will put a hand on his neck tonight to find any warm patches that might show uneven pressure. Out in the field Ruby initiated a long scratching session, both of them spitting out loose hair!

The Bennington is sensitive to driver/passenger position and has tended to go shaft-light at trot and of course uphill. I lowered one tug by one hole on the backband today, and that combined with the change to the full collar and the traces being one hole longer seems to have helped to make the balance less reactive (plus Jess being more aware of how to shift her weight!)

17 August

Eric's a people pony, no doubt about it. He hangs round the wagon-shed where Graham does his maintenance of tools and mends neighbours' machines, and when people call to see how the mending is going, he stands there as if he's taking part in the gossip. This morning as we have nobody in the holiday cottage, the ponies are on yard-grazing duty (the handmaid here got the job of tidying their stables and adding fresh bedding). Eric is roaming about now looking for mischief, pushing the stack of empty buckets about, cantering circles round the muck-heap, digging holes then deciding not to roll in them, poking his nose into the wagon-shed – but no gossip in there today so he didn't go in – then cantering up and down the yard, jumping over the dog's tether rope and periodically giving a sideways kick to tell a tree to get out of his way (he hits it too). Ruby is still in season so she is still feeling gentle!

I was planning to recuperate today after a tiring week (Centenary Ball, stewarding Fell pony exhibition, talk about my Fell Pony Centenary book *A Century of Fells*, and so on!) but I think I'm going to have to yoke him up and make use of some of that energy. Also, I think I will tell Graham that he's not to give EACH pony a full scoop of coarse mix in an evening... one between the two would be plenty to encourage them to come indoors for the night. When I feed them, Ruby gets enough to disguise her joint supplements or Bute, and Eric gets a mouthful or two just to think he's also had something.

Eric definitely felt he could use all his power properly in the full collar yesterday and he trotted everywhere, uphill and downhill, very happily. As I remarked to Jess while we jogged circumspectly *down* the bank at Beckside, this is what Ruby can no longer do: she will walk down it but she will tell me a hundred yards beforehand that she doesn't want to because it will be painful. Eric's younger legs make nothing of it.

18 August

It's been very dry, but not for so long up here in the north as in the south of England where there have been a lot of wildfires. It was extremely hot (for us!) last week. We have had heavy showers here in the past couple of days that have freshened everything up.

I took Eric out for 40 minutes at lunchtime, just a mile out and back.

He has been taught to stand with his feet rooted while he is put-to, so my requests for him to do a turn on the forehand, ie to move his hind feet to bring his quarters into line with the carriage, are foreign to him, but I think the penny dropped today. He was a very cheerful camper, trotting willingly all the way from the village up to the moor gate on Whiteham, where I gave him a chance to absorb the view while he caught his breath. Then we walked back, being overtaken by a couple of neighbours in pickups, and a cyclist who spoke, so we knew he was there. Eric wanted to chase the bike up the brow to the house, but I knew he'd overtake it much too soon so again, like the other day at Beckside, I made him stand and wait until I told him, and then he chased after it in good style. The tracker app said he did 21kph, but I take its speeds with a pinch of salt as if it has to change satellite it has been known to show me travelling in a straight line to and from a location two miles away within a few seconds but at zero mph!

Something I may do now that Eric is here is to try putting the Bennington back to its original configuration with the swingletree at the footboard. It was always heavy-on with Ruby and the axle draught helped to solve that, but with Eric it is light, despite the two ponies being the same height. It's easy enough to do and to replace, so I will try it.

Having Jess sitting up next to me has obviously affected how the carriage balances. We have the seat as far forward as we can but it goes shaft-light very easily. Of course I had previously moved the body back on the axle to get the balance right for Ruby when I drove alone, so that is another thing I can try changing back to its original position. I can always move the carriage body forward again on the axle to change the balance, then when I haven't got a passenger I can strap added weights, such as gym ankle weights, around the picnic basket to counteract any tendency to be too shaft heavy. Eric can cope with that. One thing at a time though.

Eric and I drove only a few hundred yards today but we've each learned a little more.

I thought the hames looked a bit loose at the top of the collar so I tightened them, but he began shaking his head, so I slackened them off again and he stopped.

Yesterday I had explained to Eric that he had to turn his quarters round to let me put the carriage on. He took a bit of persuading but he did it. Today he was again standing at 180 degrees to where he needed to be so I thought, I'll just walk the carriage past him and put it on him there. And he saw it and at once put himself in the right place. So I had to walk the carriage back to my usual starting point – chuckling at him and telling him he was in fact a good boy. He's a quick study, as they say.

We were not expecting Libby or Jess to join us this morning so after the normal "new-horse-wait-until-told-to-move" pause once I'd mounted the carriage, I decided to drive him straight out of the yard. This confused him because he didn't know we were not waiting for them, and he expected to do several turns up and down the yard before leaving!

So we tippytoed down the slope to the road and walked towards Greenholme, only to come to a halt on seeing two riders approaching – one on a black Fell and one on a taller chestnut. And as a result of the halt, I noticed that the right hand shaft of the carriage had yet again rotated inwards in its socket, which meant that my suspicions about the threads of the bolt last night were correct and the socket wasn't holding properly. So, with the excuse of politeness to the ridden horses, I turned Eric round and brought him back to the yard, swearing quietly to myself but telling him he was being good, because he was.

I took him out of the carriage and got Graham to use his wagon bar socket to unfasten the dodgy bolt and replace it (yes, I had a spare one in the spares basket and I'm going to stock up with another packet of them!).

Eric found it upsetting to be abandoned for engineering work without explanation, but I thought it was better to stop for the day before anything structural misbehaved and upset us both even more.

I put him out in the field and he and Ruby had a canter about before settling to graze.

Despite the short drive today, we have reached 77 miles on the FPS 100 miles challenge.

19 August

I am shattered. I've had far too many FPS Centenary activities and responsibilities this month, and taking on a new pony is not so much the icing on the cake as the final load on the barrow. I've mucked out, deloused Ruby because the heel-mites are making her itch, put Eric's collar on (with a mint) and off (without) to remind him of dropping his head while we do it, and turned them out.

I've dusted off the big 56 pound weight I used to use to balance the Quayside carriage. Hmm. I've found a possible location to put it on the Bennington if I return it to its original balance, but I'm not sure yet how I'll hold such a big weight in place when travelling. And I've also found I'm not up to lifting it with one hand any more! So I'm going to look at prices for gym weights, the kind containing iron sand, that you can strap on your ankles. I could strap them around the picnic basket and even put one flat on the floor inside it. They will distribute the weight more widely and be easier and safer to use, both on the carriage and when taking them off when I have a passenger. The added weight will be less than that of a passenger, and I don't think Eric will be that bothered. Maintaining a light weight was only a consideration for Ruby because her joints have aged.

It's mid-day now and although I haven't worked a pony today I'm seriously considering going back to bed!

Post script: I sat down in the recliner at 1pm and woke at 4:30! An afternoon snooze was obviously very much needed.

20 August 2022

Too windy today to consider driving Eric, so as #2 sprog had arrived with his motorbike we checked that Eric is not worried about them – because we have not so far met any while on the road. He isn't.

I washed off the green dapples yet again, and remade his bed, because he'd managed to drag the waterproof sheeting halfway across the box (I thought it was too good to be true that we've had almost a week of static bedding!)

Ruby whinnied at him when I put him in the field, and when I turned her out she beetled off after him at a canter. Stiff legged, but a canter none the less. There is life in the old bird yet.

23 August 2022

With Eric in Go Forward mode, the Bennington now rides quite light-on, so today Graham and I moved the body forward again to its original position with the central bolt of the spring directly above the axle. I had ordered two sets of velcro-on "ankle weights" totalling 20kg. Yesterday I fitted them on the carriage, packing them in or round the spares basket to replace the weight of a passenger. They probably more than equal it, because the weights are mainly behind the line of the axle. Three packs were easy, so the fourth is in the tack room as a spare, and that 15kg was in fact plenty today. I must remember to take them off again when a live body comes to play!

I took Eric for a quiet walk round the yard to assess the balance of the adjusted carriage-plus-weights. That was just as well, because as we were going up the yard I saw that one of the quick-releases had come undone and we were working on just one trace. I probably hadn't quite clicked the shackle shut while putting-to. I was able to quietly take Eric back to the level standing outside the stable, hop off and re-fix the trace. The beauty of the full neck collar... with a breast collar, going up the slope, I'd probably have had a shaft drop out of its tug as his distance from the carriage got longer.

Anyway, doing a circuit or two was good for Eric's patience. I turned him south towards Roundthwaite, and he immediately spotted a neighbour's cattle wagon coming back from Bretherdale, so I put him on the grass verge and asked him to "Stand and wait". He was very brave... it's a single track road so the wagon had to pass quite close, and his body rocked from side to side but his big feet were planted and didn't move until the wagon had passed (very politely and slowly) and I told him to walk on. In fact we had a nice trot just to get rid of the adrenalin. I drove him up the big hill, Pikestoll, past lots of Scary Salt Heaps and Plants That Looked At Him and Patches of New Tarmac;

took him further along a section of road he hasn't driven before and turned at a gateway we haven't previously reached.

Returning homeward, I turned him up the Bretherdale road and trotted him over more patches of tarmac. He dodged them all like a pea on a skateboard, then trotted cheerfully up to the cattle grid gate, where we turned for home and adjusted the balance of the carriage by shifting the seat back a little (sometimes the seat lever sticks, so I have to try it at different times until I find it's unstuck itself). He trotted beautifully along the level to the river and up to home, and I took him on past our gateway for a hundred yards before I turned, just to make sure he doesn't get the idea that arriving home always means "rush in".

Ruby whinnied at him as if he'd been away all day, and they are now enjoying the pasture together. She goes out at a trot; unsound, but happy. Eric, today, dived into the grass without even waiting for his headcollar to come off: "I'm a Working Man and you didn't give me enough breakfast!"

24 August 2022

A drizzly morning, but not too windy, so after Ruby and Eric had had their breakfast and some haylage, I brought Eric out for a spin up the road. Everything fits "just lovely" - neck collar, traces, breeching, carriage balance. Eric had even failed to find a poo patch to sleep in so he only needed a brief brush over before we were fit to travel.

No tootling round the yard this morning, though Eric expected it. I drove him steadily out of the yard, answering his "Which way are we going?" with "Straight on!" Down into Greenholme, round the turn to Bridge End farm, then at a trot up the hill to the railway bridge. He was still peeping at salt heaps and changes of road colour but he was much braver trotting than walking. I paused at the bridge to let our neighbour Chris go past in the farm 4x4 truck, followed by a chap with a van towing a cattle trailer – best not to get squeezed with them between the walls.

Eric was in "Let's get to market" mode and once in trot was happy to stay there. Past the motorway service entrance, over both motorway bridges – with a tucking-in of skirts as he passed the crash barriers at either end – and past the other service entrance. We went further than he has been before, past Selsmire (no event horses expressing curiosity today) and the electricity substation, and the long dark line of beech trees overarching the road. The driver of an oncoming tractor with a heavily loaded silage trailer sensibly stopped and turned off the engine, and a line of vans following waited too, while Eric paraded past, his knees and head up and his white mane flowing. There's one thing about a grey pony – you don't need much in the way of high visibility accoutrements when you're flying a two-foot-long white mane! We also stopped to chat to a neighbour in her car, and Eric was very patient and sensible until another car came along and we trotted on.

I normally "breathe" a pony when we reach the layby at the guidepost outside Orton, but Eric was having none of it. He stood there when I told him to, but he was impatient to be going, with his body swaying first one way, then the other, although his feet didn't move. So I turned him round and set off, and he went into "Let's get to market" mode again and trotted cheerfully homeward.

We met the tractor again, trailer empty, and again it stopped and he trotted past. Not pulling, not slacking, not shying, just working. Back over the motorway bridges, wagons going under him, not a foot out of place. (Salt heaps and storm drains, mind you, he was back to being a pea on a skateboard.) Over the railway bridge, heading downhill, still trotting.

I saw the van and trailer on its way back up the hill so I put Eric onto a gateway to let it go by. The driver drew up and asked, "Is it a Fell pony?" I said No, he was in fact a Dales. "A GREY Dales? Wow!" So we talked about him being grey, and not very big, and SO like a Fell pony, and Eric stood prettily and caught his breath while he waited for us to finish assessing him. (His pedigree goes back, as you'd expect, to Grey Bobbie, and so to Park End King, Scoredale Queen and Teasdale Comet.)

We trotted on down the hill, Eric listening obediently when I told him to go steady down the sharp drop to the beck, and happy to walk home the last few hundred yards up the hill to the farm gate.

What a worker I have in the shafts.

Ruby welcomed him with a whinny. Graham came over to see how he was doing and keep the dog from tangling his tether rope round him. When I turned both ponies out into the field Ruby went off with Eric at a canter. Still stiff and unlevel, but obviously very happy in her retirement.

27 August 2022

I changed the routine today. The ponies had two days off. I had been to watch the driving classes at Crosby Show (one of which I sponsor, so I get a free ticket), and to a planning meeting with two of the FPS Display Team ladies in preparation for our invitation parade at Burghley Horse Trials on 4th September; and next day I spent all day at the FPS exhibition in Shap, helping with an oral history project where we asked Fell pony breeders to talk to us about their experience of running herds on the common land on the open hill. So Eric and Ruby have been stuffing their faces with old grass and doing nothing.

I spent this morning checking the script for the FPS Display Team's performances at Black Combe Country Fair (Bank holiday Monday), and when I was happy with that and a few other bits and pieces I went out into the yard and saw Eric ambling up to the gate to meet me. So I caught him and cleaned him (though I haven't tackled his yellow tail other than brushing the shit out of it), put the harness on and put to. Eric rather wanted to follow Graham who was going by with tools to hang a gate on the new post he's put in, so I asked Graham to stand with the lad while I got into the carriage, then we set off. Ruby whinnied pathetically on seeing her pal going without her, but on the whole the grass had a stronger pull!

We trotted up Pikestoll, the big hill to the south, and turned in at the lane to The Dyke. There are Fell mares and a stallion in one of their fields but I couldn't see them and Eric was unconcerned so I assumed they were in one of the higher pastures.

Eric was more bothered about the concrete lane where there was grass growing in the junctions between the sections and he wasn't sure he could walk over it! He also dithered a bit at the storm gully that crosses the lane at the yard gate, but he hopped over it eventually and without too much coercion needed. I chatted to Felicity and Ruth in the yard for about half an hour and Eric dipped first one hind leg then the other and pretty much went to sleep except when he saw an express going up the railway line in the distance.

When we set off home he managed the storm gully much more confidently. At the top of the lane he was interested in, but not in the least upset by, the Fell stallion who came trotting along the fence line to pay his respects and if necessary warn us off. I told Eric to keep going, at a walk, and he did, with absolutely no drama – more or less implying that he'd eaten bigger boys than that, and he wasn't impressed. The stallion gave up after fifty yards and went to harass one of the mares, who kicked out and screamed at him to piss off, and the last I saw of him he was grooming with her foal. Eric got 100% for good manners there.

We trundled quietly back down the hill, and a car coming up kindly reversed to a gateway to let us go by. Ruby whinnied at Eric as he came storming up the bank to the house, but he didn't reply and he went up the yard to my taking-out position and waited to be released from his work. I brushed him off and turned him out and he had a good roll in the grass with Ruby steadily munching next to him.

A nice, quiet, educational couple of miles. As they say up here when approving something, "He'll do."

31 August 2022

Eric was fizzy this morning when I harnessed up. He was quiet for me to put to, but began tramping backwards and forwards once the carriage was on.

I let him stew for five minutes then went to the other side of the carriage and he stood quietly for me to get in. He then stood waiting – but with every muscle trembling. I wonder if the grass has had a spurt of growth and he's full of sugars. Might add some magnesium to his feed - and make sure he goes in the right stable tonight, as he and Ruby had done a bed-swap yesterday when Graham brought them in.

I left Ruby in the "inside" stable when we went out, but I forgot to shut the outer door and by the time Graham came up from the fields with the tractor, she had let herself out and was grazing on the roadside!

I had thought of taking Eric into Orton village for the first time, but he was in full-on "peeping" mode at the salt heaps and drains, although perfectly steady with the vans and road bikes and cars that we met. The only thing he scuttled at was some fat lambs running away from him across a field. I had him in trot most of the time, gave him a few breathers at walk, and decided that instead of the village we'd go partway "round the block" to Sproat Ghyll farm, turn at the cattle grid there and come back. He has done most of this distance before and it's relatively quiet for working off tickles in the toes. He liked Moor House, which he considered was a Proper Farm With Dairy Cows, and asked if he should turn in there. He was also perfectly happy to have one quad bike come at him from behind while another came at him from in front, because those were Proper Farm Traffic. However, the same farm's heaps of stone / rubble / usewood / felled timber along the roadside to Sproat Ghyll made him swerve to the opposite verge, so instead of continuing through the cattle grid gate to Scout Green I turned him round and made him see the heaps with the other eye and then trot homeward. Which he did with his usual gusto, achieving a "personal best" from the guidepost to Birk Beck of 12 and a half minutes (about 17.5kph), an average moving speed of 9kph, and clocking up 10km overall distance, his longest drive yet with me.

I'm trying to establish a gentle reminder to him to stay on the left of the road. Some horses you can "pull" over with the rein but he is capable of bending his neck and swerving anyway so I need the equivalent of a strong right leg. Gentle tapping with the whip on his flank is working, to which I'm adding a voice command.

I hope that he can overcome this urge to swerve as he becomes more familiar with our locality. I was strongly reminded today of Tom Roberts' anecdote about a cavalry horse he rode in India, who took great exception to a series of carts draped in colourful blankets that parked every day on one side of a place where he rode out. Tom let him have a loose rein and no leg aids and he used the whole width of the parade ground to avoid them. But day by day, having experienced no coercion from Tom but having passed the carts successfully each time, he made smaller and smaller swerves until eventually he walked straight past them.

I'm trusting that Eric will do the same with his salt heap aversion!

I washed the sweat off him (although quite a bit of him is still tinted green) and let him out into the field with Ruby, who came up and nibbled his neck. Then he had a good roll (and came up with green withers to add to the rest) and they are now grazing quietly together.

1 September 2022

I have been counting the miles I do with the ponies this year for the Fell Pony Society's Centenary "100 miles Challenge" – leading, riding or driving your pony. Ruby's tally crept up extremely slowly, because we often only did a couple of miles once or twice a week. Having Eric here, though, has bumped up the miles very quickly because he can cover so much more ground in each trip out. Although he's a Dales, the principle of the entrant literally buying the T shirt and so advertising the Fell breed has been extremely popular and it has been interpreted fairly generously. There are several people taking part with their children on Welsh or other small breeds – so I reason that Eric the "Fell cousin" is allowed to take part on Ruby's behalf.

Yesterday's drive with Eric took us to 99.6 miles!

This morning I gave Ruby the chance to celebrate reaching the milestone. There wasn't much to adjust on the harness other than to swap out the wide show saddle for the exercise model, adjust the racing-cup blinkered bridle back to Ruby's broader head, and lengthen the breeching straps by two holes. She dozed while I harnessed her up, but moved over easily to be put-to, and left the yard at a good walk. We went up Bretherdale for a short way, knowing that we only needed to do half a mile, so almost any distance with her would be good. She wasn't lame at walk, striding along with her ears pricked, and was happy to trot a little though only in brief bursts. I put the whip in its socket, pulled off my right glove, and took some photographs and video with my phone (not something I can spare a hand for with Eric yet!). When we got back I turned her out into the field.

Eric, who was still in the stable, was pulling horrible faces at being left, so I turned him out too, and came back indoors to work.

2 September 2022

Eric went out this afternoon modelling a pair of closed blinkers (from a bridle I borrowed back, which I used to own). We teetered down into Greenholme with Eric still peeping at changes in tarmac colour and road verge salt heaps. According to him, people were deliberately hiding behind shrubs (pruning) and walls (coming out of a farm yard), and when a big Maine Coon cat emerged from bushes, stared at him and melted back again he definitely felt he was being ganged up on.

On the other hand, we also stood and talked to two neighbours – one of whom had lent me the bridle – and he sociably went into My Driver Is Chatting mode; but when a dog materialised in the same time and place as a lawnmower starting up, he managed to leap sideways from a standstill at quite remarkable speed.

He trotted most of the way home and mostly straight. I'm not sure, though, that the closed blinker bridle improved his handling. The bridle is a lovely one and I will probably buy it back for its sentimental value to me, fondly remembering all the ponies who have worn it since it was made in the 1970s (and yes, I knew them all, including Mr T) and to reunite it with the old show set (the driving saddle that Eric wears and the collar that Ruby wears); but its blinkers sit VERY close to Eric's eyelashes, and I also think if he'd been wearing the half-cup racing blinkers today he would have seen and understood the sudden dog to be separate from the sudden lawnmower!

No work for a couple of days now as I and the Fell Pony Society Display Team are travelling south to do a fifteen minute parade, by invitation, in the Main Arena at Burghley International Horse Trials.

Eric and Ruby will be looking after Graham for 36 hours... hehe

10 September 2022

I had a very busy two weeks with the Fell Pony Society Display Team, during which we attended the Lakeland Country Fair, Black Combe Country Fair, Burghley International Horse Trials, and Westmorland County Show. Since May we had also performed at the FPS Stallion Show, Countryfest and Coniston Country Fair. It has been worthwhile, but my, it was exhausting.

This year our displays have laid heavy emphasis on the Society's Centenary, the Queen's Platinum Jubilee (70 years) and her 40 years of Patronage of the Society.

And then, on Friday afternoon, came the sad news that the Queen had died. It brought a sudden burst of work for me on Saturday, to update the society's web site and social media presence and to help deal with media approaches of various kinds: requests for interviews with people within the Fell Pony Society to pay tribute to the late Queen and her patronage of the Society: BBC Look North, BBC radio 4, BBC radio Cumbria, BBC Five Live, GB News, Sky, the local newspaper... then more requests for stories from anyone in the Society who had previously worked with the new King Charles III.

I didn't have time to go and catch Eric till mid afternoon. He came up to the field gate at my call, and Ruby trundled into the yard with him, but she went out again happily once I had tied him by the tackroom door.

Eric conveyed me cheerfully to a neighbour's farm to return the bridle and bits I had borrowed, and pay for the one I am keeping. I have put the racing half-cup blinkers back on him, with the prettily stitched noseband off T's show bridle. He's getting used to our routes now and he only peeped at one or two salt heaps today.

The visit to our neighbour was doubly sad, not only because of the death of Queen Elizabeth, but because Bracken, her Shetland driving pony for whom I had made the little bridle that I was returning, had also died. Bracken was over 30 – about 90 in human terms. Another little queen gone.

Eric waited patiently for me, tied to the yard gate, while I expressed condolences. Our neighbour, her son and daughter in law and I all hoped that the new King would continue to supply some stability behind our bonkers political system, of which we all despair.

Eric, though, went home at a cracking trot. He did one massive sideways leap when a bird flew up out of the long grass on Whiteham but that was excusable, I think. He is proving to be "a thoroughly decent chap" and Ruby greeted him with a whinny on our return.

I washed the sweat off him and turned him back out and he immediately had a roll, getting up with a green stripe of sheep muck all down one flank. Then the pair of them returned to grazing – happily unaware that we are seeing the end of the New Elizabethan era.

17th September 2022

Eric and I had That Argument this afternoon. Not quite the toddler supermarket meltdown, but the native pony equivalent in which the human asks the pony to do something it has done before, and the pony thinks about it, understands, and says, "Shan't."

I had set off with him to go over Pikey to Roundthwaite, to get him hot enough to need a bath on his return. At the top of the hill I thought I'd call in at The Dyke to see if Felicity was at home; thinking, Eric had previously dithered over the grassy junctions between concrete sections of the farm lane so it would be good practice for him to trot down there ready for the patches of tarmac in Orton tomorrow.

All went well down the lane, steady trotting with a bit of peeping but he went over all the junctions OK. Then we got to the yard gate where there is a long narrow metal drain cover that runs across the lane. Eric saw it and dithered.

Me: Walk on, Eric.

Him: No.

Me: Walk on, Eric.

Him: No. (Plants his feet.)

Me: Walk on, Eric. You've done this before.

Him: I know that. Shan't.

Me: Come on, it's not scary.

Him: I know it isn't. Shan't. (Tries to turn round. I stop him and put him back at the gateway.)

We continue in this vein, with variations in which I imitate a male driver's voice, and tap him irritatingly with the whip, and he does his Bendy Wendy act to try to get the reins around the shaft ends. When he gets too close to the gate itself I back him away (uphill) and walk him forward into place again and again he says, "Shan't."

And repeat.

I had my ride tracker app going and according to that we argued for 35 minutes before he finally consented to walk over the drain. After that he had to walk back onto the lane over it, and repeat twice more until he did it without hesitating. Then we went back to the public road, did half a mile, turned around and came back to walk over the drain again.

Give him his due, he's been here six weeks and this is the only time we've had a serious disagreement - he's done well to have gone so long without it, and he never offered to back or to kick as resistance. Still I'm glad we had the argument today and not tomorrow in Orton!

He got washed off and treated with detangler to try and keep him clean for tomorrow. He's out in the field in a waterproof rug now to try and prevent sheep poo stains, and he and Ruby are both very curious about it, as it's hers and smells of her!

18th September 2022

Fell ponies have been gathering today to say goodbye to the late Queen ahead of the funeral tomorrow. 10 Fells, including two mares and foals, came to a meet at Orton with 17 others of many breeds including Eric, the Dales, flying our flag as an "honorary Fell". 9 Fells including Marnie were at the memorial service at Tebay, plus other breeds including a Highland. Over 100 Fells in total throughout the country. All hectically organised in the last 3 days.

Eric was SO good today. He was very happy to go along with the other horses and ponies we met on the way to the memorial at Orton. We only had one eejit car driver go by unreasonably fast and Ian Pearson (who was just behind me and Eric at the time) gave it a superb mouthful of invective. I don't tend to need this reaction: Eric and his mane make a huge "silver unicorn" presence on the road, and I always have bike lamps on the carriage, so we get seen a long way off and if Eric does his dithering act the traffic anchors up fairly smartly! In Orton he stood quietly (if nosily, and constantly peering back at me either to right or left) while I spoke a tribute to the Queen and we had our minute's silence. Perfect timing by the way - two minutes of tribute and the silence began a few seconds before the church clock struck three. Good theatre! I was too focused on speaking and timing to be much moved - but will probably have a bit sniffle if I take Ruby for a quieter drive or watch the funeral tomorrow. But today everything went well - all my black/purple/red ribbons stayed in place, the harness was perfectly fitted, the carefully weighted carriage rode well, all my black clothing/shoes/helmet fitted and worked as intended and the new pair of gloves (leather, RAF surplus, officers for the use of) were comfortable, and loose enough to take off easily to use my phone to read the tribute...a big point!

On the way home Eric walked out beautifully, and when we'd parted from all the other horses he trotted home like a good 'un.

At one point there was a big black pickup sitting respectfully behind us - I wondered if it was clocking Eric's speed, to be honest, as it could have overtaken us - and when the pickup finally came up alongside Eric spotted it, decided to race, and went up yet another gear. He did a very good day's work today - considering that he has only been into the village once - when he wasn't turning his head to look at me OR sticking his tongue out. A lady helpfully told me he had his tongue over the bit... he hadn't, he just does it when he's thinking. With or without a bit. I daresay this is the first of many such observations I will hear because of this comedy habit.

The Orton memorial was on BBC Look North at 5.30pm, and ITV Border news at 6.20pm that night; Eric didn't feature in those but he was on screen during a longer ITN feature at 8.20pm on the night of the Royal funeral. I have been promised copies of the BBC "rushes" - footage that didn't make the screen - so I hope to see him on those too. All that aside, I think our meeting of so many British breeds, and their respectful silence, paid the late Queen a tribute she would have appreciated.

Drive straight, smile and trot on.

--~~~ ooo0O0ooo~~~--

Also by Sue Millard

AGAINST THE ODDS

Leaving home to work in a racing stable, Sian finds that the long hours and hard work are more than she bargained for. The only compensation is her responsibility for her favourite filly, Double Jump.

Sian is badly treated by her boyfriend, the trainer's arrogant son, Justin. When Double Jump's owner moves the filly to another yard, Sian follows so she can escape him.

At the new yard she meets stable jockey Madoc Owen, who is battling to make a National Hunt winner out of Cymru, a bored flat-race stallion. Sian and Madoc may have a future together but there will be more than steeplechase fences in their way – Justin will see to that.

GENRE: Fiction, romance, sporting, equestrian
First Published by J A Allen, 1995. ISBN 978-0-8513163-0-1
(now Remaindered - only available direct from author.) £5.00 + Postage.

2nd Edition 2018, ISBN-10: 1720047286, ISBN-13: 978-1720047285, £10.00 + Postage.

Kindle edition https://www.amazon.co.uk/dp/B00BGBIGNU

SCRATCH

Sequel to Against the Odds

A Woman. A Family. A Farm.

Sian and Madoc have borrowed heavily to buy a neglected farm, Stone Side, in the beautiful countryside of east Cumbria. They are land-rich now but short of cash and indebted not only to the bank but to members of their family.

Racehorses and Fell Ponies

In this sequel to <u>Against the Odds</u> Madoc has reluctantly had to give up his ambition to breed thoroughbreds, and instead runs the sheep farm and pre-trains young horses for National Hunt racing. Sian is a fierce mother of their three teenage children, Robbie, Cerys and Jack. In what free time she has, she buys and trains Fell ponies.

Someone is Out to Destroy Them

When Madoc's brother calls-in a big loan, the tensions begin to mount… and on the wild fellside, for someone the stakes are as high as murder.

GENRE: Fiction, family saga / thriller, sporting, equestrian

Paperback publication date: 18 September 2018. ISBN 9780957361294

£12.00 if purchased direct, plus postage.

£ 12.99 from bookshops

Kindle edition https://www.amazon.co.uk/dp/B07J6PWCS5

HOOFPRINTS IN EDEN

Winner of the Saint and Company Prize at the Lake District Book of the Year Awards, 20 June 2006. Based on a 2-year-long series of interviews with established breeders, this book explores the Fell pony breed and its traditions at the start of the new millennium.

Read about the Fell pony's Cumbrian background, the events of a typical year, its life on the fell, its traditional keeping and its links with hill farming, its characteristics and the work it can do.

Fully illustrated, and complete with a dictionary of Cumbrian farming expressions.

GENRE: Non-fiction, equestrian, history, farm & working animals

Published by Hayloft, 2005. ISBN 978-1-9045243-4-2 (available direct from author.) £17.00 plus postage.

Second edition, paperback, Jackdaw E Books.

ISBN 978-1-731565969. £12 plus postage.
www.jackdawebooks.co.uk/hoofprints.htm

Kindle edition https://www.amazon.co.uk/dp/B07KPLQ9RG

A CENTURY OF FELLS

Produced for the Centenary of the Fell Pony Society in 2022, A Century of Fells follows Hoofprints in Eden. It celebrates the 100th year of the FPS, with sequenced photographs of many families of ponies recorded in the Stud Book through the years. It also prompts consideration of how the breed may develop in the next century.

GENRE: Non-fiction, equestrian, history, farm & working animals

ISBN 978-1-913-106171. £20 plus postage

Hardback, www.jackdawebooks.co.uk/century.htm

ONE FELL SWOOP

This is where it all started, with humour, history and horses.

Norman Thelwell was Sue's hero (they both hailed from the Wirral) so when Sue moved to Cumbria and bought a Fell pony this "fellwell" book was the inevitable result.

A series of affectionate cartoons, poking gentle fun at the Fell breed and its history.

GENRE: Cartoon humour, farm & working animals.

ISBN 978-0-9573612-7-0 (Paperback) £5.00 plus postage

Kindle edition https://www.amazon.co.uk/dp/B008ZBPB14

THE FORTHRIGHT SAGA

Nothing ever happens in a small country town ... does it?

Nora Forthright and her grandson Wayne stumble through the fictional Cumbrian towns of Dangleby and Pullet St Mary, putting things right entirely by accident.

GENRE: Comedy thriller / cosy crime.

Published: 2012.

ISBN: 978-0-9573612-3-2

£5.00 plus postage

Kindle Edition https://www.amazon.co.uk/dp/B0099RQNLU

FOR CHILDREN
DRAGON BAIT

Princess Andra volunteers to act as bait for the dragon ravaging her father's lands, on condition that she is released from an arrangement to marry a foreign prince.

Unfortunately the Knight Rescuer who turns up is not the trusty old retainer she expects, but an unknown conservationist who wants the dragon, not the lady. After that very little goes according to plan.

GENRE: Comic fantasy (age 9-12). Published: 2012; 2nd edition 2021.

ISBN : 978-1-913106-15-7

Kindle   edition:
https://www.amazon.co.uk/dp/B008K8SDWG

STRING OF HORSES

Fourteen-year-old Claire Armstrong's Mum and Dad run a country pub in the Lake District. Pony trekking is part of its attractions, and Claire's love of the ponies teaches her a great deal about herself. But it's the humans in the pub who cause her the most heartache.

A coming-of-age novel set in the 1970s.

GENRE: Coming-of-age, romance, sporting, equestrian. (Teen to young adult). Published: 2021.

ISBN : 9781913106119 (paperback) £8.00

Kindle   edition
https://www.amazon.co.uk/dp/191310611X

FELL FUN and FELL FACTS

Two activity books for children relating to ponies, and Fell ponies in particular.

FELL FUN

for ages 4 to 7 years

Puzzles, counting, colouring, spot the difference, spot the same, matching, rhyming, starting letters, mazes and dot to dot, cutting and sticking – all about ponies.

GENRE: Activity book. 20 pages. £2.00 plus postage

FELL FACTS

for 7 years and upwards

Description of the Fell pony breed, what the ponies can do, where they live, crosswords, wordsearches, picture quiz, a story and lots of pictures, plus a list of other books and DVDs about Fell ponies.

GENRE: Activity book. 20 pages. £2.00 plus postage

Both books can go in one mailing for the same postage cost. **FELL FUN** and **FELL FACTS** were produced at the request of the Fell Pony Society and may also be purchased from the FPS office in Appleby, Cumbria, and at shows and events run by the Society.